Charles Yatman

Temple themes and sacred songs

With the Christian Workers' training class lessons

Charles Yatman

Temple themes and sacred songs
With the Christian Workers' training class lessons

ISBN/EAN: 9783337266394

Printed in Europe, USA, Canada, Australia, Japan

Cover: Foto ©Thomas Meinert / pixelio.de

More available books at **www.hansebooks.com**

For God so loved the world, that he gave his only
begotten Son, that whosoever believeth in him, should
not perish, but have everlasting life. For God sent
not his Son into the world to condemn the world, but
that the world through him might be saved.

—John iii. 16, 17.

TEMPLE THEMES

AND

SACRED SONGS

WITH THE

Christian Workers' Training Class Lessons,

BY

CHARLES H. YATMAN.

PHILADELPHIA:
JOHN J. HOOD
1018 ARCH ST.

GREETING.

AGAIN we present a list of Themes. Enough of them, if rightly used, to make one's soul like a watered garden. May the smile of heaven be on them and on the people who use them.

The list begins with "Jesus, the Saviour of Sinners," is held in the centre by "The Blood of Christ," and closes with the Christian's watchword, "Victory."

They begin by leading the sinner from the City of Destruction, and end by setting his face like a flint toward Mount Zion.

Their aim and object is to make the Young People's Meetings and evangelistic services so full of point and power that the attendance shall be doubled, the interest trebled, and the results fourfold greater than they have been.

They are sent forth with a prayerful God-speed, to visit and bless not only the thousands who in summer visit Ocean Grove, but the hungry and thirsty ones in home, hall, prayer circle, social meeting, and the church.

May God bless each one into whose hands the little collection shall fall, as greatly as he has blessed me in the compiling of the same.

Yours to win souls,

C. H. YATMAN.

HOW TO USE THE THEMES:

Announce beforehand the number of the Theme for the meeting.

Let the leader and the audience read in concert the seven "suggestive lines." The last two, *printed in italics*, are always in the form of a question, and are to be THE CENTRAL IDEA OF THE SERVICE.

Let the "Gems of Thought" be read by some one person who can explain them in a brief, pointed way.

The "Question" should always be asked by the leader and answered by the full congregation.

Weave in the song sayings, hymns, and proverbs.

Get your scripture out of the chapter named.

Urge that all prayers and remarks be on the lines of the Theme, and select hymns that bear directly on the subject.

LIST OF THEMES.

JESUS, THE · SAVIOUR OF · SINNERS.

I'm so glad He came to save me.
A sinner can find no Saviour but Jesus.
Saved with righteousness, peace and joy here.   Heaven and glory
First Jesus becomes a Saviour, then a helper.   [hereafter.
Not the righteous, but sinners, Jesus came to call.
Who of us can say, "He saves me"?
Who will say, "I wish He would save me"?

⊹Gems of Thought.⊹

A little girl fell into a cistern, and called loudly for help, when her mother hastened to her rescue. Telling how she was saved, she said, "I reached up as far as I could, and mother did the rest." So Christ saves the sinner.

The saddest road to hell is that which runs under the pulpit, past the Bible, and through the midst of warnings and invitations.—*Ryle.*

"Sir," said an ungodly man, "I hope to be saved at last." "It would be better,

friend, to be saved at first," was the reply. Let us go down on our knees and seek the blessing now.

When the Rev. John Newton in his old age found memory failing him, he used to say, "two things I won't forget: 1st, I am a great sinner; 2d, Jesus is a great Saviour."

Sinners, whose love can ne'er forget
The wormwood and the gall,
Go, spread your trophies at his feet,
And crown him Lord of all.

THE SOUL-SAVING PSALM—Ps. cxxvi.

QUESTION—*What must I do to be saved?*   —Acts xvi. 31.

"Believe on the Lord Jesus Christ and thou shalt be saved," for Jesus said, "Verily, verily, I say unto you, he that believeth on me hath everlasting life." It is a heart trust

in Jesus and his atoning work for YOU as a lost sinner. To be saved you must turn from all sin, receive Jesus, and give yourself, your service, your all to God.

⊹Sayings about Songs.⊹

Heaven has all the music, hell has none. In eternity a saved soul always sings, a lost soul never sings. Oh, to hear the song of Moses and the Lamb. It's worth all life's battles to hear them sing just once in heaven.

JOY TO THE WORLD.

Joy to the world! the Lord is come;
Let earth receive her King;
Let every heart prepare him room,
And heaven and nature sing.

Joy to the world! the Saviour reigns;
Let men their songs employ;   [plains,
While fields and floods, rocks, hills and
Repeat the sounding joy.

No more let sin and sorrow grow,
Nor thorns infest the ground;
He comes to make his blessings flow
Far as the curse is found.

He rules the world with truth and grace,
And makes the nations prove
The glories of his righteousness,
And wonders of his love.

PROVERB—*"A merry heart doeth good like a medicine, but a broken spirit drieth the bones."*—xvii. 22.

4

CHRIST, ···OUR··· SURE REFUGE.

Safely kept from the snare of the fowler.
Hid where no evil can betide me.
Christ, a refuge in the storm and tempest.
Jesus is the only SURE refuge.
Safe am I forever.
My brother, what is thy refuge?
Sinner, hast thou hid in Christ?

Gems of Thought.

A frightened lark was once pursued by a hawk. Round and round in narrowing cycles the scared bird flew, till it seemed as if its foe would soon plant its beak in its breast. A friend of mine standing under the birds, feeling a sympathetic interest in the chase, opened the folds of his coat, and by soothing tone and gesture wooed the weak, frightened lark, till it sank panting to his breast, safely sheltered from its ravenous foe. Its natural timidity was overcome by a greater fear, and thus its peril and its powerlessness led it to come to a sure refuge. The tempted believers will likewise seek the everlasting arms, and say, "Let me hide myself in thee!"

True Christian experience involves both hope and fear. The more we fear his justice, the more we hasten to the shelter of his mercy.—*A Contrite Heart.*

SAFETY PSALM—Psalm xci.

QUESTION—*But who may abide the day of his coming? And who shall stand when he appeareth?* —Mal. iii. 2.

The answer is, He whose transgression is forgiven, whose sin is covered.—Ps. xxxii. 1. These are they which came out of great tribulation, and have washed their robes, and made them white in the blood of the Lamb. Therefore are they before the throne of God, and serve him day and night in his temple.—Rev. vii. 14, 15.

When Christ appears we who trust and serve him shall be made like unto him.

Sayings about Songs.

Even the beasts of the field like singing. I've seen the cows listen to open-air song. Serpents like songs. The birds warble till the air rings. I wish I could get the folks to take hold of the music with the same interest that a mocking-bird does.

LED BY JESUS.

Saviour, like a shepherd lead us,
　Much we need thy tenderest care;
In thy pleasant pastures feed us,
　For our use thy folds prepare:
　　Blessed Jesus,
Thou hast bought us thine we are.

We are thine, do thou befriend us,
　Be the guardian of our way;
Keep thy flock, from sin defend us,
　Seek us when we go astray:
　　Blessed Jesus,
Hear, oh, hear us, when we pray.

Thou hast promised to receive us,
　Poor and sinful though we be;
Thou hast mercy to relieve us,
　Grace to cleanse and power to free:
　　Blessed Jesus,
We will early turn to thee.

Early let us seek thy favor,
　Early let us do thy will;
Blessed Lord and only Saviour,
　With thy love our bosoms fill:
　　Blessed Jesus,
Thou hast loved us, love us still.

PROVERB—*"Hatred stirreth up strifes: but love covereth all sins."*—x. 12.

5

THE BIBLE, OUR · GUIDE TO · HEAVEN.

The Bible, God's printed invitation to the sinner.
I believe in the full inspiration of Scripture.
The Scriptures, our only rule for faith and practice.
The key-word of the whole Bible is "Come."
To love the Bible, prove its promises.
Who trusts the promise for salvation?
Who will take Isaiah xii. 2 as theirs?

Gems of Thought.

What the Scripture forbids, avoid; what it affirms, believe; what it commands, do; what it reproves, amend. As many as walk by this rule, peace on them, and on all the Israel of God.—*Thomas Adams.*

When we have Bible conversations, our lives as rich as diamonds east a sparkling lustre in the Church of God, and are in some sense parallel with the life of Christ, as the transcript with the original.—*Watson.*

Don't think you can read the Word of God without incurring responsibility—you cannot; nor can you shirk responsibility by not reading it.

To the complaint, "I make no progress in the Christian life," Sarah Martin, the prisoner's friend, made answer, Take your Bible on your knees, plow into it, and you will not stand still.

The Bible must be the invention either of good men or angels, bad men or devils, or God. (1) It could not be the *first*, for they neither could nor would themselves invent a book meantime lying in saying, "Thus saith the *Lord*." (2) not the *second*, for they would not make a book which commands all duty, forbids all sin, and condemns their souls to hell to all eternity: (3) therefore the Bible must be given by divine inspiration.—*Wesley.*

THE GREAT PSALM—Psalm cxix.

QUESTION—*What saith the Scripture?* —Rom. iv. 3.

It says you are a sinner, and lost, and the Scripture is the word of God, but it also says, "Whosoever believeth on him shall not be ashamed."—Rom. x. 11. It repeatedly says that if thou wilt but call on the name of the Lord thou shalt be saved.

Sayings about Songs.

The Bible says much about singing. It should be with the spirit and understanding. The soul should go into every note and word. There should be worship in it. Let there be no lifeless music in our churches.

THE LOVE OF JESUS.

Jesus loves me! this I know,
For the Bible tells me so:
Little ones to him belong;
They are weak, but he is strong.

Jesus loves me! he who died
Heaven's gate to open wide,
He will wash away my sin;
Let his little child come in.

CHO.—Yes, Jesus loves me,
Yes, Jesus loves me,
Yes, Jesus loves me,
The Bible tells me so.

PROVERB—*"Hearken unto thy father that begat thee, and despise not thy mother when she is old."*—xxiii. 22.

6

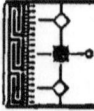

PRAYER.

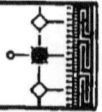

No Christian can live without prayer.
All prayer is based on the fatherhood of God.
There should be public prayer, private prayer, and family prayer.
The great prayer of Jesus is in John xvii.
The man who prays is the man of power.
Who have had answers to prayer?
Who will pray for salvation now?

⟶❦Gems of Thought.❧⟵

Prayer is not conquering God's reluctance, but taking hold of God's willingness.—*Phillip Brooks.*

Never was faithful prayer lost at sea. No merchant trades with such certainty as the praying saint. Some prayers have a longer voyage than others, but they return with a richer lading at last.—*Gurnall.*

Human prayer falls below divine resources.

The arrow of prayer that would hit the mark must be drawn with full strength. He that, in prayer for grace, *will* not be denied, *shall* not be denied.—*Swinnock.*

The power of prayer hath subdued the strength of fire; bridled the rage of lions; hushed anarchy; extinguished wars; appeased the elements; expelled demons; burst the chains of death; opened the gates of heaven; assuaged diseases; repelled frauds; rescued cities from destruction; and stayed the sun in its course; in a word, hath destroyed whatever is an enemy to man.—*St. Chrysostom.*

If tempted not to pray, pray the more. If tempted to postpone prayer, pray at that very time; most probably God has a blessing for you; Satan suspects He has. or he would not be so anxious to persuade you to put off prayer.—*Dyer.*

PRAYER CHAPTER—John xvii.

QUESTION—*Wouldst thou be spoken for to the King?*
—2 Kings iv. 13.

Yes, I would, and tell him of my many needs. If thou hast found favor at the throne of grace, pray for me.

Think of me when it shall be well with thee, and show kindness, I pray thee, unto me, and make mention of me.—Gen. xl. 14.

Thou shalt not be forgotten of me.—Isa. xliv. 21.

⟶❦Sayings about Songs.❧⟵

What an hour that will be when the entire company of redeemed souls shall take up the song "All hail the power of Jesus' name," and sing it to the listening multitude of angels who will line the streets of the heavenly city!

SWEET HOUR OF PRAYER.

Sweet hour of prayer, sweet hour of prayer,
That calls me from a world of care,
And bids me at my Father's throne
Make all my wants and wishes known!
In seasons of distress and grief
My soul has often found relief,
And oft escaped the tempter's snare
By thy return, sweet hour of prayer.

Sweet hour of prayer, sweet hour of prayer,
Thy wings shall my petition bear
To him, whose truth and faithfulness
Engage the waiting soul to bless:
And since he bids me seek his face,
Believe his word, and trust his grace,
I'll cast on him my every care,
And wait for thee, sweet hour of prayer.

PROVERB—"*Be thou diligent to know the state of thy flocks, and look well to thy herds.*"—xxvii. 23.

7

TEMPTATIONS · AND TRIALS.

In all points like we are, Christ was tempted.
Thus he knows how to succor the tempted heart.
Christ Jesus was made perfect through suffering.
Whom the Lord loveth he chasteneth.
God will not let us be over tempted or tried.
Who has been delivered in temptation?
Who have found trials a blessing?

❧Gems of Thought.☙

The hand must be steady. The arm must be strong. The soul should be well armed, so that it may be prepared for every attack, or for every expedient of the enemy. Life, honor, virtue, success, and immortality are before us.

(In persecution.) Let us sing the forty-sixth psalm in spite of the devil and all his instruments.—*Luther.*

For what ends, then, does God permit spiritual heaviness to befall so many of his children? The apostle gives a plain and direct answer to this question. (1 Pet. vii. 7.) The Lord gets his best soldiers out of the Highlands of affliction.—*Spurgeon.*

One of the greatest evidences of God's love to those that love him, is to send them afflictions, with grace to bear them.— *Wesley.*

It was a storm that occasioned the discovery of the gold mines in India. Hath not a storm driven some to the discovery of the richer mines of the love of God in Christ? —*Owen.*

When the bright temptaion lies
Glittering in thy dazzled eyes;
When the tempter's voice is near,
Whispering sweetly in thine ear,
Look not on the bright array,
Hear not the deceitful lay—
Christian, rise and flee away.

CONQUEROR'S CHAPTER—Luke iv.

QUESTION—*Whither shall I go?*   —Gen. xxxvii. 30.

Let us all answer to God, for The eternal God is thy refuge.—Deut. xxxiii. 27. I will sing of thy power; yea, I will sing aloud of thy mercy in the morning: for thou hast been my defence and refuge in the day of my trouble.—Ps. lix. 16.

❧Sayings about Songs.☙

I'm not sure but what in heaven the whistling farmer's boy will repeat his notes after the harvests have all been gathered, as he comes in with his gathered sheaves. It may seem to him as though again he were coming home for rest from work, and the habit of bygone days will creep out on the streets of the fair city.

REST FOR THE WEARY.

In the Christian's home in glory
There remains a land of rest,
Where the Saviour's gone before me,
To fulfil my soul's request.

CHO —On the other side of Jordan,
In the sweet fields of Eden,
Where the tree of life is blooming,
There is rest for you;

There is rest for the weary,
There is rest for the weary,
There is rest for the weary,
There is rest for you.

Pain or sickness ne'er can enter;
Grief nor woe my lot shall share;
But in that celestial centre
I a crown of life shall wear.

PROVERB—*"Hast thou found honey? eat so much as is sufficient for thee, lest thou be filled therewith, and vomit it."*—xxv. 16.

UTTERMOST SALVATION.

Christ alone is the author of this.
Saved from depths of sin to heights of glory.
Great to save, and mighty to keep.
When dead in sin, He brought me to life.
I will shout these words in the resurrection.
Can you say, He saves me to the uttermost?
Who wants to be saved with an uttermost salvation?

❧ Gems of Thought. ❧

Christ comes with a blessing in each hand—foregiveness in one, and holiness in the other; and never gives either to any who will not take both.

There are three sources of temptation, and only three—namely: the world, the flesh, and the devil. Provision is made in the scheme of redemption for our overcoming each of these three great enemies.

There are too many Christians now who dwell just inside the dividing line, so to speak, who are Christians, but of such a limp and feeble sort that they must be upheld continually, instead of helping others. —*Congregationalist.*

"Beyond! beyond! oh, blest beyond!
O heaven, eternal, peaceful, free!
O home on high! I haste from bonds
To find God's boundless rest in thee;
And saints beyond
Shall crowd thy gates to welcome me."

BLESSING CHAPTER—Deut. xxviii.

QUESTION—Lord God, what wilt thou give to me?
—Gen. xv. 2.

A new heart will I give you; and a new spirit will I put within you.—Ezek. xxxvi. 26.

And I will be a Father unto you, and ye shall be my sons and daughters, saith the Lord Almighty.—2 Cor. vi. 18.

When we have the Giver, we have all his gifts.

❧ Sayings about Songs. ❧

Think of listening to the morning stars as they sing together. The hum of ten thousand thousand spinning worlds all set to music will make shouting Methodists of every soul in heaven. Hallelujah!!!

THE LORD WILL PROVIDE.

Though troubles assail,
  And dangers affright,
Though friends should all fail,
  And foes all unite:
Yet one thing secures us
  Whatever betide,
The Scripture assures us
  The Lord will provide.

The birds, without barn
  Or storehouse, are fed;
From them let us learn
  To trust for our bread:
His saints, what is fitting,
  Shall ne'er be denied,
So long as 'tis written,
  The Lord will provide.

PROVERB—"*He becometh poor that dealeth with a slack hand: but the hand of the diligent maketh rich.*"—x. 4.

9

ADOPTION— THE CHILDREN OF GOD.

Members of the household of faith.
Christ our elder brother, hence God is *our* Father.
Beloved, now are we sons of God.
It doth not yet appear what we shall be,
We know, at last we shall be like Jesus.
Who can say, "I am a child of God?"
Who will say, "I want to be?"

Gems of Thought.

God has promised to feed us with the heritage of Jacob our Father; but I find the thorns of affliction and briers of disappointment grow plentifully thereon; consequently such things should be expected: "In the world ye shall have tribulation." The truest proof of a man's religion is the quality of his companions.—*Baile.*

Man, being as he is, must have a Church. Christianity without order and authority is a dream, an enthusiasm, a desolation.- *Wilson.*

The moment a heart touches the heart of Christ in living faith, he becomes, whether he knows it or not, the brother of every other, in heaven or on earth, who has come into the same relationship with Christ.

All sects are merely pockets in the garments of the Lord Jesus Christ. And it does not make any difference whether you go to heaven in a side-pocket or in a skirt-pocket. To get into heaven is the main thing, after all.—*Beecher.*

CHRISTIAN'S CHAPTER—1 Peter ii.

QUESTION—Is there room in thy Father's house for us?
—Gen. xxiv. 23.

There is room.—Luke xiv. 22.
In my Father's house are many mansions: if it were not so, I would have told you. I go to prepare a place for you.—John xiv. 2. Heaven is big enough for the whole

world, and furthermore God wants the whole human race to dwell there with him. The invitation means all; it says, "Whosoever will may come."

Sayings about Songs.

Mother, wife, and children, when the men folks come home at night, dont let the latch-key get fully turned before the piano plays and you sing. Greet the weary worker for your bread with music, you can drive the "tiredness" out with a note of song. Then when you sit down to sup together sing grace, 'twill flavor the meat.

CHILDREN OF GOD.

Around the throne of God in heaven
Thousands of children stand,
Children whose sins are all forgiven,
A holy, happy band,

CHO.—Singing glory, glory,
Glory be to God on high.

What brought them to that world above—
That heaven so bright and fair,
Where all is peace, and joy, and love—
How came those children there?
Because the Saviour shed his blood,
To wash away their sin;
Bathed in that pure and precious flood,
Behold them white and clean!

PROVERB—*"Say unto wisdom, thou art my sister; and call understanding thy kinswoman,"*—vii. 4.

Theme 8.

CHRIST, THE ROCK OF AGES.

The Rock was cleft for the whosoever.
Read Deuteronomy xxxii. and 1 Cor. x. **4**.
Also read Isaiah xxvi. 3, 4.
There is no safety off this great Rock.
Hide Thou me.
Is your house built upon the Rock or sand?
What sinner will hide in the cleft to-day?

❧Gems of Thought.☙

The believer resting on his Rock may smile at the billows of trouble foaming at his feet.   Isa. xxviii. 16.

God's Israel never receives a drop of spiritual joy or comfort but through the Smitten Rock.

When Satan first comes to tempt he is modest, and asks but a little. He digs about and loosens the roots of faith, and then the tree falls the easier on the next gust of temptation.—*Gurnall.*

Down to the grave comes the millionaire. "How much are you worth?" says Death.

"Men call me worth thirty millions." It is not enough to pay his ferriage! But he goes through; and when he has got through, his wealth having been taken from him, he is no bigger than a mosquito. There is hardly enough of him for a nucleus to start on in the next life.—*Beecher.*

"My hope on nothing less is built
Than Jesus, and the blood He spilt;
I dare not trust the sweetest frame,
But wholly lean on His great Name:
On Christ, the solid Rock, I stand,
All other ground is sinking sand."

CHARACTER CHAPTER—Job xxix.

QUESTION—When he giveth quietness, who then can make trouble?
—Job xxxiv. 29.

None, for the peace of God is beyond the reach of the world when hid in the heart that loves God devotedly.   What joy there is in these words of Jesus, "Peace I leave with you, my peace I give unto you."

❧Sayings about Songs.☙

I am willing to give life's blood, drop by drop, if at the end I can listen just once to a million sinners singing "Rock of ages, cleft for me," or "Jesus, Lover of my soul."

CHRIST, THE ROCK OF AGES.

Jesus, the weary wanderer's rest,
   Give me thy easy yoke to bear;
With steadfast patience arm my breast,
   With spotless love and lowly fear.

Thankful, I take the cup from thee,
   Prepared and mingled by thy skill;
Though bitter to the taste it be,
   Powerful the wounded soul to heal.

Be thou, O Rock of ages, nigh!   [gone,
   So shall each murmuring thought be
And grief, and fear, and care shall fly,
   As clouds before the midday sun.

Speak to my warring passions, "Peace,"
   Say to my trembling heart, "Be still;"
Thy power my strength and fortress is,
   For all things serve thy sovereign will.

PROVERB—"*As the whirlwind passeth, so is the wicked no more: but the righteous is an everlasting foundation.*"—x. 25.
11

RIGHTEOUSNESS, THE CHRISTIAN'S BREASTPLATE.

Not self-righteousness, but Christ's righteousness.
Our breast-plate is from heaven's armory.
The breast-plate covers the heart.
We are complete only in Christ.
Say ye to the righteous it shall be well with them.
Are you wearing this breast-plate?
In whose righteousness are you trusting?

Gems of Thought.

One day I was climbing a mountain in the Alpine range near the boundary line between France and Switzerland. By and by we came upon snow and icicles and all the usual attendants in the train of winter; but when we got higher we found delightful flowers, blooming in all the beauty of floral loveliness. I said to myself, How is this? Down yonder are icicles and snow; up here are these exquisite flowers. The secret of the matter was that this part of the mountain had a southern aspect, and faced the sun, while the other was turned from it. Even so it is with ourselves. When our hearts are turned toward Him who is the fountain of love and of marvelous spiritual beauty, we bring forth the fruits and the flowers of Christian character, and show the world what a blessed and beautiful thing it is to be a disciple of Christ. It is when our affections and thoughts are turned from Him that the graces which would otherwise abound in us languish and die.—*Dr. Clemance.*

" Lord, let the dead now hear thy voice,
And bid thy chosen ones rejoice.
Their beauty this, their glorious dress,
Jesus, ' the Lord our Righteousness.' "

ADMONITION CHAPTER—Hebrews xiii.

QUESTION—And now, what doth the Lord thy God require of thee? —Deut. x. 12.

The Bible puts it very plain. None need mistake the voice of duty and the will of the Most High. To fear the Lord thy God, to walk in all His ways, and to love Him, and to serve the Lord thy God with all thy heart and with all thy soul.—Deut. x. 12.

The God of peace make you perfect in every good work to do His will, working in you, that which is well-pleasing in His sight, through Jesus Christ.—Heb. xiii. 20, 21.

Sayings about Songs.

Make your singing appropriate. Dont sing funeral hymns at a praise meeting, nor " Hold the fort " at a memorial service. Many leaders leave the selection of hymns for the last moment, and have no connection between the theme and the songs. This is not right. Let's do better.

THE ARMOR OF GOD.

Soldiers of Christ, arise,
 And put your armor on;
Strong in the strength which God supplies
 Through His eternal Son.
Strong in the Lord of Hosts,
 And in His mighty power;
Who in the strength of Jesus trusts,
 Is more than conqueror.

Stand, then, in His great might,
 With all His strength endued;
But take, to arm you for the fight,
 The panoply of God.
Your foes, not flesh and blood,
 But powers of hell and night;
Nought but the weapons of your God
 Can put these foes to flight.

PROVERB—*"Can one go upon hot coals and his feet not be burned?"*—vi. 28.

12

THE GRACE OF GOD.

By grace are ye saved, through faith.
God wants to make His grace abound towards you.
When Jesus came He brought grace with Him.
When He left he took it not away.
All-sufficient grace for all needful work.
What has grace done for you?
What will you do for God by his assisting grace?

Gems of Thought.

Grace does not come to the heart as we set a cask at the corner of the house, to catch the rain in the shower. It is a pulley fastened to the throne of God, which we pull, bringing the blessing.—*Talmage.*

Grace is free in all and for all. It does not depend upon any power or merit in man, neither in whole nor in part; neither upon good works, nor good tempers, nor good desires, nor good intentions. These are the fruits of free grace, not the root.

We want not time to serve God, but zeal; we have not too much business, but too little grace.—*Hamilton.*

Grow in grace, because this is the only way to be certain that you have any grace at all. If we aim not at growth in grace, we have never been converted to goodness. He that is satisfied with his attainments has attained nothing.—*Robert Hall.*

GIFT CHAPTER—1 Cor. xii.

QUESTION—*Behold, the Lord God will help me; who is he that shall condemn me?* —Isa. l. 9.

The world may say much against us. Let us care little for that. One smile of God towards us is better than the approving words of the whole race. Romans viii. 1 says, "There is therefore now no condemnation to them which are in Christ Jesus." Be sure your life is hid with Christ's in God. Then rest.

Sayings about Songs.

The delight of a soul as with redeemed men made perfect they walk up the streets, lined on either side by angels and archangels, singing Redemption's Song, or the "Old, Old Story," can be thought of but not described. Will you be amongst the number?

THE GOSPEL STORY.

I love to tell the story,
Of unseen things above,
Of Jesus and his glory,
Of Jesus and his love.
I love to tell the story,
Because I know 'tis true;
It satisfies my longings,
As nothing else can do.

I love to tell the story;
For those who know it best
Seem hungering and thirsting
To hear it like the rest.
And when, in scenes of glory,
I sing the new, new song,
'Twill be the old, old story
That I have loved so long.

CHO.—I love to tell the story,
'Twill be my theme in glory
To tell the old, old story
Of Jesus and his love.

PROVERB—*"The soul of the sluggard desireth, and hath nothing: but the soul of the diligent shall be made fat."*—xiii. 4.

WORK, THE + CHRISTIAN'S + PRIVILEGE AND DUTY.

Work here, rest hereafter.
As our work is so shall our reward be.
Saved by grace and work by love.
God wants heart service.
And wants no idle Christians.
Are you one of God's workmen?
Will thou be a servant of Jesus?

Gems of Thought.

If you do not wish for His kingdom, dont pray for it. But if you do, you must do more than pray; you must work for it.— *J. Ruskin.*

I hate to see a thing done by halves: if it be right, do it boldly; if it be wrong, leave it alone.—*Gilpin.*

If we are prepared to shine, God will find the candlestick; if we are prepared to work, God will find us something to do. Only be ready and willing for anything.—*Milne.*

It is not worth while to think too much about being good. Doing the best we know, minute by minute, hour by hour, we insensibly grow to goodness as fruit grows to ripeness.

A good action never perishes, neither before God nor before men.—*Asiatic Proverb.*

When you go forth to do a good deed, put on the slippers of silence.—*F. B. Ginty.*

He who would build high must lay the foundation deep.—*John Crook.*

WORK CHAPTER—James ii.

QUESTION—*Which is the first commandment of all?*
—Mark xii. 28.

Exodus xx should be learned by all, as it is the commandment chapter of the Bible, but the answer to this question, answered in the New Testament, is especially pointed. The first of all the commandments is, Hear, O Israel; The Lord our God is one

Lord: and thou shalt love the Lord thy God with all thy heart, and with all thy soul, and with all thy mind, aud with all thy strength.—Mark xii. 29, 30.

He that loveth not, knoweth not God; for God is love.—1 John iv. 8.

Sayings about Songs.

How singers live! Long after they are gone their songs bring them back. Beethoven and Handel, Haydn and Mozart, they live yet. Many of their songs born of grief have taken grief away. Many a hymn is but the reflex of the writer. Many a word and note of song is but crystalized tears set to music.

WORK FOR THE NIGHT IS COMING.

Work, for the night is coming,
Work through the morning hours;
Work, while the dew is sparkling,
Work 'mid springing flowers;
Work, when the day grows brighter,
Work in the glowing sun;
Work, for the night is coming,
When man's work is done.

Work, for the night is coming,
Work through the sunny noon;
Fill brightest hours with labor,
Rest comes sure and soon,
Give every flying minute
Something to keep in store:
Work, for the night is coming,
When man works no more.

PROVERB—"*A good name is rather to chosen than great riches, and loving favor rather than silver and gold.*"—xxii. 1.

Theme 12.

JOY, THE ✛ CHRISTIAN'S STRENGTH.

Get more of Jesus and you will have more joy.
Joy on earth as well as in heaven.
It is the joy of doing good.
It is the joy of the Lord, not the joy of yourself.
This is the second fruit of the Spirit.
Are you a joyful or joyless Christian?
Who will draw with joy from the wells of salvation?

Gems of Thought.

The test of your Christian character should be that you are a joy-bearing angel to the world.—*Beecher.*

Christ takes no more delight to dwell in a sad heart than we do to live in a dark house.—*Gurnall.*

There is no heaven either in this world or in the world to come for people who do not praise God.—*Dr. Pulsford.*

Cheerfulness is an excellent wearing quality. It has been called the bright weather of the heart.—*Smiles.*

The child of God should live above the world, moving through it as some quiet star moves through the blue sky, clear, serene, joyous.—*Bowman.*

I wonder many times that ever a child of God should have a sad heart, considering what the Lord is preparing for him.

What is our life without joy? Without joy we can do nothing. We are like an instrument out of tune. An instrument out of tune it yields but harsh music. Without joy we are a member out of joint.—*Sibbes.*

PASSOVER CHAPTER—Exodus xii.

QUESTION—*Should I wait for the Lord any longer?*
—2 Kings vi. 33.

Yes, "Rest in the Lord and wait patiently for Him." The hour will come when He will wipe away all tears from off all faces. If He tarry in coming it is for your good and His own glory. It is written "The just shall live by FAITH," and not by feeling or sight.

Sayings about Songs.

What holy joy it will be to hear P. P. Bliss singing his praises of Jesus on the streets of gold. I'm persuaded that processions with banners and songs are not infrequent scenes in the celestial city.

O HAPPY DAY.

O happy day, that fixed my choice
On thee, my Saviour and my God!
Well may this glowing heart rejoice,
And tell its rapture all abroad.

CHO.—Happy day, happy day,
When Jesus washed my sins away;
He taught me how to watch and pray,
And live rejoicing every day;
Happy day, happy day,
When Jesus washed my sins away.

'Tis done, the great transaction's done—
I am my Lord's and he is mine;
He drew me, and I followed on,
Charmed to confess the voice divine.

Now rest, my long divided heart:
Fixed on this blissful center, rest,
Nor ever from thy Lord depart,
With him of every good possessed.

PROVERB—*"Better is a dinner of herbs where love is, than a stalled ox and hatred therewith."*—xv. 17.

15

JESUS, THE · MAN · OF · SORROWS.

Thus He knows our griefs.
Hence He can carry our burdens.
He has balm for every wound.
Heaven knows every heart-beat.
He had sorrow that we might have joy.
Do you know the sympathy of Jesus?
Will you let Him save you, then sympathize with you?

Gems of Thought.

The best defence against sin at any time is the remembrance of Christ's sufferings.—*Horneck.*

Prayers and tears are the weapons with which the saints have obtained the most glorious victories.—*Henry.*

How many a christian pilgrim would never have seen anything of the spiritual manna, and the spiritual stream from the rock, had God listened to him when, with fear and trembling, he besought Him not to lead him into a desert.—*Krummacher.*

Christians resemble travellers in a stage-coach. We are full of our plans and schemes, but the coach is moving rapidly forward: it passes one milestone, and then another; and no regard is paid to the plots or plans of the passengers.—*Cecil.*

"Let those that sow in sadness wait
    Till the fair harvest come:
They shall confess their sheaves are great,
    And shout the blessings home."
"When storms of fierce temptation beat,
    And furious foes assail,
My refuge is the mercy seat,
    My hope within the vail."

SUFFERER'S CHAPTER—Isaiah liii.

QUESTION—*Hath God forgotten to be gracious?* —Ps. lxxvii. 9.

It seems so sometimes, but is never really so.

Can a woman forget her sucking child, that she should not have compassion on the son of her womb? Yea, she may forget, yet will I not forget thee, saith the Lord.—Isa. xlix. 15.

Thy love to me was wonderful, passing the love of women.—2 Sam. i. 26.

God never neglects or forgets His children.

Sayings about Songs.

"Other refuge have I none" was born out of suffering. Mr. Wesley was under severe trials, and when a bird flew through his window for refuge from the hawk and he sheltered it, then came this immortal hymn from his pen.

WHITE ROBES.

Who are these in bright array,
    This exulting, happy throng,
Round the altar night and day,
    Singing one triumphant song?
CHO.—They have clean robes, white robes,
    White robes are waiting for me!

Yes, clean robes, white robes,
    Washed in the blood of the Lamb.
These through fiery trials trod,
    These from great affliction came,
Now before the throne of God,
    Sealed with His almighty name.

PROVERB—"*Say not unto thy neighbor, Go, and come again, and to-morrow I will give; when thou hast it by thee.*"—iii. 28.

THE CROSS OF CHRIST.

In the cross of Christ I glory.
Only at the cross is there pardon for the sinner.
No cross—no crown.
Because Christ died we shall live.
Salvation and self-denial go together.
Saved sinner, what did you find at the cross?
Lost sinner, when will you come to the cross?

Gems of Thought.

O what a cross to have no cross!
The cross is easier to him who takes it up than to him who drags it.
The best way to bear crosses is to consecrate them all in silence to God.—*Fletcher.*
I find the doing of the will of God leaves me no time for disputing about his plans.—*George MacDonald.*
Christ's cross is the sweetest burden that ever I bore: it is such a burden as wings are to a bird, or sails to a ship, to carry me forward to my harbor.—*Rutherford.*

"Nothing, either great or small,
Nothing, sinner, no;
Jesus did it, did it all,
Long, long ago.
'It is finished!' yes, indeed,
Finished every jot;
Sinner, this is all you need—
Tell me, is it not?"

FIERY FURNACE CHAPTER—Dan. iii.

QUESTION—*How shall this man save us?*   —1 Sam. x. 27.

Many query thus, but the answer is pointed and plain. It is by the sacrifice of Himself. "He gave himself a ransom for all."—1 Tim. ii. 6. Christ died that we might live. "Be it known unto you, therefore, men and brethren, that through this man is preached unto you the forgiveness of sins."—Acts xiii. 38.

Sayings about Songs.

With the old hymns and tunes dont fail to add some new ones. I can't listen to a harp of one string very long. There are churches that would be swept into a mighty revival if some of the grand new songs would be introduced and well sung. Put them in quick.

IN THE CROSS OF CHRIST.

In the cross of Christ I glory,
Towering o'er the wrecks of time;
All the light of sacred story,
Gathers round its head sublime.

When the woes of life o'ertake me
Hopes deceive and fears annoy,
Never shall the cross forsake me;
Lo! it glows with peace and joy.

When the sun of bliss is beaming
Light and love upon my way,
From the cross the radiance streaming,
Adds new lustre to the day.

Bane and blessing, pain and pleasure,
By the cross are sanctified;
Peace is there that knows no measure,
Joys that through all time abide.

PROVERB—*"He that walketh with wise men shall be wise: but a companion of fools shall be destroyed."*—xiii. 20.

COME, THE + KEY - WORD + OF + THE + BIBLE.

Come *out* from the world,—"Be ye separate."
Come *into* the fold,—"There shall be one fold."
Come *up* to reward,—"Enter into the joy of your Lord."
God's precious message to the sinner lost.
It is to-day given to you.
Have you been to Jesus?
Will you trust and follow Him?

Gems of Thought.

Christ says to every lost sinner, "Come;" to every redeemed sinner, "Go." The world says, "Come to me and I will fail you;" the flesh says, "Come to me and I will destroy you;" Christ says, "*Come to me and I will give you rest.*"—*St. Bernard.*

Sin has the awful power of self-propagation. It grows stronger with every indulgence. And the awful possibility is this—the final victory in our hearts of the sin which we play with, but which will yet become our master and tyrant. If not turned in time, we *must* be what we once chose to be. And if we do not desire to be forever what we are to-day, let us see to it that we be to-day what we wish to be forever.

How long may it take a man to embrace Christ as his Saviour? As long as it takes a drowning man to let go a straw and lay hold of an offered rope.

COME CHAPTER—Isaiah lv.

QUESTION—*Who can tell whether God will be gracious to me?* —2 Sam. xii. 22.

You are in deep trouble: nothing but clouds and storms; nothing but trials and sore trouble; you reason that it is a strange dealing that God has with you. Listen to His voice in Hebrews xii, and read this, " He will be very gracious unto thee at the voice of thy cry; when he shall hear it, he will answer thee."—Isa. xxx. 19.

Sayings about Songs.

How to get the sinners to come? you ask. Why "sing them in;" singing attracts sinners like clover heads draw bees. But its got to be of the right kind, hearty, full, with heart-beat and not baton. Let it be varied, too, old tunes and new ones. Solos, quartets, and the full congregation.

THE GOSPEL INVITATION.

Blow ye the trumpet, blow,
The gladly-solemn sound!
Let all the nations know,
To earth's remotest bound,
The year of jubilee is come!
Return, ye ransomed sinners, home.

Jesus, our great High Priest,
Hath full atonement made:
Ye weary spirits, rest:
Ye mournful souls, be glad:
The year of jubilee is come!
Return, ye ransomed sinners, home.

Extol the Lamb of God,
The all-atoning Lamb;
Redemption in his blood
Throughout the world proclaim:
The year of jubilee is come!
Return, ye ransomed sinners, home.

Ye slaves of sin and hell,
Your liberty receive,
And safe in Jesus dwell,
And blest in Jesus live:
The year of jubilee has come!
Return, ye ransomed sinners, home.

PROVERB—"*How much better is it to get wisdom than gold, and to get understanding rather to be chosen than silver?*"—xvi. 16.

18

CHRIST, THE CRUCIFIED.

The Lord laid on Him all my sins. Hallelujah!
The law tells me what a sinner I am.
The cross tells me what a Saviour I have.
Its only at the cross the sinner and God can meet.
He died for me so I could live for Him.
Can you say, Jesus died for me?
Sinner, trust in Christ the crucified.

Gems of Thought.

One earnest gaze upon Christ is worth a thousand scrutinies of self. The man who beholds the cross, and beholding it weeps, cannot be really blind nor perilously self-ignorant.—*Dean Vaughan.*

Christians are often employed in digging wells to find comfort, and the deeper they go the darker they get; the fountain of life, salvation, and comfort, is above; call upon thy God, and look up, and the light of his love will soon cheer thee.

Look at Jehovah in his infinite love, omnipotent power, unsearchable riches, universal dominion, unsullied holiness, eternal veracity, and unspeakable glory; and then you may say, "This God is my God forever and ever, and all that he has is mine: why then am I cast down?"

CHASTENING CHAPTER—Heb. xii.

QUESTION—*Is my hand shortened at all, that it cannot redeem?* —Isa. l. 2.

No, no, Lord, we believe as thou hast written, "The Lord's hand is not shortened, that it cannot save; neither his ear heavy, that it cannot hear."—Isa. lix. 1; but keep us from sin.

That thy beloved may be delivered; save with thy right hand, and hear me.—Ps. lx. 5.

Sayings about Songs.

John the revelator, from the isle of Patmos, says he heard a new song in heaven. How his ear must have listened to that wondrous music! There will come a day when the same shall be heard by us. The thought makes one homesick for heaven.

MORE LOVE TO THEE.

More love to thee, O Christ!
More love to thee;
Hear thou the prayer I make
On bended knee;
This is my earnest plea,
More love, O Christ, to thee,
||: More love to thee! :||

Once earthly joy I craved,
Sought peace and rest;
Now thee alone I seek,
Give what is best;
This all my prayer shall be,
More love, O Christ, to thee!
||: More love to thee! :||

Let sorrow do its work,
Send grief and pain;
Sweet are thy messengers,
Sweet their refrain,
When they can sing with me,—
More love, O Christ, to thee,
||: More love to thee! :||

Then shall my latest breath
Whisper thy praise,
This be the parting cry
My heart shall raise;
This still its prayer shall be;
More love, O Christ, to thee,
||: More love to thee! :||

PROVERB—"*A talebearer revealeth secrets: but he that is of a faithful spirit concealeth the matter.*"—xi. 13.

19

THE ATONEMENT.

At - one - ment.

Blood alone makes an atonement for the soul.

This blood was shed for the whole world.

Only believe that He died for you.

Believe and be saved. Believe not and be lost.

Do you now believe in Jesus?

Who will accept Christ Jesus as Saviour?

Gems of Thought.

Dont grasp the shadow and miss the substance as, alas, many do. What do you know of atonement, reconciliation, peace, victory?

What must I do to be lost? It is not necessary to do anything; you are lost already! If you do nothing, just simply neglect salvation, you will assuredly perish.

The man in the water has but to refuse to grasp the life-buoy, and he is drowned; the person in the fire has only to remain where he is, and he is destroyed; the sick one has only to reject the remedy and he dies. So it is in like manner with the soul. Neglect is ruin; stay where you are, and

you perish. Lay not hold of eternal life, and you die. It needs not positive rejection, but simple neglect of the way of escape. There may be an admiration or an approval of God's remedy for sin, but unless there be acceptance of it all is lost.

See to it then, that you make not the fatal mistake, but believe, receive, accept, and salvation is yours, even life eternal and the glory that fadeth not away.

How extensive is the atonement! so extensive that none will be lost by reason of any deficiency in it: so extensive that if all would accept it all would be saved.

ATONEMENT CHAPTER—Heb. ix.

QUESTION—*O wretched man that I am: who shall deliver me from the body of this death?* —Rom. vii. 24.

Here we get the beauty of the G pel. Listen to these gracious words: We had the sentence of death in ourselves, that we should not trust in ourselves, but in God which raiseth the dead: who delivered us

from so great a death, and doth deliver: in whom we trust that he will yet deliver us. —2 Cor. i. 9, 10.

He shall send them a Saviour, and a great one, and he shall deliver them.—Isa. xix. 20.

Sayings about Songs.

The music teaching of the present day is faulty in that it does not teach the people to start a hymn without an instrument to give the right pitch. Every prayer meeting that has one or two persons that can start a tune off hand is mightily blessed, especially if they have good sense to know when is just the right time to do it.

CHRIST CRUCIFIED.

Alas! and did my Saviour bleed?
And did my Sovereign die?
Would he devote that sacred head
For such a worm as I?

Was it for crimes that I have done
He groaned upon the tree?
Amazing pity! grace unknown!
And love beyond degree!

Thus might I hide my blushing face
While his dear cross appears;
Dissolve my heart in thankfulness,
And melt mine eyes to tears.

But drops of grief can ne'er repay
The debt of love I owe:
Here, Lord, I give myself away,—
'Tis all that I can do.

PROVERB—*"Seest thou a man wise in his own conceit? there is more hope of a fool than of him."*—xxvi. 12.

DEATH, ·· THE ·· CONQUERED ✦ FOE.

As Jesus rose from the dead so shall we.
In Christ we have no fear of death.
They "fall asleep" who believe in God.
Death can but let the soul free to mount to heaven.
What mighty victories the resurrection will reveal.
Dead in sin, have you found life through Christ?
Is death your conquered foe through Christ?

Gems of Thought.

Death is the waiting-room where we robe ourselves for immortality.—*Spurgeon.*

Death is the dropping of the flower that the fruit may swell.—*Beecher.*

The sublimity of wisdom is to do those things living which are to be desired when dying.—*Bishop Taylor.*

Believers should not have a slavish dread of death; for where is the infant that feared to go to sleep in his nurse's arms.—*Toplady.*

The accurate work of salvation, upon which hangs eternity, can hardly be done in the dim-soul light of dying—*Gauden.*

It is not exile, rest on high;
It is not sadness, peace from strife;
To fall asleep is not to die;
To dwell with Christ is better life.
—*John Mason Neale.*

ASCENSION CHAPTER—Acts i.

QUESTION—*How wilt thou do in the swelling of Jordan?*
—Jer. xii. 5.

I will not be anxious, for thus saith the Lord, Fear not: for I have redeemed thee I have called thee by thy name; thou art mine. When thou passest through the waters, I will be with thee; and through the rivers, they shall not overflow thee.—Isa. xliii. 1, 2.

Hold thou me up, and I shall be safe.

Sayings about Songs.

How sad it will be to sing here, to sing gospel hymns, anthems, oratorios, and at death to have one's voice hushed forever. O singer, trust this Jesus about whom thou dost sing so beautifully. Trust Him to save thee.

TRIUMPH O'ER THE GRAVE.

My faith shall triumph o'er the grave,
And trample on the tomb;
I know that my Redeemer lives,
And on the clouds shall come.

I know that he shall soon appear
In power and glory meet;
And death, the last of all his foes,
Lie vanquished at his feet.

PROVERB—"*For by wise counsel thou shalt make thy war: and in multitude of counsellors there is safety.*"—xxiv. 6.

21

JESUS, ··OUR·· BURDEN ✦ BEARER.

The whole world needs such a Saviour.
He wants to relieve every burdened heart.
The chastisement of our peace was upon Him.
The Lord laid on Him all our sin.
Let us cast on Him our every care.
Do you know Jesus by this name?
Have you cast your burden on the Lord?

❧Gems of Thought.❧

There never has been, and never will be, a believing prayer unanswered.—*McCheyne.*

O most grateful burden, which comforts them that carry it. The burdens of earthly masters gradually wear out the strength of those who carry them; but the burden of Christ assists the bearers of it: because we carry not grace, but grace us.—*St. Chrysostom.*

I have never seen anybody that didn't make mistakes, except babies, and they always died early.—*Beecher.*

I know not by what methods rare,
But this I know, God answers prayer.
I now not when he sends the word
That tells us fervent prayer is heard.
I know it cometh soon or late:
Therefore, we need to pray and wait.
I know not if the blessing sought
Will come in just the guise I thought.
I leave my prayers with him alone
Whose will is wiser than my own.
—*Christian Register.*

BOTTOMLESS CHAPTER—Eph. iii.

QUESTION—*Are the consolations small with thee?* —Job xv. 11.

No, for without them we could not live; many of us know this full well. He has made true these precious promises: God, even our Father, hath loved us, and hath given us everlasting consolation.—2 Thess. ii. 16. Consolation in Christ.—Phil. ii. 1.

❧Sayings about Songs.❧

One may love music dearly without being able to render it: Such is my case. This lays an extra burden on those who can sing to double their power and sing for others as well as themselves.

HEAVEN IS OUR HOME.

We are but strangers here;
Heaven is our home!
Earth is a desert drear;
Heaven is our home!
Dangers and sorrows stand
Round us on every hand;
Heaven is our Fatherland,
Heaven is our home!

What though the tempest rage;
Heaven is our home!
Short is our pilgrimage;
Heaven is our home!
This life's wild wintry blast
Soon will be overpast:
We shall reach home at last;
Heaven is our home!

PROVERB—"*The fear of the Lord is the beginning of wisdom: and the knowledge of the Holy is understanding.*"—ix. 10.

THE MESSIAH, PRINCE OF PEACE.

There are many Princes, but one Messiah.
Jesus alone can give heart-peace.
The peace and power of Christ is unlimited.
They dwell in peace who dwell in Christ.
Peace in life, in death, in heaven.
Who has the gift of Christ's peace?
Who will receive the Prince of Peace?

❧ Gems of Thought. ❧

Be assured that sin is not a light thing, either as you find it in yourself, or see it in others. It is hateful to God; it is ruinous to man. If not confessed to God, forsaken in practice, and pardoned, it will shut the soul out of heaven. But Christ is a Saviour. He came into the world to save us from the guilt and power of all sin. Go to Him with faith in His atoning sacrifice, and though your sins have been great, and your example only for evil, you shall find that He is able to save even you.

If you think you can trust in Christ's sacrifice for salvation, without obeying his precepts as a rule of sanctification, you are greatly mistaken: trust in Christ will lead you to take the yoke of Christ.

"A little while to tell the old, *old* story,
  How Jesus came, the glorious Prince of Peace;
Oh, then the heights from glory unto glory,
  In the bright realm where joy shall never cease."

THE GOLDEN PSALM—Psalm xvi.

QUESTION—*Is thy heart right?* —2 Kings x. 15.

A mighty question this, and how answer you it? You may say "yes" to the world, but what say you to God? Unless it be a "new heart" *it is not* right, for the natural heart is deceitful and desperately wicked above all things.

God alone can give you a new heart; ask Him for it.

❧ Sayings about Songs. ❧

I think Jesus must have sang with the rest at the last supper in the upper room. How grand it will be to have Him join with us in our songs on high. With His humanity He can unite with our devotions to His divinity.

CHRIST OUR KING.

Hark! the herald angels sing,
"Glory to the new-born King!
Peace on earth, and mercy mild;
God and sinners reconciled."

Joyful, all ye nations, rise;
Join the triumphs of the skies;
With th' angelic hosts proclaim,
"Christ is born in Bethlehem."

Mild he lays his glory by;
Born that man no more may die;
Born to raise the sons of earth;
Born to give them second birth.

Let us, then, with angels sing,
"Glory to the new-born King!
Peace on earth, and mercy mild;
God and sinners reconciled!"

PROVERB—*"A man that hath friends must show himself friendly: and there is a friend that sticketh closer than a brother."*—xviii. 24.

23

CHRIST, + THE + GIVER · OF · LIFE.

To have Christ is to have eternal life.
Dead souls live when Christ speaks the word of life.
There is life for a look at the Crucified One.
Faith is the channel by which life flows.
Everlasting life cannot be bought, it is a gift.
Have you the gift of God—eternal life?
Who will pass from death unto life to-day?

Gems of Thought.

Dost thou love life? then do not squander time: for that is the stuff life is made of.—*Franklin.*

Few are they who by faith *touch* Christ; multitudes are they who throng about him.

The whole of the Christian religion is this: The grace of God as the source of mercy; faith in Christ as the way of salvation; the Spirit of God as our guide; the love of God as our law; and eternal life as our end.

The wages that sin bargains for with the sinner are life, pleasure and profit; but the wages it pays him with are death, torment, and destruction. He that would understand the falsehood and deceit of sin, must compare its promises and its payments together.

No other hope shall intervene:
To Him we look, on Him we lean:
Other foundations we disown,
And build on Christ, the " Living Stone."

LIFE CHAPTER—Luke vii.

QUESTION—*For what dost thou make request?* —Neh. xi. 4.

Let us join the great apostle, and ask with him the following: That I may know Christ, and the power of his resurrection.—Phil. iii.

10. And know the love of Christ, which passeth knowledge.—Eph. iii. 19.

Sayings about Songs.

If you want to be an ever welcome messenger go with a song on your lips. A song will subdue a tempest within the breast. A strain of music will often curb a passion that would have spent its force to great harm. The Sailors' Hornpipe has helped to weather many a gale.

CHRIST'S PRAISES.

O could I speak the matchless worth,
O could I sound the glories forth,
Which in my Saviour shine,
I'd soar and touch the heavenly strings,
And vie with Gabriel while he sings
In notes almost divine.

I'd sing the precious blood he spilt,
My ransom from the dreadful guilt
Of sin, and wrath divine;
I'd sing his glorious righteousness,
In which all-perfect, heavenly dress
My soul shall ever shine.

I'd sing the characters he bears,
And all the forms of love he wears,
Exalted on his throne;
In loftiest songs of sweetest praise,
I would to everlasting days
Make all his glories known.

Well, the delightful day will come
When my dear Lord will bring me home,
And I shall see his face;
Then with my Saviour, Brother, Friend,
A blest eternity I'll spend,
Triumphant in his grace.

PROVERB—"*When pride cometh, then cometh shame: but with the lowly is wisdom.*"—xi. 2.

FAITH, THE · CHRISTIAN'S ✛ SHIELD. ✛

Above all take the shield of faith.
Then no darts of Satan can reach us.
Faith cometh by hearing and hearing by the word of God.
Faith is a wee bit of no doubt.
Faith is taking God at His word.
Have you saving faith in Christ Jesus?
Are you a big or little faith Christian?

Gems of Thought.

Faith puts a strengthening plaster to the back of courage.—*Spurgeon.*

Be careful for *nothing*, in the calm and holy assurance that God is, for our sakes, caring for *everything.*—*Pridham.*

Faith is the soul's eye, which must be fixed upon Christ; the soul's hand, to lay hold upon Christ; the soul's mouth, to feed upon Christ.—*Bury.*

It is not for us, who are passengers, to meddle with the chart and with the compass. Let that all-skillful Pilot alone with his own work.—*Hall.*

Faith trembling, but holding fast! The firmest thing in this inferior world is a believing soul.—*Wilberforce.*

Faith says to me generally, "Vast and unspeakable blessings are prepared by God for his faithful servants." Hope says, "Those blessings are for *me.*" Love says, "I will therefore run to receive them."—*St.Bernard.*

We must trust God where we cannot trace him.—*Adam.*

There is nothing like faith to help at a pinch: faith dissolves doubt as the sun drives away mists. There are times when some graces may be out of use, but there is no time wherein faith can be said to be so. Faith, though weak, is still faith; a glimmering taper if not a glowing torch; but the taper may give light as truly as the torch, though not so brightly.—*H. Muller.*

FAITH CHAPTER—Hebrews xi.

QUESTION—*How can man be justified with God?*—Job xxv. 4.

By faith, for it is written, "A man is justified by faith."—Rom. iii. 28. Christ having died for us, God can justify the vilest sinner and yet He Himself be just. If there had been no cross this could never have been. Hence our glory in the "Christ crucified."

Sayings about Songs.

Please don't *over sing.* Now and then I hear a voice so far above the rest that the melody is spoiled. Loud singing is not the most effective, lest it be by the entire company, who must "shout as they sing." The low, rich, full, round, penetrating notes strike the heart chords quickest.

O FOR A FAITH.

O for a faith that will not shrink,
Though pressed by every foe,
That will not tremble on the brink
Of any earthly woe;

That will not murmur or complain
Beneath the chast'ning rod,
But, in the hour of grief or pain,
Will lean upon its God;—

A faith that shines more bright and clear
When tempests rage without;
That when in danger knows no fear,
In darkness feels no doubt;—

Lord, give us such a faith as this,
And then, whate'er may come,
We'll taste. e'en here, the hallowed bliss
Of an eternal home.

PROVERB—"*Withhold not good from them to whom it is due, when it is in the power of thine hand to do it.*"—iii. 27.

J<u>ESUS</u>, LOVER · OF MY · SOUL.

I know He loves me, for He died for me.
Oh, the heights and depths, length and breadth of the love of Jesus!
He loves me with all my faults.
He saves me from all my sins.
He keeps me when I cannot keep myself.
Friend, dost thou love Him?
Wilt thou love and serve Him from this hour?

Gems of Thought.

The holy Sabbath, the house of the Lord, the preaching of the word, the melody of psalms, the offering of prayers, the sacraments, are green pastures, where the Shepherd feeds his flock.—*Stevenson.*

Art thou a Christian? Then art thou wedded to Christ, and the law of marriage binds thee to him: let all see that you love your husband, his house, his provision, his company, and his commands.

The *habit* of telling Jesus everything is of itself an incalculable blessing. The effect of thus telling him brings us into his immediate presence, and is the greatest possible safeguard and protection.

A Christian is the best commentary on the New Testament. But there are not enough such commentaries to send out. The edition is small.—*Beecher.*

VICTORIOUS CHAPTER—Luke xxiv.

QUESTION—*Doth not he see my ways and count all my steps?*
—Job xxxi. 4.

Every step he counts, and all our ways are known unto him. More than that, we take no step without he himself being by our side. God is not only our guide but our rearward.

Sayings about Songs.

What joy it will be to have a family reunion in heaven, and once more gather about for an hour's sacred song. To invite at such a time David, Paul and Silas, indeed all the singers of the Bible, will add much to the occasion.

JESUS, LOVER OF MY SOUL.

Jesus, lover of my soul.
    Let me to thy bosom fly,
While the nearer waters roll.
    While the tempest still is high:
Hide me, oh, my Saviour, hide,
    Till the storm of life is past;
Safe into the haven guide.
    Oh, receive my soul at last.

Other refuge have I none,
    Hangs my helpless soul on thee;
Leave, oh, leave me not alone,
    Still support and comfort me,
All my trust on thee is stayed,
    All my help from thee I bring;
Cover my defenceless head
    With the shadow of thy wing.

Thou, O Christ, art all I want:
    More than all in thee I find:
Raise the fallen, cheer the faint,
    Heal the sick, and lead the blind.
Just and holy is thy name,
    I am all unrighteousness;
Vile and full of sin I am,
    Thou art full of truth and grace.

Plenteous grace with thee is found—
    Grace to cover all my sin;
Let the healing streams abound;
    Make and keep me pure within.
Thou of life the fountain art,
    Freely let me take of thee;
Spring thou up within my heart,
    Rise to all eternity.

PROVERB—*"Faithful are the wounds of a friend; but the kisses of an enemy are deceitful."*—xxvii. 6.

THE GLORIOUS GOSPEL.

"Gospel" means, Good news for the lost.
It's not the Gospel of man, but the Gospel of Christ.
Believe the Gospel and win heaven.
Reject the Gospel and lose heaven.
This must be the message of every Christian.
Are you a believer in the Gospel of Christ?
Do you receive or reject Christ?

✧Gems of Thought.✧

The gospel of salvation is the world's only hope. Ethical teaching can never reach to the depth of the evil. I have no harsh word to utter against any who are honestly trying to do good to their fellow men; but when you can dispense with sunlight, and make your wheat fields flourish by the agency of moonshine, then you may expect to break the power of sin by mere ethical culture.—*Prof. Fisher, of Yale College.*

The beauty of that holiness which is enshrined in the four brief biographies of the Man of Nazareth has done more, and will do more to regenerate the world and bring in everlasting righteousness, than all the other agencies put together.—*Chalmers.*

If we do not see the golden thread through all the Bible marking out Christ, we read the Scripture without the key.—*Cecil.*

Love strong as death, nay, stronger,
Love mightier than the grave;
Broad as the earth, and longer
Than ocean's widest wave:
This is the love that sought us,
This is the love that bought us,
This is the love that brought us
To gladdest day from saddest night,
From deepest shame to glory bright.

MILLENNIUM CHAPTER—Rev. xx.

QUESTION—*Is it well with thee?* —2 Kings iv. 26.

That is, is it well with thy soul; if there be illness there, if the soul be sin-sick, the whole man is wrong. In such case no one can help but the Great Physician.

Thou hast dealt well with thy servant, O Lord, according unto thy word.—Ps. cxix. 65.
It shall be well with them that fear God.—Eccles. viii. 12.

✧Sayings about Songs.✧

Some can't sing here. I doubt if it will be so in heaven. There it will be as natural to sing as here it is to breathe. I can't tell one note from another now. It will not always be so. There I shall vie with the best of them.

HAIL TO THE BRIGHTNESS.

Hail to the brightness of Zion's glad morning!
Joy to the lands that in darkness have lain!
Hushed be the accents of sorrow and mourn-
Zion in triumph begins her mild reign. [ing;

Hail to the brightness of Zion's glad morning!
Long by the prophets of Israel foretold:
Hail to the millions from bondage returning;
Gentiles and Jews the blest vision behold.

PROVERB—"*Look not thou upon the wine when it is red, when it giveth his color in the cup, when it moveth itself aright. At the last it biteth like a serpent, and stingeth like an adder.*"—xxiii. 31, 32.

CHRIST OUR KEEPER.

Kept in temptation, not from temptation.
Preserved blameless and presented faultless.
Kept from the snares of Satan.
Preserved from the spotting of the world.
We cannot keep ourselves, but Christ can keep us.
Is Christ your keeper?
Will you let him save, then keep you?

Gems of Thought.

As the most dangerous winds may enter at little openings, so the devil never enters more dangerously than by little unobserved incidents, which seem to be nothing, yet insensibly open the heart to great temptations.
— *Wesley.*

Rather do what is nothing to the purpose than be idle; that the devil may find thee doing. The bird that sits is easily shot, when flyers 'scape the fowler.— *Quarles.*

He was tempted that he might triumph, and he triumphed that "He might teach by his example those whom he defends by his power."— *Ford.*

Nothing relative to God's children is too great, nothing too little for his attention. He has his eye continually, as upon every individual person of his family, so upon every circumstance that relates either to their souls or bodies.— *Wesley.*

My Saviour, 'mid life's varying scenes
　　Be thou my stay;
Guide me through each perplexing path
　　To perfect day.
In weakness and in sin I stand;
Still faith can clasp its mighty hand,
And follow at thy dear command.
　　　　—*Elizabeth E. A. Godwin.*

FEAR NOT CHAPTER—Isaiah xli.

QUESTION—*Who is he that will harm you, if ye be followers of that which is good?*　　—1 Pet. iii. 13.

No one, for God will make our very enemies to be at peace with us. "The righteous shall never be moved. The angel of the Lord encampeth round about those who fear God, and delivereth them."

Because thou hast made the Lord, which is my refuge, even the Most High, thy habitation, there shall no evil befall thee.—Ps. xci. 9, 10. There shall no evil happen to the just.—Prov. xii. 21.

Sayings about Songs.

I hate to see a man look hard and savage and cold when singing. Put cheer and good humor into your face, my friend. It's not a nice thing to see a man's face in a rage when singing of love and God. I think it must be habit. Well, let's quit now looking sour.

SUN OF MY SOUL.

Sun of my soul, thou Saviour dear,
It is not night if thou be near:
O may no earthborn cloud arise
To hide thee from thy servant's eyes.

When the soft dews of kindly sleep
My wearied eyelids gently steep,
Be my last thought, how sweet to rest
Forever on my Saviour's breast.

Abide with me from morn till eve,
For without thee I cannot live;
Abide with me when night is nigh,
For without thee I dare not die.

If some poor wandering child of thine
Have spurned to-day the voice divine,
Now, Lord, the gracious work begin;
Let him no more lie down in sin.

PROVERB—"*When a man's ways please the Lord, he maketh even his enemies to be at peace with him.*"—xvi. 7.

THE FRUIT OF THE SPIRIT.

The first fruit of the Spirit is LOVE.
Where the Spirit is, there is joy and peace.
Our bodies are the temple of the Holy Spirit.
We all are to be rooted and grounded in love.
By our fruit bearing we are known.
What has been the fruitage of your life?
Who wants to "be filled with the Spirit?"

Gems of Thought.

Sour godliness is not the fruit of the love of Christ. Sweetness, gentleness, and pity, are the qualities with which he endows his disciples. It is imperfect virtue which is sour, severe, and implacable. Perfect virtue is meek, affable, and compassionate. It thinks of nothing but doing good, "of bearing one another's burdens." There is no acidity in pure Christ love.

Fruit might as well be expected from a tree without a root, as meekness and temperance without the indwelling Spirit. Gal. v. 23. Religion, in the very essence of it, is nothing short of holy tempers.—*Wesley.*

Pure religion and undefiled is "minister-ing;" not the other thing, "being ministered unto." It is handing over the morning paper to another for first perusal. It is vacating a pleasant seat by the fire for one who comes in chilled. It is giving the most restful arm-chair or sofa-corner for one who is weary. It is "moving up" in the pew to let the new-comer sit down by the entrance. It is rising from your place to darken the blind when the sun's rays stream in too brightly upon some face in the circle. It is giving up your comfort and convenience every time for the comfort and convenience of another. This is at once true courtesy and real Christianity.—*Rev. A. L. Stone.*

PROFESSOR'S CHAPTER—Luke xii.

QUESTION—*How oft shall my brother sin against me, and I forgive him?* —Matt. xviii. 21.

Four hundred and ninety times, at least, then as often as you would like to be forgiven yourself. I say not unto thee, Until seven times seven; but, Until seventy times seven —Matt. xviii. 22. Forgive, and ye shall be forgiven; . . . with the same measure that ye mete withal it shall be measured to you again.—Luke vi. 37, 38.

Sayings about Songs.

I want to hear the seven great songs of the Bible repeated by the original authors. No one can sing them like they. In heaven voices never wear out, and Miriam's song of the Red Sea will be as fresh as the day when sung to the Israelitish host.

FRUIT BEARING.

A charge to keep I have,
A God to glorify;
A never-dying soul to save,
And fit it for the sky.
To serve the present age,
My calling to fulfil,—
O may it all my powers engage,
To do my Master's will.

Arm me with jealous care,
As in thy sight to live;
And oh, thy servant, Lord, prepare,
A strict account to give.
Help me to watch and pray,
And on thyself rely,
Assured, if I my trust betray,
I shall forever die.

PROVERB—*"Surely the churning of milk bringeth forth butter, and the wringing of the nose bringeth forth blood: so the forcing of wrath bringeth forth strife."*—xxx. 33. 29

ALL · FOR · JESUS.

Three mighty words.

If truly spoken they make mighty men.

God is never satisfied with half-hearted service.

A life thus lived "All for Jesus" is a very happy one.

Write these words on the opening fly leaf of your Bible.

From to-day who will make it ALL FOR JESUS?

Who here, unsaved, will join the number?

Gems of Thought.

Lean on Jesus, and he will rest you. Labor for Jesus, and he will bless you. Live for Jesus and your soul shall mount up as on an eagle's wing; you shall run and never weary, you shall walk arm in arm with him and never faint.

To expect a young tree to produce abundance of fruit, before the branches are come forth, and spread with strength to bear it, is not reasonable.—*John Churchman.*

Avoid society, books, thoughts which would prove temptations to you. This is to *watch.*— *Wesley.*

Remember, an Achan in the camp troubled Israel, and they were smitten before their enemies. So one idol left in your heart may trouble you.—*McCheyne.*

Whate'er I fondly counted mine,
  To thee, my Lord, I here restore;
Gladly I all for thee resign;
  Give me thyself, I ask no more.
    —*Charles Wesley.*

BEAUTIFUL CHAPTER—Matt. v.

QUESTION—*Why doth thy heart carry thee away?*—Job xv. 12.

Because it is not right. It is of the world, worldly. Its loves are all of the world. Its desires are all of the flesh. Its thoughts are all of self and sense. Pray now this prayer of the Psalmist, "Create in me a clean heart, O God."

Sayings about Songs.

If our ears were open we would hear the music of light, the song of the wind, and the melody of the hills and the mountains as they break forth into strains of quiet praise. There is singing about us that we can never hear till our vile body is changed and made like unto His own glorious body.

NONE OF SELF.

O the bitter pain and sorrow
  That a time could ever be,
‖: When I proudly said to Jesus,
  ‖: "All of self and none of thee." :‖

Yet he found me; I beheld him
  Bleeding on th' accursed tree;
‖: And my wistful heart said faintly,
  ‖: "Some of self and some of thee." :‖

Day by day his tender mercy
  Healing, helping, full and free,
‖: Brought me lower, while I whispered,
  ‖: "Less of self and more of thee." :‖

Higher than the highest heaven,
  Deeper than the deepest sea,
‖: Lord, thy love at last has conquered,
  ‖: "*None* of self and *all* of thee." :‖

PROVERB—*"He that hath pity upon the poor lendeth unto the Lord; and that which he hath given will he pay him again."*—xix. 17.

ASSURANCE.

Look up the "we knows" of Scripture.
Assurance and Peace are fellow travellers.
Assurance is not a look at self, but a look at Christ.
The first epistle of John should be read with this theme.
Doubters and idlers deserve no assurance.
Upon what does your assurance of salvation rest?
Can you say, "I know I am saved?"

Gems of Thought.

The Bible stands like a way-mark on the high road to eternity, and is intended simply to announce what is truth, and the way to its dwelling-place, but not to make known to the traveller all the details of the city to which he is journeying.—*J. A. James.*

How is it possible to *receive the seal* without feeling the impression.—*Downhame.*

If a man would know whether the sun shines or not, he need not climb to the sky, for he may behold the beams on earth. So, wouldst thou know whether thy name be written in heaven, never essay to get the view of God's own book; thou shalt find the beams of that grace in thyself.

The testimony of the Spirit is an *inward impression on the soul*, whereby the *Spirit of God directly* witnesses to *my* spirit, that I am a child of God.—*Wesley.*

ASSURANCE CHAPTER—1 John iii.

QUESTION—*On whom dost thou trust?* —Isa. xxxvi. 5.

O Lord God, thou art my trust. — Ps. lxxi. 5.

Trust in him at all times; ye people, pour out your heart before him: God is a refuge for us.—Ps. lxii. 8.

The Lord will be a refuge for the oppressed, a refuge in times of trouble: and they that know thy name will put their trust in thee: for thou, Lord, hast not forsaken them that seek thee.—Ps. ix. 9, 10.

Sayings about Songs.

To sing one don't have to know all the notes and bars and clefs, with sharps and flats. To be sure it is good to know them, but instinctively with nearly every one there is a tendency to song. Just keep at it and you will be able to carry a tune by and by.

KNOWLEDGE OF SALVATION.

Amazing grace! how sweet the sound,
That saved a wretch like me!
I once was lost, but now am found,
Was blind, but now I see.
'Twas grace that taught my heart to fear,
And grace my fears relieved;
How precious did that grace appear
The hour I first believed!

Through many dangers, toils, and snares,
I have already come;
'Tis grace hath brought me safe thus far,
And grace will lead me home.
The Lord has promised good to me,
His word my hope secures;
He will my shield and portion be
As long as life endures.

PROVERB—"*Better is a little with fear of the Lord, than great treasure and trouble therewith.*"—xv. 16.

HOPE, THE · ANCHOR OF · THE · SOUL.

My hope is in Christ alone.
Hopes never fail when founded on the Rock.
A sure hope makes a sure heaven.
A false hope makes a sure hell.
Be able to say, "Mine is a steadfast hope."
Upon what is thy hope founded, my friend?
Sinner, hast thou a hope in Jesus Christ?

Gems of Thought.

"A *lively* hope," because it makes the Christian active and zealous for God. They are men of metal who have it; you may expect more from them than from many others, and not be deceived.—*Gurnall.*

If thy hope be anything worth it will purify thee from thy sins.—*Joseph Alleine.*

The Bible writes hope over the darkest fields of life. Man, above all things, needs hope, and the Bible is the character of hope, the message of the God of revelation, who alone is the God of hope.—*Canon Westcott.*

When St. Augustine's mother lamented the ill courses that her son took in his youth, the priest (St. Ambrose) to whom she imparted her sorrows said, "The son of such tears cannot perish."—*Donne.*

What a blessed hope is ours! it serves as an anchor at sea and a helmet in battle.

Hope which on God is firmly grounded,
Will never fail, nor be confounded.
—*Thomas Ellwood.*

HOPE CHAPTER—Hebrews vi.

QUESTION—*Men and brethren, what shall we do?*—Acts xi. 37.

There is but one thing to do in this world of need and place of helplessness. The saint and the sinner in their distresses should turn to the omnipotent and loving God. Hear their words: Come, and let us return unto the Lord; for he hath torn, and he will heal us; he hath smitten, and he will bind us up.—Hosea vi. 1. He healeth the broken in heart, and bindeth up their wounds.—Ps. cxlvii. 3.

Sayings about Songs.

The Alpine herdsman at sunset from his horn gives forth "Praise the Lord God," which is taken up by others, till far and near the hills echo the words, then at last as the sound dies away "Good night" sounds forth, and the day is closed with this benediction.

THE GREAT HOPE.

Watchman, tell me, does the morning
Of fair Zion's glory dawn?
Have the signs that mark its coming
Yet upon thy pathway shone?
Pilgrim, yes, arise, look round thee,
Light is breaking in the skies;
Gird thy bridal robes around thee,
Morning dawns, arise, arise!

Watchman, see, the light is beaming,
Brighter still upon the way;
Signs through all the earth are gleaming,
Omens of the coming day
When the Jubal trumpet sounding,
Shall awake from earth and sea,
All the saints of God now sleeping,
Clad in immortality.

PROVERB—"*Hope deferred maketh the heart sick: but when the desire cometh it is a tree of life.*"—xiii. 12.

BACKSLIDING.

There is no peace to a backslidden heart.
God says, "I would thou wert cold or hot."
Read Hosea xiv. 4 with Psalm li.
Hear the trumpet call of grace—"Return."
God can be satisfied with nothing but the whole heart.
Have you wandered from Christ's fold?
Who will return from their backslidings now?

❖Gems of Thought.❖

Israel's apostasy began when she made affinity with the people of the land, and confessed that she was not strong enough to drive them out. The apostasy of the Church begins at the same point. Whenever the Church makes affinity with the world, and becomes a respecter of persons, going after one class to the neglect of another, and confesses, either by declaration or action, that she is not equal to the task of evangelizing the world, her power is gone, and she must from that point decline.—*G. F. Pentecost.*

A Christian never falls suddenly from an advanced Christian life to barrenness or open sin. The stages in the descent are slow and often almost imperceptible.

Don't let the heart backslide; if it does, the life will soon show it. Things always go wrong *inside* first, then the evidence is not long wanting.

None will have such a dreadful parting with the Lord at the last day as those who went half way with him and then left him. Even after the shipwreck we try the sea again.—*Seneca.*

Lot's wife looked back, and God never gave her leave to look forward again.—*Donne.*

BACKSLIDER'S CHAPTER—Jer. iii.

QUESTION—*How much owest thou unto my Lord?*
—Luke xvi. 5.

Without doubt all we have, for it is written, "Thou owest me even thine own self besides." Our money belongs to him, our time and strength are his. When wilt thou pay what thou owest? answer, "Now!"

❖Sayings about Songs.❖

Every revival usually has its one battle hymn, one song that touches the hearts more than any other, often it is a new hymn, sometimes an old one. Music plays no small part in the scheme of redemption.

A CLOSER WALK WITH GOD.

O for a closer walk with God,
 A calm and heavenly frame;
A light to shine upon the road
 That leads me to the Lamb.

Where is the blessedness I knew
 When first I saw the Lord?
Where is the soul-refreshing view
 Of Jesus and his word?

What peaceful hours I once enjoyed!
 How sweet their memory still!
But they have left an aching void
 The world can never fill.

The dearest idol I have known,
 Whate'er that idol be,
Help me to tear it from thy throne,
 And worship only thee.

PROVERB—"*The fruit of the righteous is a tree of life; and he that winneth souls is wise.*"—xi. 30.

SINNERS SEEKING CHRIST.

They find Him who seek prayerfully and earnestly.
Take the path of humility and reach for the cross.
All *may* find Him, some do find Him.
It is a heart search with the lamp of faith.
Some seek Him too late.
Have you found the Saviour?
Will you seek Him this hour?

❖Gems of Thought.❖

A number of young men were walking down Princes street, Edinburgh, one evening, all of them treading the path that leadeth to death. As they passed along, a church clock suddenly struck ten. The thought instantly occurred to one of them, "This is the time when at home father is taking down the Bible for family prayers." He stopped short, and said, "I can't go with you." They enquired why not, and tried to laugh him into going; but he turned and went home, and there on his knees he prayed and wept before God. It was the sinner arrested, convicted, saved. The voice of the clock was God's voice to him; he heard, and obeyed. But how many there are who stop their ears to every call, and rush on to eternal ruin! Yet a little longer the voice still cries to the unsaved: "To-day, if ye will hear his voice, harden not your hearts."

A man may go to heaven without health, without riches, without honors, without learning, without friends; but he can never get there without Christ.—*Dyer.*

SEEKING CHAPTER—Amos v.

QUESTION—*To whom will ye flee for help?* —Isa. x. 3.

To the Mighty to Save, of course.
In the shadow of thy wings will I make my refuge, until these calamities be overpast.—Ps. lvii. 1.

He shall cover thee with his feathers, and under his wings shalt thou trust: his truth shall be thy shield and buckler.—Ps. xci. 4.

❖Sayings about Songs.❖

A word for the organ boy. He will have no pumping in the New Jerusalem, and it's quite likely his place will be as high, if not higher, than he or she who now handles the keys. What if all the strains ever heard by him should there be reproduced by his own hand? It may be so.

FAVORED BY JESUS.

1 Arise, my soul, arise;
  Shake off thy guilty fears;
  The bleeding sacrifice
  In my behalf appears:
Before the throne my Surety stands,
My name is written on his hands.

2 He ever lives above
  For me to intercede,
  His all-redeeming love,

His precious blood, to plead;
His blood atoned for all our race,
And sprinkles now the throne of grace.

3 My God is reconciled;
  His pard'ning voice I hear:
  He owns me for his child;
  I can no longer fear:
With confidence I now draw nigh,
And Father, Abba, Father, cry.

PROVERB—"*He that gathereth in summer is a wise son: but he that sleepeth in harvest is a son that causeth shame.*"—x. 5.

Theme 32.

REGENERATION, OR·THE NEW·BIRTH.

Ye must be born again.
The Spirit alone is the author of the new birth.
We believe, He regenerates.
By regeneration we get Christ's nature.
Truth is God's instrument in this great work.
Have you been born again?
"How old art thou in Christ?"

Gems of Thought.

"No obstacle can close the kingdom of heaven against him who desires to enter it.
Some persons, instead of "putting off the old man," dress him up in a new shape.—*St. Bernard.*
If religion has done nothing for your temper it has done nothing for your soul.—*Clayton.*
A christian mother does not give birth to a christian child; it is not a natural but a spiritual birth which makes a Christian.—*Tertullian.*
What are marks of the new birth? So to *believe* in God, through Christ, as "not to commit sin," and to enjoy at all times " the peace of God;" so to *hope* in God, through Christ, as to have not only the "testimony of a good conscience," but also the Spirit of God "bearing witness with yours;" so to *love* God as you never loved any creature, and "all men as ourselves."—*Wesley.*
The calm and quiet conversions of the eunuch and Cornelius stand in contrast with the violent conversion of St. Paul. There is the same contrast between the conversion of Lydia and that of the jailer. According to the diversity in the recipient is the Spirit's working. Why, then, insist upon the same process for every individual? Or why judge others by ourselves?—*Ford.*

NEW BIRTH CHAPTER—John iii.

QUESTION—*What sayest thou of thyself?* —John i. 22.

So many profess to be good when they know they are sinful that this question has special weight. Let the same come home to the individual heart. How answer you?
Why not adopt the prodigal's words, "Father, I have sinned against heaven and before thee, and am no more worthy to be called thy son."—Luke xv. 18, 19.

Sayings about Songs.

I'd not have a singer in my church that sang "Just as I am, without one plea" on Sunday night to the congregation, and Monday night in "Pinafore" at the theatre. It's the devil's advertisement for the sale of tickets.

YE MUST BE BORN AGAIN.

How solemn are the words,
And yet to faith how plain,
Which Jesus uttered while on earth—
"Ye must be born again."

"Ye must be born again!"
For so hath God decreed:
No reformation will suffice—
'Tis life poor sinners need.

"Ye must be born again!"
And life in Christ must have:
In vain the soul elsewhere may go—
'Tis he alone can save.

"Ye must be born again!"
Or never enter heaven;
'Tis only blood-washed ones are there—
The ransomed and forgiven.

PROVERB—*"Buy the truth, and sell it not; also wisdom, and instruction, and understanding."*—xxiii. 23.

35

SANCTIFICATION.

Sanctification, consecration, and holiness are one.
Christ is our Sanctification.
The Holy Ghost is our Sanctifier.
It means "set apart for service."
Romans xii. is to be read with this theme.
Have you studied this bible subject?
Do you know its full meaning?

✥Gems of Thought.✥

The true test of love to God is joyful obedience and self surrender.

How wise and happy is the man who continually endeavors to be as holy in the day of life as he wishes to be found in the day of death.—*Thomas a Kempis.*

Holiness is an unselfing of ourselves.—*F. W. Faber.*

A man's life is an appendix to his heart.—*South.*

Christian perfection is *not* freedom from ignorance, infirmities, nor temptation.

There may be growth in knowledge without a growth in holiness, but there can be no growth in holiness without a growth in knowledge; there is, indeed, a connection between a growth in knowledge of gospel truth and real progress in holiness; hence the apostle said: "This I pray, that your *love* may *abound* yet more and more in all knowledge and in all judgment, that ye may approve the things that are excellent, that ye may be sincere and without offense till the day of Christ, being *filled with the fruits of righteousness* which are by Jesus Christ to the praise and glory of God."

SEPARATION CHAPTER—2 Cor. vi.

QUESTION—*Wherewith shall I come before the Lord, and bow myself before the high God?* —Micah vi. 6.

This is a great question. Many come before God irreverently. Let us not do so. There must be humility, contrition of heart, a broken spirit instead of pride. Ps. li. 17 is a verse for this question, and with it should go Ps. xxxiv. 18.

✥Sayings about Songs.✥

What music is proper for the church? I answer, all that is devotional, all that has in it the power of uplifting the soul, and rule out all else. Especially keep from the organ keys the silly, frivolous pieces of the world, which may call to some minds the dance or the theatre.

A PURE HEART.

O for a heart to praise my God,
A heart from sin set free!
A heart that always feels thy blood,
So freely spilt for me!

A heart resigned, submissive, meek,
My great Redeemer's throne;
Where only Christ is heard to speak,
Where Jesus reigns alone.

O for a lowly, contrite heart,
Believing, true, and clean,
Which neither life nor death can part
From him that dwells within!

A heart in every thought renewed,
And full of love divine;
Perfect, and right, and pure, and good,
A copy, Lord, of thine.

PROVERB—"*The curse of the Lord is in the house of the wicked: but he blesseth the habitation of the just.*"—iii. 33.

THE RESURRECTION.

Because Christ lives we shall live also.
Resurrection—a word for three worlds to read.
With this theme the grave loses its victory.
Our bodies made like unto His glorious body.
At the last—both soul and body redeemed.
What part will you have in the resurrection?
Will yours be a resurrection unto life?

❧ Gems of Thought. ❧

He raises the daughter of Jairus from the dead, the widow's son from his coffin, Lazarus from his grave, the dead saints at Jerusalem from their rottenness; that it might appear no degree of death can hinder his overruling, *divine* command.—*Hall.*

If man can by art make, of ashes, the curious glass, why cannot an omnipotent God, of dust and ashes, make glorified bodies as fair as crystal.—*Lowe.*

There will then be the reappearance of every human being that ever moved on the face of the earth. The old man who sunk beneath the burden of years, and the young man who perished in his prime, and the infant who just opened his eyes on a sinful and sad world, and then closed them as though terrified—all reproduced, though all had been dispersed like chaff before the hurricane—all receiving their original elements, though these elements had been the playthings of the winds, and the fuel for the flames, and the foam upon the waters.—*Melvill.*

RESURRECTION CHAPTER—1 Cor. xv.

QUESTION—*How are the dead raised up?* —1 Cor. xv. 35.

With bodies that never tire; with brain that never wearies; with limbs that never ache. The same kind of body that Jesus rose with we shall have. It will be a glorified body. All this will be done at the voice of him who raised the dead when with us on earth. He will come again thus to speak.

❧ Sayings about Songs. ❧

I wish God had let us hear the singing of the angels, though he kept our eyes from seeing them. This he has reserved for our glad surprise in the day when we shall see him. Maybe if we could hear them we would be discouraged and not try our hand at it.

THE RISEN CHRIST.

Look, ye saints! the sight is glorious,
  See the "Man of sorrows" now;
From the fight return victorious,
Every knee to him shall bow.
  Crown him! crown him!
Crowns become the victor's brow.

Crown the Saviour, angels crown him,
  Rich the trophies Jesus brings;
In the seat of power enthrone him,
While the vault of heaven rings.
  Crown him! crown him!
Crown the Saviour "King of kings."

Hark! those bursts of acclamation!
  Hark! those loud, triumphant chords!
Jesus takes the highest station:
Oh, what joy the sight affords!
  Crown him! crown him!
"King of kings, and Lord of lords."

Sinners in derision crowned him,
  Mocking thus the Saviour's claim;
Saints and angels crowd around him,
Own his title, praise his name,
  Crown him! crown him!
Spread abroad the Victor's fame.

PROVERB—"*Honor the Lord with thy substance, and with the first fruits of all thine increase: so shall thy barns be filled with plenty, and thy presses shall burst out with new wine.*"—iii. 9, 10.

37

CHRISTIAN GIVING.

Some give little, some give much.
Many give nothing at all.
The first giving is the giving of our heart.
God loveth a cheerful giver.
Everything we have comes from God.
Who will make an offering unto the Lord?
What sinner will give God his heart?

Gems of Thought.

The generous never enjoy their possessions so much as when others are made partakers of them.—*Sir W. Jones.*

Had the widow not given her mite the day she did to the treasury, but delayed it a week, how much would she herself, and the whole Christian Church, have lost by the delay!

The best thing to give to your enemy is forgiveness; to an opponent, tolerance; to a friend, your heart; to your child, a good example; to a father, deference; to your mother, conduct that will make her proud of you; to yourself, respect; to all men, charity.—*Mrs. Balfour.*

Yes! you will find people ready enough to do the "Good Samaritan" without the oil and the twopence.—*Sydney Smith.*

God does not say he loves an open-handed, liberal, munificent giver, but a *cheerful* giver. Boaz did not give Ruth a quantity of corn at once, but kept her gleaning. That is the best charity which so relieves another's poverty as still continues their industry.—*Fuller.*

"I have known," says St. Basil, "men who have fasted, and prayed, and groaned, and yet would not give the afflicted a farthing." But God said to Cornelius, "Thy prayers *and thine alms* are come up for a memorial before God."—*Barrow.*

TITHING CHAPTER—Malachi iii.

QUESTION—*Shall we give, or shall we not give?* —Mark xii. 15.

How answer you here; with your money, with your time, with your talents, with your service. Freely ye have received, freely give. —Matt. x. 8.

Not grudgingly, or of necessity; for God loveth a cheerful giver. And God is able to make all grace abound toward you; that ye, always having all sufficiency in all things, may abound to every good work.— 2 Cor. ix. 7, 8.

Sayings about Songs.

There will be "no trouble in the choir" up in heaven. In the passing of Jordan that will be all washed out of the peculiar saints. We will need to get to the City of Gold before singers will all prefer one above another.

GIVE TO JESUS.

Bring the tithes into the storehouse;
  Let there be a bounteous store;
Then I'll pour you out a blessing
  Till you have no room for more.
Prove me now, ye doubting children,
  Let your faith attest my word;
Trust your welfare to the Saviour,
  Seek to glorify your Lord.

Stand no longer idly waiting;
  Prayer unproved hath little power;
Vain your longing, without effort,
  To advance the promised hour.
Bring your offerings to the altar;
  Tithes of money, work and prayer;
Yea, with earnest consecration,
  Give yourselves to service there.

PROVERB—"*He that giveth to the poor shall not lack: but he that hideth his eyes shall have many a curse.*"—xxviii. 27.

L‒OVE, THE NAME OF G‒OD.

There is no love like the love of God.
Christ died for jerusalem sinners.
"I have loved thee with an everlasting love."
If you love Christ keep his commandments.
Behold what love, "we are the sons God."
Who will pray, "More love to thee, O Christ"?
Do you love God? If not, why not?

‒❖Gems of Thought.❖‒

In love feel that you owe so much that you cannot pay all at once; be always paying as you are always owing.

Tenderness of affection toward the most abandoned sinners is the highest instance of a godlike soul.—*Law.*

Tell men that God is love; that right is right, and wrong is wrong.—*Robertson.*

Our Saviour places the love of God at the head of all morality, telling us that it is *"the first and great commandment."* St. Paul places it at the rear, telling us that *"the end of the commandment is charity."* So, then,

it is first and last, the beginning and the end.

Those who love the Lord find in our hearts a home.—*Robertson.*

The devils, we are told, believe and tremble. Our part is to believe and love. But it is hard to convince people that nothing short of this can be true Christian faith.—*Guesses at Truth.*

So when we are weak and wretched,
By our sins weighed down, distressed,
Then it is that God's great patience
Holds us closest, loves us best.
—*Saxe Holm.*

CHARITY CHAPTER—I Cor. xiii.

QUESTION—*Will God in very deed dwell with men on the earth?*
—2 Chron. vi. 18.

Yes, he will; the Comforter abides with us forever. Jesus dwells in the heart of the believing one. "Thus says the high and lofty One that inhabiteth eternity, whose name is holy; I dwell in the high and holy place, with him also that is of a contrite and humble spirit, to revive the spirit of the humble, and to revive the heart of the contrite ones."
—Isa. lvii. 15.

‒❖Sayings about Songs.❖‒

When the tide of song rolls up from the pew to the pulpit with majestic swell there is a courage and boldness given to the preacher he knew not of before. His sermon will have enthusiasm in it. There will be in that discourse meat for men and milk for babes.

THE LOVE OF GOD.

How tedious and tasteless the hours
When Jesus no longer I see! [flowers,
Sweet prospects, sweet birds, and sweet
Have all lost their sweetness to me;
The midsummer sun shines but dim,
The fields strive in vain to look gay;
But when I am happy in him,
December's as pleasant as May.

His name yields the richest perfume,
And sweeter than music his voice;
His presence disperses my gloom,
And makes all within me rejoice;
I should, were he always thus nigh,
Have nothing to wish or to fear;
No mortal so happy as I,
My summer would last all the year.

PROVERB—*"He that is slow to anger is better than the mighty, and he that ruleth his spirit than he that taketh a city."*—xvi. 32.

CHRIST SEEKING SINNERS.

This was His business in coming to the world.
Unless He finds us we are lost forever.
He knocks at the door of every human heart.
Many have opened and let Him in.
A sheep lost—a Shepherd seeking—a wanderer found.
Has Jesus found you?
What soul desires to be found of Him to-day?

Gems of Thought.

Roofs arched with gold, and palaces adorned with marble, are no fit abode for the Most High; but the humble, contrite spirit he has chosen as his temple; there the Holy Ghost dwells.

The Lord's call to the Presence Chamber means only that further work here was not ours to do.—*Anna Warner.*

The God who loves the penitent sinner hates his sins, and is determined that he shall hate them, and be separated from them: this is good news to a sin-sick soul.

Wonder of wonders, Jesus loved me—
A wretch—lost, ruined, sunk in misery;
He sought me—found me—raised me—set me free.

SHEPHERD'S CHAPTER—John x.

QUESTION—*Lord, what wilt thou have me to do?* —Acts ix. 6.

Here is a question that thousands of Christians, now idle, need to ask. The perishing are all about us; the needy are on every hand; the heathen world now stretch out their hands to us for gospel light. Paul asked the question, and in the fulfilment of the answer thousands heard the story of the cross by him and those whom he set at work.

Sayings about Songs.

I want the time to come, and come quick, when the songs of the sanctuary shall be the songs of the street. Singing kindles emotion, but sad are some of these emotions, for the same is produced by low, vulgar songs of the hall. Let us get more of the people singing good songs.—Songs of Zion.

LOVE DIVINE.

Love divine, all love excelling,
Joy of heaven, to earth come down!
Fix in us thy humble dwelling;
All thy faithful mercies crown.
Jesus, thou art all compassion,
Pure, unbounded love thou art;
Visit us with thy salvation;
Enter every trembling heart.

Breathe, O breathe thy loving Spirit
Into every troubled breast!
Let us all in thee inherit,
Let us find that second rest.
Take away our bent to sinning;
Alpha and Omega be;
End of faith, as its beginning,
Set our hearts at liberty.

PROVERB—"*A word fitly spoken is like apples of gold in pictures of silver.*"
—xxv. 11.

Theme 38.

THE BLOOD OF CHRIST SHED FOR ME.

Great sinners saved by the great sacrifice.
Scarlet sins made white as wool.
Blood must be shed for remission of sins.
The Lamb of God is the Lion of Judah.
He is our Passover, who believe.
Who can say, "I know He died for me"?
Are you washed in the blood of the Lamb?

❖Gems of Thought.❖

Christ put away sin by the sacrifice of himself, and we have nothing more to add to that work; we have but to come as vile sinners, just as we are, and accept a full salvation. The gift of God is eternal life, and, if a gift, we have not to earn it, or pay towards it, but to take it because God gives it, and just as he gives it. "This is the record, that God hath given to us eternal life, and this life is in his Son."

No amount of sin, no depth of guilt of which men can be guilty, prevents God from receiving them, if they come to him through Christ. His blood has atoned for all sins, and his righteousness will hide the iniquities of all who accept his offers of mercy.

Gone for ever, all my guilt, cancelled by the blood; [God.
Peace is mine, and pardon, perfect peace with
Gone for ever, every spot, every mark and All pollution, never to be seen again. [stain,
Gone for ever, every charge Satan now can raise; [matchless grace!
For the blood has answered—wondrous,
Gone for ever, judgment gone, condemnation too!
Christ, my Surety, bore it, giving me his due.
Gone for ever, every cloud, rent the veil is now;
In God's very presence peacefully I bow.

PURIFICATION CHAPTER—Num. xix.

QUESTION—*What profit shall I have, if I be cleansed from my sin?* —Job xxxv. 3.

There be many strange questions in Job, and this is one of them. The question might well be reversed, "What profit shall I have if I be not cleansed from my sin?" "Blessed are the pure in heart, for they shall see God." No cleansing—no heaven.

❖Sayings about Songs.❖

In solo singing everything depends on expression. The expression of the words, the facial expression of the sentiment, the soul expression of the song. A piece may be perfectly rendered, so far as the notes are concerned, but fall cold ,and chill on the listener. There must be more than mere mechanical execution.

THERE IS A FOUNTAIN.

There is a fountain filled with blood,
Drawn from Immanuel's veins,
And sinners, plunged beneath that flood,
Lose all their guilty stains.

The dying thief rejoiced to see
That fountain in his day,
And there may I, though vile as he,
Wash all my sins away.

Thou dying Lamb, thy precious blood
Shall never lose its power,
Till all the ransomed Church of God
Are saved, to sin no more.

E'er since by faith I saw the stream
Thy flowing wounds supply,
Redeeming love has been my theme,
And shall be till I die.

PROVERB—*"For the drunkard and the glutton shall come to poverty: and drowsiness shall clothe a man with rags."*—xxiii. 21.

41

SIN — AND·ITS·· CONSEQUENCES.

All have sinned,—I have sinned.
The blood of Christ is the only remedy for sin.
God hates sin,—so should I.
Secret sins,—scarlet sins.
Sin and Satan for others.—Christ for me.
Are you working for the wages of sin?
Will you give up sin and serve Christ now?

✦Gems of Thought.✦

Satan does with sinners as the Philistines did with Samson; first puts out their eyes, then makes them grind in his mill. God touches the eyes, and the scales fall from them.—*Halyburton*

Notwithstanding all the strikes and lock-outs, the wages of sin have not been cut down.

The Spirit convinces us of the *fact* of sin, that we have done so and so; of the *fault* of sin, that we have done ill in doing so; of the *folly* of sin, that we have acted against right, reason, and our true interest; of the *filth* of sin, that by it we are become odious to God; of the *fountain* of sin, the corrupt nature; and lastly, of the *fruit* of sin, that the end thereof is death.—*Matthew Henry*.

"Thou hast cast all my sins behind thy back," and therefore they are no more "in the light of thy countenance;" thou lookest on them no more.

Use sin as it will use you; it is your murderer, and the murderer of the whole world. Kill it, before it kill you.—*Baxter*.

One leak in a ship will sink her, though she be tight every way else.—*Mead*.

DUTY CHAPTER—Ezekiel xxxiii.

QUESTION—*What shall the end be of them that obey not the gospel of God?*
—1 Peter iv. 17.

Good were it for that man if he had never been born, so says the Bible in Mark xiv. 21. Their end must be death and woe, eternal separation from God and the good. Gospel disobedience brings death, while gospel obedience brings LIFE.

✦Sayings about Songs.✦

Hell never had one song, and never will, lest it be the echo of the songs of heaven, heard across the great gulf fixed. What woe to thus know that in these songs they might have had a part had they only believed and followed Jesus.

THE GOSPEL CALL.

In the silent midnight watches,
List,—thy bosom door!
How it knocketh, knocketh, knocketh,
Knocketh evermore!
Say not 'tis thy pulse is beating;
'Tis thy heart of sin;
'Tis thy Saviour knocks, and crieth,
Rise, and let me in!

Death comes down with reckless footstep,
To the hall and hut;
Think you death will stand a-knocking
Where the door is shut?
Jesus waiteth, waiteth, waiteth;
But thy door is fast!
Grieved, away thy Saviour goeth:
Death breaks in at last.

PROVERB—"*An high look, and a proud heart, and the ploughing of the wicked, is sin.*"—xxi. 4.

THE CHRISTIAN WARFARE.

Every soul has its battles.
Every one may have victory.
Put on the *whole* armor of *God.*
Let your shield be large and strong.
The sword of the Spirit is the Word of God.
Are you one of Christ's soldiers?
Who will enlist "for life" in the King's army?

❧ Gems of Thought. ❧

Providence has a thousand keys to open a thousand doors for the deliverance of his own.—*Rutherford.*

It is not enough to break with sin, unless you break with sinners too.—*Lovington.*

The Christian must not only mind heaven, but attend to his daily calling, like the pilot who, while his eye is fixed upon the star, keeps his hand upon the helm.—*Watson.*

Don't think the battle won when first you put your armor on.

The point between lawful pleasure and vice is like a boundary between two kingdoms at war with each other. It is there- fore most prudent, weak and defenceless as we are, not to venture to the very edge of our side, lest an insidious enemy surprise and capture us unawares.— *Townson.*

God never permits the disciple to fall into the hands of an enemy, except when by that means some good to the Church or to the suffering disciple himself is to be accomplished by it.—*Watson.*

It is no great matter to live lovingly with good-natured, humble, and meek persons; but he who can do so with the froward, wilful, ignorant, peevish, and perverse, hath true charity.—*Thomas a Kempis.*

THE SOLDIER'S CHAPTER—Eph. vi.

QUESTION—*What shall we do, that we might work the works of God?* —John vi. 28.

Let the Scriptures answer this: This is the work of God, that ye believe on him whom he hath sent.—John vi. 29. Now the God of peace make you perfect in every good work to do his will, working in you that which is well pleasing in his sight, through Jesus Christ; to whom be glory for ever and ever.—Heb. xiii. 20, 21.

❧ Sayings about Songs. ❧

No army ever marches without its music. If the christian soldier would fight well let there be music all around him. The Spartan's were led to victory by the lays of the minstrel. Let us keep our music always going.

MY SOUL, BE ON THY GUARD.

My soul, be on thy guard;
Ten thousand foes arise;
The hosts of sin are pressing hard
To draw thee from the skies.

Oh, watch, and fight, and pray!
The battle ne'er give o'er;
Renew it boldly every day,
And help divine implore.

Ne'er think the victory won,
Nor once at ease sit down;
Thy arduous work will not be done
Till thou obtain thy crown.

Fight on, my soul, till death
Shall bring thee to thy God!
He'll take thee at thy parting breath,
Up to his blest abode.

PROVERB—*"Wealth gotten by vanity shall be diminished: but he that gath-ereth by labour shall increase."*—xiii. 11.

THE COMMANDMENTS OF GOD.

The Great Psalm is the cxix.
Its whole theme is the law of God.
God's commandments are never grievous.
Great peace have they that love thy law.
What commandment did Christ add?
Who can repeat the ten commandments?
Who will obey Christ's command—Follow me?

Gems of Thought.

An effort to injure your neighbor is regarded by Jesus as containing the moral elements of murder.

A great many persons are more ready to excuse their outbursts of passion by appealing to the difficult passage, "Be ye angry and sin not," than they are to find out and apply to themselves the real meaning of "Thou shalt love thy neighbor as thyself."

"Now for the world, dear child, I know it too well to persuade thee to dive into the practices of it; rather stand upon thy guard against all those that tempt thee to it, or may practice upon thee, whether in thy conscience, thy reputation, or thy estate. Be assured that no man is wise or safe but he that is honest."—*Sir Walter Raleigh's letter to his son.*

COMMANDMENT CHAPTER—Ex. xx.

QUESTION—*Who hath warned you to flee from the wrath to come?*
—Matt. iii. 7.

Was it thy guilty conscience, or the drawings of the cross, or what?

God commandeth all men everywhere to repent; because he hath appointed a day, in the which he will judge the world in righteousness by that man whom he hath ordained; whereof he hath given assurance unto all men, in that he hath raised him from the dead.—Acts xvii. 30, 31.

Sayings about Songs.

These foreludes and afterludes and interludes of the organist are enough to kill half the singing in our meetings. Let's away with them all. Leave the flourishes off. Give us just enough of the instrument to lead the people, and let them do the work of worship.

OBEDIENCE.

How happy are they
Who the Saviour obey,
And have laid up their treasures above!
O what tongue can express
The sweet comfort and peace
Of a soul in its earliest love?

'Twas heaven below
My Redeemer to know,
And the angels could do nothing more,
Than to fall at his feet,
And the story repeat,
And the Lover of sinners adore.

O the rapturous height
Of that holy delight,
Which I felt in the life-giving blood!
Of my Saviour possessed,
I was perfectly blest,
As if filled with the fulness of God.

Then, all the day long,
Was my Jesus my song,
And redemption, thro' faith in his name;
O that all might believe,
And salvation receive,
And their song and their joy be the same.

PROVERB—*"He that tilleth his land shall have plenty of bread: but he that followeth after vain persons shall have poverty enough."*—xxviii. 19.

CONFESSION OF CHRIST.

Confess him *here*, confessed by him *hereafter*.
Let it be both a word and a work confession.
Don't shout louder than you live.
To deny him is to be denied by him.
I will let the whole world know I love him.
Who will pray, "O Lord, open thou my lips"?
Who will now confess him as Saviour?

⟶ Gems of Thought. ⟵

A child of God should be a visible beatitude for joy and happiness, and a living doxology for gratitude and adoration.—*Spurgeon.*

Some confess, but believe not, as hypocrites; others believe, but profess not, as timorous; others do neither profess nor believe, as atheists; others both believe and confess, and they be true Christians.— *Willet.*

Had the faith of the heart been sufficient, God would not have given you a mouth.— *T. Aquinas.*

If we must give account of every "idle word," take care also lest you have to answer for an idle silence.—*Ambrose.*

It is the way of lovers to be unable to conceal their love.—*St. Augustine.*

The very core of healthy and happy discipleship is the willingness to deny self, and to let the Master have his way. This principle runs through all the deepest, richest experience of the blood-bought and consecrated believer.—*T. L. Cuyler.*

HUMILITY CHAPTER—Luke xviii.

QUESTION—*What think ye of Christ?* —Matt. xxii. 42.

Not what others think, but what YOU think of him. He, the only Saviour for the soul, given but a passing, idle thought, while the world and its follies have all your time and brain. Stop; think; meditate; read his life; look at your lost soul, which only he can save: What think you of him?

⟶ Sayings about Songs. ⟵

" I love to tell the story" will live long after scientists and their notions and their infidel books have become dust. "Now I lay me down to sleep" will live in memory when the very names of Paine, Voltaire, Rosseau, Bradlaugh, and Ingersol have been forever forgotten.

I'M NOT ASHAMED.

I'm not ashamed to own my Lord,
　Or to defend his cause;
Maintain the honor of his word,
　The glory of his cross.

Jesus, my God! I know his name;
　His name is all my trust;
Nor will he put my soul to shame,
　Nor let my hope be lost.

Firm as his throne his promise stands,
　And he can well secure
What I've committed to his hands,
　Till the decisive hour.

Then will he own my worthless name
　Before his Father's face,
And in the New Jerusalem
　Appoint my soul a place.

PROVERB—*"There is that maketh himself rich, yet hath nothing: there is that maketh himself poor, yet hath great riches."*—xiii.

45

REST FOR THE WEARY.

If you would find rest, go to Jesus.
For "rest," seek the closet of prayer.
Rest for to-day, for mind, for soul.
Rest forever.
Rest in Heaven.
Have you rest from the bondage of sin?
Who has found rest at the cross?

⸙ Gems of Thought. ⸙

The aching head may well cease to throb when laid upon that softest pillow for human pain,—"God knows!"

Lord, I have tried how this thing and that thing will fit my spirit. I can find nothing to rest on, for nothing here hath any rest itself. O Center and Source of light and strength! O Fulness of all things! I come back to join myself to thee.—*Arthur H. Hallam.*

What is resignation? It is putting God between one's self and one's grief.—*Madame Swetchine.*

Upon thy word I rest
So strong, so sure;
So full of comfort blest,
So sweet, so pure—
The word that changeth not,
That faileth never!
My King, I rest upon
Thy word forever.
—*F. R. Havergal.*

REST CHAPTER—Hebrews iv.

QUESTION—*What is thy request?* —Esther vii. 2.

When answering to the King's voice as he thus speaks, let us ask great things, for he thus invites, "Open thy mouth wide, and I will fill it." Let us ask for great grace and mighty salvation, for revivals all over the world, for a hastening of the day when the earth shall be full of the knowledge of the glory of the Lord.

⸙ Sayings about Songs. ⸙

Many a one has left earth with a cry of pain only to pass out and up and in with the bitter cry broken into a merry laugh, followed by the song, "I'm saved, oh, I'm saved." How often God has made the night of sorrow to be followed by the joy of morning.

THERE IS A HAPPY LAND.

There is a happy land,
  Far, far away,
Where saints in glory stand,
  Bright, bright as day;
Oh, how they sweetly sing,
Worthy is our Saviour King,
Loud let his praises ring,
  Praise, praise for aye.

Come to that happy land,
  Come, come away;
Why will ye doubting stand,
  Why still delay?
Oh, we shall happy be,
When from sin and sorrow free,
Lord, we shall live with thee,
  Blest, blest for aye.

PROVERB—*"Riches profit not in the day of wrath: but righteousness delivereth from death.*

COME·TO·JESUS.

Come to him with your burdens of sin.
Come to him for uttermost salvation.
Come to him for all your needs.
The invitation is to the whole world.
Especially does it mean YOU.
How many here have come unto him?
Who will come to Jesus and be saved?

Gems of Thought.

If the hypocrites are in your way, it is because they are ahead of you; and if I were you, I would not confess that I was hindered from serving God by a hypocrite. Let me tell you in all candor that I think you are *lying* when you talk about being kept from serving God by us poor fellows who are in the Church.—*Sam Jones.*

I am persuaded if Judas had said unto Christ what he said to the high priest, "*I have sinned in that I have betrayed innocent blood,*" he might have been saved.

"Look unto me, and be ye saved," Christ said,
"Trust in thy God," and he shall lift thy head.
"Come unto me," when burdened and dismayed,
"Believe on Jesus," and thou shalt be saved.
"Hear, and your soul shall live," he says again,
"Wait on the Lord," and you shall strength obtain.
'Tis not thy look that saves; 'tis not thy trust;
'Tis not thy coming, and yet come you must;
'Tis not believing which can save the soul,
It is not hearing which can make thee whole;
It is the Object upon which you rest
That brings contentment to your longing breast.

CONVERT'S CHAPTER—Isaiah xii.

QUESTION—*Who then can be saved?* —Mark x. 26.

All who will, for the promise is to the "whosoever." There is a wide open door for the whole world, and inside is safety, outside is wrath. As it is written, "We shall be saved from wrath through him." You can be saved.

Sayings about Songs.

Put more soul-power into your church songs. Let *the heart* take hold of the music. Let the anthems come from lips which have confessed the Nazarene as Son of God. Make the building echo the well sung songs.

COME, SINNERS, COME.

Come, ye sinners, poor and needy,
  Weak and wounded, sick and sore;
Jesus ready stands to save you,
  Full of pity, love, and power.
    He is able,
    He is willing; doubt no more.

O ye needy, come and welcome,
  God's free bounty glorify;
True belief and true repentance,
  Every grace that brings us nigh,
    Without money,
    Come to Jesus Christ and buy.

PROVERB—"*As vinegar to the teeth, and as smoke to the eyes, so is the sluggard to them that send him.*"—x. 26.

THE HOLY SPIRIT ··OUR·· COMFORTER.

Jesus is in heaven. The Holy Spirit is here.
In thought, and word, and work, honor the Holy Ghost.
The Holy Spirit alone administer's redemption.
Guided by the Spirit through the Word of God.
He alone can regenerate the heart.
Who will let him reveal Christ as Saviour now?
Who will pray, "Lord, fill me with thy Spirit"?

⊹Gems of Thought.⊹

Without the Spirit St. Peter trembled at the voice of a maid-servant; with the Spirit he withstood kings and princes. (Eph. vi. 10-18.)—*St. Jerome.*

The devil, the father of lies, hath added this lie to those which he hath told thee before, namely, that thou hast committed the *sin against the Holy Ghost.* For that sin is ever attended with these two symptoms, namely, absence of all *contrition* and of all *desire* of forgiveness.—*Fuller.*

When the Holy Spirit is forced away the evil spirit takes his place. (1 Sam. xvi. 14.)—*Allestry.*

Sometimes the Holy Spirit is "like a hammer that breaketh the rock in pieces," (Jer. xxiii. 29; sometimes it distils, as "the small rain upon the tender herb," (Deut. xxxii. 2.)—*Ford.*

He that hath the witness in himself cannot explain it to one who hath it not.—*Wesley.*

Religion is the best armor a man can have, but it is the worst cloak.—*Bunyan.*

HOLY SPIRIT CHAPTER—John xvi.

QUESTION—*Have ye received the Holy Ghost since ye believed?* —Acts xix. 2.

Thousands of church members must answer, "No," and this is the reason of their bearing no fruit and living such unsatisfactory lives both to themselves and to others. The Spirit in us to help us believe unto salvation is one thing, and the anointing of the Spirit for service is quite another. As with the disciples who received power after the Holy Ghost came upon them, so with us when baptized with the same Spirit of power. Oh, pray much for power from on high!

⊹Sayings about Songs.⊹

Song study is one of the useful arts. Few have it. Why not learn more about the writers of hymns, their lives, and their work? Then, too, why not learn more hymns by heart? It's quite impossible now to get a congregation to sing five hymns all through without a book.

HOLY SPIRIT, FAITHFUL GUIDE.

Holy Spirit, faithful guide,
Ever near the Christian's side;
Gently lead us by the hand,
Pilgrims in a desert land;
Weary souls fore'er rejoice,
While they hear that sweetest voice
Whisp'ring softly, wanderer, come;
Follow Me, I'll guide thee home.

Ever present, truest Friend,
Ever near thine aid to lend,
Leave us not to doubt and fear,
Groping on in darkness drear,
When the storms are raging sore,
Hearts grow faint, and hopes give o'er—
Whisper softly, wanderer, come!
Follow Me, I'll guide thee home.

PROVERB—"*Where no counsel is, the people fall: but in the multitude of counsellors there is safety.*"—xi. 14.

48

TO-DAY, ··THE·· TRUMPET CALL.

God's voice speaks only of To-day.
To-day—repent, believe, be saved.
To say, "to-morrow" is presumption. Prov. xxvii. 1.
Some day will surely be your last.
This *may* be your last day.
Can you say to-day—now—I am saved?
Will you THIS DAY turn to God with all your heart?

❧Gems of Thought.❧

Help us to dismiss to-morrow from our thoughts; may we be men of to-day.

Do not say, "I will help thee to-morrow;" perchance that poor soul may not need thee to-morrow; perchance thou mayest have nothing to give to-morrow; perchance there shall be no such day as to-morrow.—*Donne.*

We can easily manage if we will only take each day the burden appointed for it. But the load will be too heavy for us if we add to its weight the burden of to-morrow before we are called to bear it.

How often you come to the house of God, and see the minister preaching of eternal things, but your heart is full of cares, and plans, and pleasures. One thing is plain, that thorns and wheat cannot grow on the same spot of ground; so that, if you will keep to your thorns, you must burn with them.—*McCheyne.*

Salvation without money,
Salvation without price,
Salvation without labor,
Believing doth suffice;
Salvation now—this moment!
Then why, oh, why delay?
You may not see to-morrow;
Now is salvation's day!

TO-DAY CHAPTER—Hebrews iii.

QUESTION—*Why sleep ye?* —Luke xxii. 46.

When sleep is death, while you slumber in the bed of ease many are being lost that might be saved.

Awake! thou that sleepest, and arise from the dead, and Christ shall give thee light.—Eph. v. 14. And with the light given go forth to dark corners of the earth to tell of a risen Christ.

❧Sayings about Songs.❧

I am led to believe that we shall have orchestral music in heaven. What a day that will be when flute and trumpet, horn and harp, bugle and bell, shall be handled by thousands of apt players, and we listen to their marshalled music.

SINNERS, COME.

To-day, if ye will hear his voice,
Now is the time to make your choice;
Say, will you to the Saviour go?
Say, will you have this Christ, or no?
Ye wand'ring souls, who find no rest,
Say will you be forever blest?
Will you be saved from sin and hell?
Will you with Christ in glory dwell?

Come now, dear youth, for ruin bound,
Obey the gospel's cheerful sound;
Come, go with us, and you shall prove
The joy of Christ's redeeming love.
Once more we ask you in his name—
For yet his love remains the same—
Say, will you to the Saviour go?
Say, will you have this Christ, or no?

PROVERB—"*The sluggard will not plough by reason of the cold; therefore shall he beg in harvest, and have nothing.*"—xx. 4.

SAVED OR LOST—WHICH?

A mighty question.
Put to great sinners.
By a precious Saviour.
Who would have all men saved.
By the offering of himself once made.
How do you answer it?
Who will trust "the Mighty to Save"?

Gems of Thought.

A city missionary called at a house. The door was opened by a woman, to whom he said that he had come to converse with her on the salvation of her soul. She seemed uneasy at his words, and replied: "I am too busy to speak to you to-day; call another time." He gave a kind parting word, and retired. On a second visit the missionary found the woman preparing to go to the theatre. The same excuse was made. "I am very busy; come another time." "Ah! my friend," said the faithful visitor, "death will one day come to the house, and it will not do to tell him to call another time." The woman went to the play-house, returned home seeming in her usual health, was taken ill in the night, and died the next morning.

Almost persuaded, harvest is past!
Almost persuaded, doom comes at last!
Almost cannot avail; almost is but to fail;
Sad, sad that bitter wail—Almost, *but lost!*

SINNER'S CHAPTER—Luke xix.

QUESTION—*Whither goest thou?* —Gen. xxxii. 17.

There are but two places in eternity for the abode of the soul. Which of these will be yours? Are you a pilgrim and a stranger now seeking a city built by God? Will we meet you on those streets paved with gold? Directly to the question will you answer "to heaven" or "to hell."

Sayings about Songs.

I take it that when we listen to all the children from every clime, numbered by the millions, singing the praises of our mighty God there will come a sense of recompense for all the sufferings endured on earth.

THE TRUMPET CALL.

To-day the Saviour calls;
Ye wand'rers, come;
O ye benighted souls,
Why longer roam?
To-day the Saviour calls:
Oh, listen now;
Within these sacred walls
To Jesus bow.

To-day the Saviour calls:
For refuge fly;
The storm of justice falls,
And death is nigh.
The Spirit calls to-day:
Yield to his power;
Oh, grieve him not away;
'Tis mercy's hour.

PROVERB—"*There is a way which seemeth right unto a man; but the end thereof are the ways of death.*"—xiv. 12.

Theme 48.

SOWING AND REAPING.

Every one is both sower and reaper.
As the sowing is, so shall the harvest be.
We reap far more than we sow.
The good seed is the Word of God.
Sow no tares for Satan.
What sowing of the good seed have you done?
What will your eternal harvest be?

Gems of Thought.

It is an awful moment when the soul meets God in private, to stand the test of his all-seeing eye.—*Adam.*

One action is able to undo the whole host of Israel. Up, Joshua, and ferret out the thief.—*Sanderson.*

'Tis not so much a man's outward condition, as his inward disposition and temper of mind, that makes temptation prevalent or unsuccessful. Joseph was chaste in Potiphar's house, Reuben incestuous in good Jacob's: Lot temperate and chaste in Sodom, drunk and incestuous in a cave.—*Boyle.*

The end will come—the end of your life: it may be to-day—it has come to many quite as unexpectedly. But whether to-day or not, *it will come,*—and if you go on as you are going, what will your end be? I know not how you are going on. Perhaps you are walking in the ways of the Lord: perhaps you are walking in the counsels of your own heart. If you are following Christ, your end will be peace: if you are following your own heart, unless you repent, and believe the gospel, your end will be *everlasting destruction!*

SAD CHAPTER—Luke xxii.

QUESTION—*Who hath sorrow and who hath woe?*—Pr.xxiii.29.

They that tarry long at the wine. They who taste the awful cup. At the last it biteth like a serpent and stingeth like an adder. A drunkard's hell must be an horrible pit of woe. The burning fires of an unconsumed conscience that remembers its own doom and the wreck of others' hopes in the crash of character is sorrow born of torment. Let us neither touch, taste, or handle the liquid brewed by death.

Sayings about Songs.

"Old Hundred!" Ah! there is a tune that can never be buried. Sinner and saint alike sing it as the years roll on, and they ever will. Is there a saved sinner on earth that has not sung that? Few; if any. Children lisp it; old men rejoice in it; all love it.

THE GOOD SEED.

Almighty God, thy word is cast
Like seed upon the ground;
O let the dew of heaven descend,
And shed its influence round.

Let not the foe of Christ and man
This holy seed remove;
May it take root in every heart,
And grow in faith and love.

Let not this life's deceitful cares,
Nor worldly wealth and joy,
Nor scorching beam, nor stormy blast,
The rising plant destroy.

Where'er the word of life is sown,
A large increase bestow;
That all who hear thy message, Lord,
Its saving power may know.

PROVERB—*"Burning lips and a wicked heart are like a potsherd covered with silver dross."*—xxvi. 23.

51

JESUS, ··THE·· MIGHTY TO SAVE.

He saves the sinner from sin.
He saves the sinner from death.
He saves the sinner from hell.
He delivers him in trouble.
He keeps him in perfect peace.
Are you one of the sinners saved?
Will you trust "the Mighty to Save" now?

Gems of Thought.

You may be a dreadful failure. Christ is a divine success.—*Edward Thomson.*

A man undertakes to jump across a chasm that is ten feet wide, and jumps eight feet; and a kind sympathizer says, "What is going to be done with the eight feet that he did jump?" Well, what *is* going to be done with it? It is one of those things which must be accomplished in whole, or it is not accomplished at all.—*Beecher.*

The grave is God's bankrupt court, which clears a man of his property and his debts at the same time.—*Beecher.*

Good ground, good seed, good weather, and a good crop, prove that we have a good God; but a good heart, good purposes, good works, and a good end, prove that we have a gracious God.

Fierce was the wild billow;
Dark was the night;
Oars labored heavily;
Foam glimmered white;
Mariners trembled;
Peril was nigh;
Then said the God of might,
"Peace, it is I!"

MARVELOUS CHAPTER—Luke ix.

QUESTION—*Is not thy wickedness great?* —Job xxii. 5.

Very great. "O my God, I am ashamed and blush to lift up my face to thee, my God; for our iniquities are increased over our head, and our trespass is grown up unto the heavens."—Ezra ix. 6. But remember this, that "God's mercy is great above the heavens." Turn to him; this is thine only refuge.

Sayings about Songs.

"Sing unto the Lord!" that's a Bible injunction and should be heeded. The choir usually "sings unto the people," and half the time the people think the words are Latin or Chinese. Oh, for common sense in the organ loft! Thus pray at the next prayer meeting.

THE REDEEMER'S PRAISE.

From all that dwell below the skies
Let the Creator's praise arise:
Let the Redeemer's name be sung
Through every land, by every tongue.

Eternal are thy mercies, Lord;
Eternal truth attends thy word;
Thy praise shall sound from shore to shore,
Till suns shall set and rise no more.

PROVERB—"*Wine is a mocker, strong drink is raging: and whosoever is deceived thereby is not wise.*"—xx. 1.

53

HEAVEN, THE HOME OF THE REDEEMED.

There I shall see Jesus.
There the weary are at rest.
Mother, Home, Heaven,—all for me.
Tell the sinner of Jesus and Heaven.
No tears or sorrow or pain up there.
Who is now there that you know?
Will you be there at the last?

Gems of Thought.

God would never let us long for our friends with such a strong and holy love, if they were not waiting for us.—*Mountford.*

Lord, I am not solicitous of the passage, so that I get to thee.—*Jeremy Taylor.*

Blessed are they who are home-sick, for they shall come at last to their Father's house.—*Heinrich Stilling.*

Be not dismayed at the prospect of getting home. Where is the man that would be sorry to be ejected from a cottage, in order to his living in a palace?—*Toplady.*

I know not the way that I'm going,
But well do I know my Guide;
With a childlike trust I give my hand
To the mighty Friend at my side.
And the only thing that I say to him,
As he takes it, is "Hold it fast,
Suffer me not to lose my way,
And bring me home at last!"

Like a bairn to its mother, a wee birdie to its nest,
I wad fain be ganging noo unto my Saviour's breast;
For he gathers in his bosom witless, worthless lambs like me,
An' be carries them himself to his ain countree. —*Miss M. A. Lee.*

HEAVEN CHAPTER—Rev. xxi.

QUESTION—*Are there few that be saved?* —Luke xiii. 23.

"Many are called, but few are chosen." It is for YOU to strive to enter in at the straight gate. You must determine to be amongst the number of the redeemed. There will be no doubt of God's having chosen you, when there is no doubt of your having chosen him. Then when saved carry the gospel to other hearts that are just as needy as was yours.

Sayings about Songs.

Will the rapture be complete till we hear Charles Wesley sing some of his own inspired songs? If our hymn books can't go with us to heaven the hymns will, for they are written on the heart.

NEARER HOME.

One sweetly solemn thought
Comes to me o'er and o'er,
Nearer my parting hour am I
Than e'er I was before.

Nearer my Father's house,
Where many mansions be;
Nearer the throne where Jesus reigns—
Nearer the crystal sea;

Nearer my going home,
Laying my burden down,
Leaving my cross of heavy grief,
Wearing my starry crown;

Nearer that hidden stream,
Winding through shades of night,
Rolling its cold, dark waves between
Me and the world of light.

PROVERB—"*The liberal soul shall be made fat: and he that watereth shall be watered also himself.*"—xi. 25.

THE PROMISES OF GOD.

They are many and mighty.

They cover all our needs for time and eternity.

Not one has ever been broken.

Everything depends on our meeting their conditions.

In Christ all the promises are yea and amen.

Who will trust God's promises for salvation?

Who have proven the promises true?

Gems of Thought.

All the saints who have gone to heaven went there living upon the promises. Every step of Abraham's life he walked with a promise in it.—*A. Gray.*

Faith feeds on the promise when no relief is in view, or no bread in the cupboard. Rom. i. 17.

The promises of God never fail when the conditions on which they are made to depend are perseveringly performed.—*Watson.*

Be not disheartened, as if comfort would not come at all, because it comes not all at once; but patiently attend God's leisure: they are not styled the swift, but "the sure mercies of David." Be assured when grace patiently leads the front, glory at last will be in the rear.—*Fuller.*

Jehovah's covenant shall endure
All-ordered, everlasting, sure;
O child of God, look up, and trace
Thy portion in its glorious grace.
  —*F. R. Havergal.*

PEACE AND PROMISE CHAPTER—John xiv.

QUESTION—*Now in whom dost thou trust?* —2 Kings xviii. 20.

Not in self, or even in princes, but my soul trusteth in thee: be merciful unto me, O God, be merciful unto me.—Ps. lvii. 1.

He that trusteth in the Lord, mercy shall compass him about.—Ps. xxxii. 10.

Sayings about Songs.

The perfection of song is not for earth; we go not to the organ factory to hear the sweet, bewildering sounds of that far famed instrument. There we hear but poundings, sawings, planings; the noise of tools. This world is God's workshop for building singers, and we hear but tunings, and that mixed with the noise of hammer and file, sand paper and chisel. Heaven will be the place for the instrument finished and tuned.

THE UNBROKEN PROMISES.

Glorious things of thee are spoken,
  Zion, city of our God;
He whose word cannot be broken,
  Formed thee for his own abode;
On the Rock of ages founded,
  What can shake thy sure repose?
With salvation's walls surrounded,
  Thou mayst smile at all thy foes.

See the streams of living waters,
  Springing from eternal love,
Still supply thy sons and daughters,
  And all fear of want remove:
Who can faint while such a river
  Ever flows our thirst to assuage?
Grace, which, like the Lord, the giver,
  Never fails from age to age.

PROVERB—*"As a jewel of gold in a swine's snout, so is a fair woman which is without discretion."*—xi. 22.

Theme 52.

CONSECRATION FOR · CHRIST'S SERVICE.

Saved ourselves, let us help to save others.
Christ is no hard taskmaster.
We serve God as sons and not as servants.
Consecration to the Lord's work, not our work.
Consecration is our part, Sanctification is God's part.
Who will consecrate their all now to God?
Who will give their hearts to Jesus?

⊹Gems of Thought.⊹

Pious impulses are no proof of consecration. What we need is grace to resolve such impulses into permanent principle.

Write nothing you would not like God to read.—Heb. iv. 13.

Go to no place where you would not like God to find you.—Job xxxiv. 21.

Example is more forcible than precept. People look at my six days in the week to see what I mean on the seventh.—*R. Cecil.*

We must be ready to go out of our way if God calls us out of our way; or, in other words, to have our little plans so modified and corrected as to be brought into the scheme of his great and all-wise plan.

No man ever achieved anything for Christ who did not, when necessary, trample both self and selfish enjoyment under foot.

CONSECRATION CHAPTER—Rom. xii.

QUESTION—*Who then is willing to consecrate his service this day unto the Lord?* —1 Chron. xxix. 5.

Consecration means set apart for the Lord's service. This is but a reasonable service. "The spirit indeed is willing, but the flesh is weak. . . . O Lord God, remember me, I pray thee, and strengthen me."—Matt. xxvi. 41; Judges xvi. 28.

Take hold of my strength.—Isa. xxvii. 5.

⊹Sayings about Songs.⊹

When you sing open your mouth; let the words come out clear and strong. Get the sense of what you are singing. Some hymns have no sense in them; dont sing them. They should have been buried before they were born.

WORK FOR JESUS.

One more day's work for Jesus,
One less of life for me!
But heaven is nearer,
And Christ is dearer
Than yesterday, to me;
His love and light
Fill all my soul to-night.

One more day's work for Jesus!
How sweet the work has been,
To tell the story,
To show the glory,
Where Christ's flock enter in!
How it did shine
In this poor heart of mine!

One more day's work for Jesus!
Oh, yes, a weary day;
But heaven shines clearer
And rest comes nearer
At each step of the way;
And Christ in all,
Before his face I fall.

O blessed work for Jesus!
O rest at Jesus' feet!
There toil seems pleasure,
My wants are treasure,
And pain for him is sweet.
Lord, if I may,
I'll serve another day!

PROVERB—"*A man's gift maketh room for him, and bringeth him before great men.*"—xviii. 16.

55

SALVATION FOR ALL WHO BELIEVE.

I believe, therefore it is for me.
There is no song like the song of salvation.
Salvation for every tribe, tongue, people, and nation.
Saved from sin and the power thereof.
The greater the sinner the greater the salvation.
Who can testify, "I have salvation"?
What soul will seek salvation NOW?

Gems of Thought.

There will never be a second Saviour to atone for the guilt of rejecting the first.
"*Mine eyes have seen thy salvation.*" Simeon had nothing greater to see on earth; he desires to depart. *Salvation* is one of the names of Messiah. Gen. xlix. 18; Isa. xlix. 6.—*Watson.*

Mark xii. 40. When our Saviour rakes up the bottom of hell, who do you find there? The drunkard, the unclean? No; the Pharisee, who "*for pretence makes long prayers;*" proud, hard hypocrites.—*Hopkins.*

Colonel Ethan Allen, of Vermont, openly rejected the Christian religion, and wrote several works against it. But how little faith he possessed in his own principles when put to the test, will be seen from a fact related by Dr. Dwight: While the Colonel was engaged in reading some of his own writings to a friend, a message was brought that his daughter was at the point of death. His wife, a pious woman, had instructed her child in the truths of the Bible. When the father appeared at the bedside, the daughter affectionately looked at him and said: "Father, I am about to die: shall I believe in the principles you have taught me, or shall I believe in what my mother has taught me? On hearing the question, the Colonel was much distressed, and, after a pause, replied: "BELIEVE IN WHAT YOUR MOTHER HAS TAUGHT YOU."

I WILL CHAPTER—Hosea ii.

QUESTION—*Where is any other that may save thee?*
—Hosea xiii. 10.

"There is none other name under heaven given among men, whereby we must be saved." This is the Scripture; our good works will not save us; our giving up sin wont save us; not even faith saves us, nor repentance. These may all be means for salvation, but there is only one Saviour, and his name is JESUS. Trust him now.

Sayings about Songs.

It may be that some other world will need to hear the Gospel Story, and to them we will be sent to preach. I hope so, for with me shall go a chorus choir, both of angels and men, and such music as we will give them will win them to Christ's service forever.

SALVATION! OH, THE JOYFUL SOUND!

Salvation! oh, the joyful sound;
'Tis pleasure to our ears;
A sovereign balm for every wound,
A cordial for our fears.

Buried in sorrow and in sin,
At hell's dark door we lay;

But we arise by grace divine
To see a heavenly day.

Salvation! let the echo fly
The spacious earth around;
While all the armies of the sky
Conspire to raise the sound.

PROVERB—"*The lips of the righteous feed many: but fools die for want of wisdom.*"—x. 21.

CHRIST, ··THE·· GREAT PHYSICIAN.

By faith he heals the sin-sick soul.
There is no case he cannot cure.
Jesus is the only GREAT physician.
Who forgiveth all thine iniquities.
Who healeth all thy diseases.
Have you been healed by him?
Who will call for the Great Physician?

Gems of Thought.

Dear soul, you are not the doctor: you are the patient. What a mistake you have been making all this time! Put it to rights quickly; give yourself entirely into the hands of Jesus—into his heart, I should rather say —and he will take you along with himself, and cure you as you go, doing all for you.

A clean heart will choose clean company and clean ways, and delight in clean subjects and clean employments.

Those diseases which, upon their first seizure, have, without any great peril of the patient, been cured, after a relapse have threatened death.—*Hall.*

It is no compliment to divine grace for a man who has been forty years in the church to get up, and say, "I feel as though I was a vile and filthy rag." He *is* a vile and filthy rag to say that.—*Beecher.*

THE MERCY PSALM—Psalm cxxxvi.

QUESTION—*Dost thou believe on the Son of God?*—John ix. 35.

Your friends believe and those of your household believe, but dost *thou* believe? Have you a personal trust in the Saviour of sinners? With a childlike faith do you lay hold of him as the Great Deliverer? Lord, I believe; help thou mine unbelief. —Mark ix. 24. Fear not; I will help thee, saith the Lord.—Isa. xli. 14.

Sayings about Songs.

I take it that Gabriel and his chorus choir will be outsung by the host that will gather on the sea of glass before the throne to praise the Son of Man who came to seek them when they were lost.

CLING TO JESUS.

Cling to the Mighty One,
  Cling in thy grief;
Cling to the Holy One,
  He gives relief;
Cling to the Gracious One,
  Cling in thy pain,
Cling to the Faithful One,
  He will sustain.

Cling to the Living One,
  Cling in thy woe,
Cling to the Loving One,
  Through all below;
Cling to the Pardoning One,
  He speaketh peace;
Cling to the Healing One,
  Anguish shall cease.

PROVERB—"*Stolen waters are sweet, and the bread eaten in secret is pleasant: but he knoweth not that the dead are there; and that her guests are in the depths of hell.*"—ix. 17, 18.

SONGS · OF · ZION.

Come, let our songs abound.
Sing with the Spirit and with the understanding.
We worship the Lord in holy song.
Sing much of Christ and heaven.
We shall sing through all eternity.
Can you sing Redemption's Song?
Who will march with us to Zion?

Gems of Thought.

But though we may speak of the wonders of heaven, and the glory of the Lord Jesus and the redeemed, it is far better if we know ourselves to be seated in heavenly places with Christ even now. This we can know, by being born again of the Spirit through the Word of God. None but those who have been washed in the blood of Jesus can ever enter heaven or see the wonders there.

SONG CHAPTER—Luke i.

QUESTION—*Can God furnish a table in the wilderness?*
—Psa. lxxviii. 19.

He can furnish a table anywhere, and especially does he like to do the impossible.
The Lord shall comfort Zion: he will comfort all her waste places; and he will make her wilderness like Eden, and her desert like the garden of the Lord; joy and gladness shall be found therein thanksgiving, and the voice of melody.—Isa. li. 3.
God shall supply all your need.—Phil. iv. 19.

Sayings about Songs.

The first thing I expect to hear when the soul leaves the body is singing. They will sing as I pass out, they will sing as I pass up, and as I pass in they will sing the wonders of his grace. I'll join them.

SONGS FOREVER.

When shall we meet again,
Meet ne'er to sever?
When will peace wreathe her chain
Round us forever?
Our hearts will ne'er repose,
Safe from each blast that blows,
In this dark vale of woes,
Never—no, never!

When shall love freely flow
Pure as life's river?
When shall sweet friendship glow
Changeless forever?
Where joys celestial thrill,
Where bliss each heart can fill,
And fears of parting chill
Never—no, never!

Up to that world of light
Take us, dear Saviour;
May we all there unite,
Happy forever;
Where kindred spirits dwell,
There may our music swell,
And time our joys dispel
Never—no, never!

Soon shall we meet again,
Meet ne'er to sever;
Soon shall peace wreathe her chain
Round us forever;
Our hearts will then repose
Secure from worldly woes;
Our songs of praise shall close
Never—no, never!

PROVERB—*"As cold waters to a thirsty soul, so is good news from a far country."*—XXV. 25.

THE TWO WAYS.

One way leads to the City of God.
Another way leads to hell.
The entrance way of each stands wide open.
You make your own choice of destiny.
Many stand now at the fork of these two roads.
Do you tread the broad or narrow road?
Will you turn from the paths of sin now?

❖Gems of Thought.❖

Though we know not where the road winds, we know where it ends.—*Spurgeon.*

I read of my Saviour that, when he was in the wilderness, then the devil leaveth him; and behold, angels came and ministered unto him. A great change in a little time. No twilight betwixt night and day. When out devil, in angel.—*Fuller.*

If you have been tempted into evil, fly from it! It is not falling into the water, but lying in it, that drowns.

Beloved, God meets those who are in the way; Satan meets those who are out of it. —*Harrington Evans.*

Eternity is crying out to you louder and louder as you near its brink. Rise, be going! count your resources; learn what you are not fit for, and give up wishing for it; learn what you can do, and do it with the energy of a man.—*Robertson.*

Jonah did but change his vessel when he entered the whale; he was not shipwrecked. God was his pilot then, as well as in the ship.—*Donne.*

WISDOM CHAPTER—Prov. iii.

QUESTION—*Seekest thou great things for thyself?*
—Jer. xiv. 5.

Seek them not; but rather seek great things for thy God. The humble soul shall be exalted, the proud heart will be brought low. Of love we cannot have too much, neither can we have too much of the Spirit's power. On these two lines seek great things for thyself and others.

❖Sayings about Songs.❖

The old lullaby and cradle song, if rightly sung, can move an entire audience to tears. 'Tis like the meeting of long parted friends, or the coming back to the old church where in childhood we gathered at the ringing of the bell.

I'M A PILGRIM.

I'm a pilgrim, and I'm a stranger;
I can tarry, I can tarry but a night;
Do not detain me, for I am going
To where the rivers are ever flowing.

Of the country to which I'm going,
My Redeemer, my Redeemer is the light;
There is no sorrow, nor any sighing,
Nor any sinning, nor any dying.

REF.—I'm a pilgrim, and I'm a stranger,
I can tarry, I can tarry but a night.

PROVERB—"*The memory of the just is blessed: but the name of the wicked shall rot.*"—x. 7.

CHRIST · FOR · ME.

Many say, "The world for me."
Others say, "Honor for me."
Some say, "Pleasure for me."
A few say, "Heaven for me."
Let us all say, "Christ for me."
Who, for the first time, to-day, will thus speak?
What sinner present will choose Christ now?

❧ Gems of Thought. ☙

Prof. Henry Drummond, of Edinburgh, in one of his admirable talks at the Northfield Conference, gave this bit of Bible reading on Life: "Christ is our examplar. *His object:* 'I come to do thy will, O God.' *His food:* 'My meat is to do thy will.' The *society* he gives: 'He that doeth my will, the same is my brother, my sister, my mother.' *Education*—'Teach me to do thy will.' *Pleasure*—'I delight to do thy will.' He that doeth my will abideth forever.'"

Oh! arouse yourself from your state of false security. You have neglected your salvation too long. Years of life have been spent, and seasons of grace have been lost. Consider the great work you have to do. It does not admit of delay. You live in a dying world: time is short: eternity is at hand. Every moment of delay adds to your danger. What is not done now, may never be done. And if neglected, there is no coming back to this world to recover what you have lost. There is no place for repentance beyond the grave.

HUMILITY CHAPTER—Luke xiv.

QUESTION—*If God so clothe the grass, shall he not much more clothe you?* —Matt. vi. 30.

How sweetly comes the answer to this: He that overcometh, the same shall be clothed in white raiment; and I [Christ] will not blot his name out of the book of life, but I will confess his name before my Father, and before his angels.—Rev. iii. 5.

I will greatly rejoice in the Lord, my soul shall be joyful in my God; for he hath clothed me with the garments of salvation, he hath covered me with the robe of righteousness.—Isa. lxi. 10.

❧ Sayings about Songs. ☙

Every church ought to have its song service, where the old folks and young folks gather to learn the hymns and practise new pieces. Much depends on the leader: get one who knows music, who knows hearts, and can get the most out of the congregation.

ASHAMED OF JESUS.

Jesus, and shall it ever be,
A mortal man ashamed of thee?
Ashamed of thee, whom angels praise,
Whose glories shine through endless days!

Ashamed of Jesus! sooner far
Let evening blush to own a star;
He sheds the beams of light divine,
O'er this benighted soul of mine.

Ashamed of Jesus! just as soon
Let midnight be ashamed of noon;
'Tis midnight with my soul, till he,
Bright Morning Star, bid darkness flee.

Ashamed of Jesus! that dear friend
On whom my hopes of heaven depend!
No, when I blush, be this my shame,
That I no more revere his name.

PROVERB—"*There is no wisdom nor counsel nor understanding against the Lord.*"—xxi. 30.

SOUL WINNERS AND THEIR WORK.

The soul winners' work is to win souls.

"They that turn many to righteousness shall shine as the stars."

"He that winneth souls is wise."

To win souls you must know God, the Scriptures, and men.

Hard work and God's blessing go hand in hand.

Do you desire to be a winner of souls?

Have you ever won a soul to Christ?

✦Gems of Thought.✦

He put a high value on the souls of men; for them he had an unmanageable passion, often crying out, "Oh, what a glorious thing! how rich a prize for the expense of a man's whole life, were it to be the instrument of rescuing any one soul."—*Life of Dr. Hammond, by Dr. Fell.*

A man arose in one of Moody's meetings and gave his experience. "I have been for five years on the Mount of Transfiguration." "How many souls did you lead to Christ last year?" was the sharp question that came from Mr. Moody in an instant. "Well,

I don't know," was the astonished reply. "Have you saved any?" persisted Mr. Moody. "I don't know that I have," answered the man. "Well, we don't want that kind of mountain-top experience. When a man gets so high that he can't reach down and save poor sinners, there is something wrong."

"*Paul and Barnabas return again to Lystra,*" (Acts xiv. 21,) to the scene of their former persecution," not counting their lives dear unto themselves." What boldness! What determination! What love to souls!

SERVICE CHAPTER—Luke x.

QUESTION—*What doth it profit, my brethren, though a man say he hath faith, and have not works? Can faith save him?* —James ii. 14.

No, for faith, if it hath not works, is dead, being alone.—James ii. 17. But whoso looketh into the perfect law of liberty, and continueth therein, he being not a forgetful hearer, but a doer of the work, this man shall be blessed in his deed.—James i. 25.

✦Sayings about Songs.✦

One prays better after song. I would advise that at all home altars there be song. Let the children sing; let mother and father sing; let grandma and grandpa sing; bring in the servants, let all sing, then talk with God. 'Tis thus there come refreshing showers of grace.

SOW IN THE MORN THY SEED.

Sow in the morn thy seed;
  At eve hold not thy hand;
To doubt and fear give thou no heed—
  Broadcast it o'er the land.

Thou know'st not which shall thrive—
  The late or early sown;
Grace keeps the precious germ alive,
  When and wherever sown:

And duly shall appear,
  In verdure, beauty, strength,
The tender blade, the stalk, the ear,
  And the full corn at length.

Thou canst not toil in vain:
  Cold, heat, and moist, and dry,
Shall foster and mature the grain
  For garners in the sky.

PROVERB—"*Ointment and perfume rejoice the heart: so doth the sweetness of a man's friend by hearty counsel.*"—xxvii. 9.

GOD · OUR · GUIDE.

How he guides,—by his Word and Spirit.
Where he guides,—to service and heaven.
Whom he guides,—the whosoever that will let him.
When he guides,—always.
Guided by his Word and his providences.
Who is your guide—Christ or Satan?
Who will follow Jesus from now?

Gems of Thought.

We should *follow* Providence, and not attempt to *force* it, for that often proves best for us which was least our own doing.—*Henry.*

Providence brings good out of evil. The neglect of certain widows leads to the institution of deacons. Stephen's death prepares the way for Paul's conversion. The subsequent Jewish persecution scatters the sowers of the Word far and wide, not to waste, but to harvests.—*Ford.*

The chariot of God's providence runneth not upon broken wheels.—*Rutherford.*

Providence, like Hebrew letters, must be read backward.—*John Flavel.*

I do not ask my cross to understand,
　My way to see:
Better in darkness just to feel thy hand
　And follow thee. —*A. A. Proctor.*

The way is dark, my child, but leads to light,
I would not have thee always walk by sight,
My dealings now thou canst not understand,
I meant it so; but I will take thy hand,
And through the gloom lead safely home,
　My child! —*Henry M. Cobb.*

Where our banner leads us,
　We may safely go;
Where our Chief precedes us,
　We may face the foe.
　　—*John Mason Neale.*

COURAGE CHAPTER—Joshua i.

QUESTION—*Who will lead me?* —Psa. lx. 9.

Some of the sweetest names in the Bible refer to God as the Leader of his people, and to this question we simply say—Christ. I will go before thee, and make the crooked places straight.—Isa. xlv. 2. I will even make a way in the wilderness, and rivers in the desert, . . . to give drink to my people, my chosen.—Isa. xliii. 19, 20.

Sayings about Songs.

Let it be understood once and forever that operatic music is not for the house of God. When the church attempts to compete with the artistic world in music she will fail every time, and ought to. That is not her mission. Her music is for devotion, worship, and praise.

GOD'S GUIDANCE.

Guide us, O thou great Jehovah!
　Pilgrims through this barren land;
We are weak, but thou art mighty;
　Hold us by thy gracious hand:
Bread of heaven!
　Feed us now and evermore.

Open wide the living fountain
　Whence the healing waters flow;
Be thyself our cloudy pillar
　All the dreary desert through:
Strong Deliverer!
　Be thou still our strength and shield.

PROVERB—"*Whoso diggeth a pit shall fall therein: and he that rolleth a stone, it will return upon him.*"—xxvi. 27.

REDEMPTION FOR SOUL AND BODY.

Redemption alone by the blood of Christ.
There are many helpers, but only one Redeemer.
He redeems us from the curse of the law.
And from the power of the grave.
Redeemed forever.
Is Christ your Redeemer?
Who can save you but Jesus?

❧ Gems of Thought. ☙

There will be no Christian but will have a Gethsemane: but every praying Christian will find that there is no Gethsemane without its angel.—*Rev. T Birney.*

"Blessed is he whose sin is *covered.*" Where God has put a covering, shall man dare to lift it off? Yet he has covered the sins of his pardoned ones.

Receive Christ with all your heart; as there is nothing in Christ that may be refused, so there is nothing in you from which he must be excluded.—*John Flavel.*

The humble, the more he approaches to be a saint, the more he apprehends himself to be a sinner.—*J. H. Newman.*

Great the work by Christ completed!
Sin forever put away;
Satan vanquished, death defeated!
Opened wide the realms of day!
See the Victor, crowned with glory,
Seated on the throne of God!
Shout aloud the joyful story
Of redemption through his blood.

REDEMPTION CHAPTER—Luke xxiii.

QUESTION—*Should not a people seek unto their God?*
—Isa. viii. 19.

Blessed are they that keep his testimonies, and that seek him with the whole heart.—Ps. cxix. 2. With my whole heart have I sought thee: O let me not wander from thy commandments.—Ps. cxix. 10.

A people without prayer is a powerless people. Let the church pray more. Let there be more prevailing prayer. That word "seek" is big in meaning.

❧ Sayings about Songs. ☙

The chiming bells, heard across the water, what magic spell they give. How the notes struck one by one lift the heart heavenward. At eventide many a weary soul has found fresh courage as amidst the gloom there suddenly rung out the chimes. The bells of old Trinity will forever be remembered by millions.

DEAR JERUSALEM.

O mother, dear Jerusalem,
When shall I come to thee?
When shall my sorrows have an end?
Thy joys when shall I see?

O happy harbor of God's saints!
O sweet and pleasant soil!
In thee no sorrows can be found
No grief, no care, no toil.

In thee no sickness is at all,
Nor hurt, nor any sore;
There is no death nor ugly sight,
But life forevermore.

No dimming cloud o'ershadows thee,
No cloud nor darksome night:
But every soul shines as the sun,
For God himself gives light.

PROVERB—*"Rejoice not when thy enemy falleth, and let not thine heart be glad when he stumbleth."*—xxiv. 17.

63

PEACE, ·· THE ·· GIFT OF GOD.

There is no peace to the wicked.
The righteous shall have abundance of peace.
There is a false and a true peace.
The Christian's peace was made at the cross.
Read John xiv. 27.
Have you peace—peace with God?
Is it well with thy soul?

✦ Gems of Thought. ✦

There is a blessed peace in looking for nothing but our daily task and our portion of Christ's cross between this day and the appointed time when we shall fall asleep in him.—*Bishop Wilberforce.*

It is a great mercy to enjoy the Gospel of peace, but a greater to enjoy the peace of the Gospel.

Renounce all kinds of peace, till thou hast found peace of conscience. Discard all joy, till thou feelest the joy of the Holy Ghost.—*Mede.*

Like a river glorious,
　Is God's perfect peace,
Over all victorious,
　In its glad increase.

I asked for peace with suppliant knee,
　And peace was given; not peace alone,
　But *love* and *joy* and *ecstasy.*

Peace upon peace, like wave upon wave,
This is the portion that I crave;
The peace of God which passeth thought,
The peace of Christ which changeth not.
　　　　　　　　　—*H. Bonar.*

HOUSEHOLD CHAPTER—Col. iii.

QUESTION—*To whom will ye flee for help?* —Isa. x. 3.

The question is for the time of trouble, and at the grave, and before the judgment seat of Christ. For we who trust in the living God, we say, "To him who is our refuge and strength, a very present help in time of trouble." "The Lord God will help me."
　　　　　　　　　—Isa. l. 7.

✦ Sayings about Songs. ✦

"Home, sweet home!" what a mighty chorus will take up that song on the other side. Here they had no home, they were but pilgrims and strangers, there they will be "at home." 'Twill be rest forever. God knew it could not be "home" where there was no song, so abundance of music will be found in "our Father's house."

THE PLACE OF PEACE.

From every stormy wind that blows,
From every swelling tide of woes,
There is a calm, a sure retreat—
'Tis found beneath the mercy seat.

There is a place where Jesus sheds
The oil of gladness on our heads,
A place than all besides more sweet—
It is the blood-bought mercy seat.

PROVERB—*"A soft answer turneth away wrath, but grievous words stir up anger."*—xv. 1.

PRAISE FOR GOD'S GREAT GIFTS.

Praise him first for Jesus.
Praise him next for the Comforter.
Then praise him for spiritual blessings.
Next praise him for temporal supplies.
Last praise him for everything.
Who will speak of God's goodness?
Who will take God's Son as Saviour?

Gems of Thought.

When prayer cannot unlock heaven, praise will often do it.

Prayer purchaseth blessings, giving praise keeps the quiet possession of them.—*Fuller.*

The spirit of melancholy would often take its flight from us if only we would take up the song of praise.—*Power.*

Praise as well as pray. If you would arm yourselves for trouble and duty, recount the marvelous acts of the Lord, as well as supplicate the communications of his grace. Before they departed—the Redeemer to the terrible agony, the disciples to the dreaded separation—the last thing was to sing a hymn—a chant of thankful psalms.—*Melville.*

The slender returns of gratitude which we make are many times a formal ceremony, a preface to usher in petitions for what we want, rather than thankfulness for what we have received.—*Scougal.*

LAME MAN'S CHAPTER—Acts iii.

QUESTION—*What sayest thou of him?* —John ix. 17.

Amidst the praises of him from others, what sayest THOU of him? Hast thou known him as a personal Saviour? Is he thy companion and friend? In the meeting, in the home, in the marts of trade—what sayest thou? What sayest thou of him to-day?

Sayings about Songs.

A congregation that don't sing won't pray. A music-loving people in the Lord's house will draw heaven down with mighty blessings. You can never hire a choir to do what the Spirit lays upon the congregation to perform.

PRAISE TO GOD.

All people that on earth do dwell,
Sing to the Lord with cheerful voice;
Him serve with mirth, his praise forth tell,
Come ye before him and rejoice.

Know that the Lord is God indeed;
Without our aid he did us make;
We are his flock, he doth us feed,
And for his sheep he doth us take.

O enter then his gates with praise,
Approach with joy his courts unto:
Praise, laud, and bless his name always,
For it is seemly so to do.

For why? the Lord our God is good,
His mercy is forever sure;
His truth at all times firmly stood,
And shall from age to age endure.

PROVERB—"*Let another man praise thee, and not thine own mouth; a stranger, and not thine own lips.*"—xxvii. 2.

JESUS, THE SINNER'S FRIEND.

Yes, the *sinner's* Friend.
While yet sinners, he died for us.
Thus he proved his wonderful love.
He changes sinners to saints.
He lives with sinners here.
Will you live with him hereafter?
Who will call him "Friend" and Saviour?

Gems of Thought.

Anything is too much to be expected while we look at ourselves; nothing while we look at Christ.—*Venn.*

Fear not is the first word in the first annunciation of his conception; the first word in the first annunciation of his birth; the first word in the first annunciation of his resurrection; and almost the last word in his last exhortation.—*Mallerus.*

"*Go tell my brethren.*"—Matt. xxviii. 10. Blessed Lord, thou hast not called angels brethren; but men thou art pleased to call so.

A little negro boy, when on his death-bed, was visited by a missionary to whom he spoke of the happiness he felt, and the longing desire to be with Jesus. "I am going to heaven soon, and then I shall see Jesus, and be with him forever," said the little fellow. "But," rejoined the missionary, "if Jesus were to leave heaven, what would you do?" "I would follow him," replied the boy. "But, suppose," said the missionary, "Jesus went to hell, what would you do then?" In an instant, with a look of triumph, he replied, "Then I'd go too; there is no hell where Jesus is."

There's a refuge in God for the sin-burdened soul,
In the peace-giving fountain, whose streams make us whole;
There's a refuge in Jesus, the sinner's rich Friend,
Who pardons, and cleanses, and keeps to the end.

LOST AND FOUND CHAPTER—Luke xv.

QUESTION—*Wilt thou be made whole?* —John v. 6.

Yes, Lord, for this is THY question to me who art broken; both mind and heart have gone to pieces. Sin has wounded me, by its power I am undone. Make true thy promise unto me this day—"I will heal thee."

Sayings about Songs.

Mother hushes the babe to sleep with song. The last hour of many a child of God is soothed with strains from the portals of glory. How many in dying have said, "Listen! don't you hear them singing"? The ears of the soul begin to open as the ears of the body begin to close.

THE GREAT NAME.

Jesus! the name that charms our fears,
That bids our sorrows cease;
'Tis music in the sinner's ears,
'Tis life, and health, and peace.

He breaks the power of cancelled sin,
He sets the prisoner free;

His blood can make the foulest clean,
His blood availed for me.

He speaks, and, listening to his voice,
New life the dead receive;
The mournful broken hearts rejoice,
The humble poor believe.

PROVERB—"*Can a man take fire in his bosom, and his clothing not be burned?*"—vi. 27.

66

ABIDING IN CHRIST.

Christ the true vine, we the branches.
We abide in Christ and he in God.
To abide in Christ is to abide in love.
There is no fruit-bearing apart from Christ.
Branches that bear no fruit are taken away.
Do you now abide in Jesus?
From to-day who will abide in Christ?

Gems of Thought.

The serene, silent beauty of a holy life is the most powerful influence in the world next to the almightiness of the Spirit of God. —*Spurgeon.*

Remember, you are not a tree, that can stand alone—you are only a "branch"; and it is only while you abide in him as a branch that you will flourish.—*McCheyne.*

Christian, wouldst thou fruitful be? Jesus says, "abide in me"; From him all thy fruit is found; May it to his praise abound!

Christian, wouldst thou holy be? Jesus says, "abide in me"; Sanctified in him thou art; Sanctify him in thy heart.

ABIDING CHAPTER—John xv.

QUESTION—*Who shall separate us from the love of Christ?*
—Rom. viii. 35.

I am persuaded that neither death, nor life, nor angels, nor principalities, nor powers, nor things present, nor things to come, nor height, nor depth, nor any other creature, shall be able to separate us from the love of God, which is in Christ Jesus our Lord.—Rom. viii. 38, 39. Yea, I have loved thee with an everlasting love.—Jer. xxxi. 3.

Sayings about Songs.

That grand old hymn, "Come, ye disconsolate," has done more to lift the world into sunshine and out of the fog than all the simple pleasures of the world put together. There is felt every time you sing it an upward pull, like as though an omnipotent hand had hold of you and your burdens.

JESUS IS MINE.

Fade, fade, each earthly joy,
Jesus is mine;
Break, every tender tie,
Jesus is mine.
Dark is the wilderness,
Earth has no resting-place,
Jesus alone can bless,
Jesus is mine.

Tempt not my soul away,
Jesus is mine;
Here would I ever stay,
Jesus is mine.
Perishing things of clay,
Born but for one brief day,
Pass from my heart away,
Jesus is mine.

Farewell, ye dreams of night,
Jesus is mine;
Lost in this dawning bright,
Jesus is mine.
All that my soul has tried
Left but a dismal void;
Jesus has satisfied,
Jesus is mine.

Farewell, mortality,
Jesus is mine;
Welcome, eternity,
Jesus is mine.
Welcome, O loved and blest,
Welcome, sweet scenes of rest,
Welcome, my Saviour's breast,
Jesus is mine.

PROVERB—*"Before destruction the heart of man is haughty; and before honor is humility."*—xviii. 12. **67**

PAUL, THE SINNER SAVED.

The chief of sinners made the chief of saints.
Saul the persecutor made Paul the preacher.
Paul would know nothing but Christ and him crucified.
Let us follow his example.
Read Romans viii. with Ephesians iii.
Do you know Paul's mighty Saviour?
Who will change from sinner lost to sinner saved?

Gems of Thought.

Art thou an unjust person? Think upon the publican. Hast thou lived in uncleanness? Think upon the harlot. Hast thou defrauded? Consider the thief upon the cross. Art thou a profane person? Think upon St. Paul, once a blasphemer, afterward an apostle. Do not therefore frame vain excuses, or pretend difficulties where there are none.—*Chrysostom.*

If St. Paul had feared the *mockers*, he would not have reached the believers.—*St. Augustine.*

The apostles were as burning coals scattered throughout the nations, blest incendiaries of the world.—*Leighton.*

The apostles were very full, because very empty; full of the Spirit of God because empty of the spirit of the world. — *St. Augustine.*

Those that are bound for heaven must be willing to swim against the stream, and must not do as *most* do, but as *the best* do. —*Henry.*

The peace of God leads you to war with every thing that is opposed to his holy will and way.

SAUL OF TARSUS CHAPTER—Acts ix.

QUESTION—*If God be for us, who can be against us?*
—Rom. viii. 31.

Yes, indeed, who? Strength and deliverance is with our God.

He doeth according to his will in the army of heaven, and among the inhabitants of the earth: and none can stay his hand.—Dan. iv. 35.

Alleluia! for the Lord God Omnipotent reigneth.—Rev. xix. 6.

Sayings about Songs.

" How firm a foundation, ye saints of the Lord!" My brother, just you get your people singing that old hymn as it ought to be sung, and there will be more piety in the pews than has been known heretofore. One such song as that is worth a bushel of the nonsense we find set to music now-a-days.

ALL FOR JESUS,

Jesus, I my cross have taken,
   All to leave and follow thee;
Naked, poor, despised, forsaken,
   Thou from hence my all shalt be.
Perish every fond ambition,
   All I've sought, or hoped or known:
Yet how rich is my condition!
   God and heaven are still my own.

Let the world despise or leave me:
   They have left my Saviour, too.
Human hearts and looks deceive me—
   Thou art not, like them, untrue.
Oh, 'tis not in grief to harm me,
   While thy love is left to me;
Oh, 'twere not in joy to charm me,
   Were that joy unmixed with thee.

PROVERB—*"He that hath a bountiful eye shall be blessed; for he giveth of his bread to the poor."*—xxii. 9.

ROMANS, THE · BOOK · OF DOCTRINES.

This book is the quintessence of the Gospel.
The eighth chapter is the "Victory" chapter.
Chapter fourteen is to be the rule of your life.
Verse twenty-eight of chapter eight is a diamond.
This is not Paul's, but God's Epistle to the church at large.
Is verse sixteen of chapter one your experience?
Who knows the truth of verse one, chapter eight?

Gems of Thought.

Surely, it is a great deal to avoid wrong-doing; but what would you account that husbandry worth which succeeded only in keeping down weeds? A man goes on ploughing and ploughing, harrowing and harrowing, hoeing and hoeing; and he rejoices, as July comes on, saying, "There is not a weed on my farm—not a weed." Round and round he goes, looking into every corner, and under every hedge, to spy out any weeds that may have been left; and he says, "Not one weed shall grow on this farm." But where is thy corn, O farmer? "I have no corn." Where is thy wheat? "I have no wheat." Where are thy fruits? "I have no fruits" What hast thou? No weeds!—*Beecher.*

If you have really given up your heart to God in private, your life will show forth the praise of God in public: if God has the heart, he is sure of the life.

JUDGMENT CHAPTER—Romans xiv.

QUESTION—*If a man die, shall he live again?* —Job xiv. 14.

He will. "There shall be a resurrection of the dead, both of the just and unjust." Not one will be left in the grave, for all shall come forth, some to life others unto a resurrection of damnation. How will it be with thee, my brother, my sister?

Sayings about Songs.

Some hymns are very unscriptural. They should never be sung. Let there be truth in the words. Let the theology be right. Let the teaching be as by the Bible. Cut out all unsound pieces. The old hymns of the church can never be supplanted, because they are so sound and scriptural.

WALK IN THE LIGHT.

Walk in the light! so shalt thou know
  That fellowship of love,
His Spirit only can bestow
  Who reigns in light above.

Walk in the light! and thou shalt find
  Thy heart made truly his,
Who dwells in cloudless light enshrined,
  In whom no darkness is.

Walk in the light! and thou shalt own
  Thy darkness passed away,
Because that light hath on thee shone
  In which is perfect day.

Walk in the light! and e'en the tomb
  No fearful shade shall wear;
Glory shall chase away its gloom,
  For Christ hath conquered there.

PROVERB—"*A whip for the horse, a bridle for the ass, and a rod for the fool's back.*"—xxvi. 3.

DAVID, GOD'S CHOSEN · MAN.

The shepherd boy made king.
Out of sinners God makes sons.
We are chosen, in Christ, by God.
Some day we shall see David and hear him sing.
God's chosen ones are not earth's chosen ones.
Can you say, "The Lord is my Shepherd"?
Who will trust in David's God?

Gems of Thought.

As we put our hand to the sacred Book, be our prayer with David: "Open mine eyes, that I may see wondrous things out of thy law."

A thousand sermons can't put down heresy so fast as a hundred hymns.—*Beecher.*

From David, learn to give thanks in everything. Every furrow in the book of Psalms is sown with seeds of thanksgiving.—*Jeremy Taylor.*

I have seen persons who have so exhausted themselves by religious emotions that they had no strength left for religious duties.—*Beecher.*

Deliver me from premature saintship! I cannot endure to see a girl forty years old before she is five, or to see a boy imitating Isaiah or Dante when he is not yet out of his pantalets.—*Beecher.*

PRODIGAL'S PSALM—Psalm li.

QUESTION—*Wherewithal shall a young man cleanse his way?* —Ps. cxix. 9.

"By taking heed thereto according to thy Word," and the way of thousands needs to be cleansed. Let the young men put more trust in their mothers' Bible, and less in their own mistaken judgments. "Though your sins be as scarlet, they shall be white as snow."

Sayings about Songs.

'Twill be a happy day, I reckon, when we with the others washed in the blood, gather about David and his harp, and listen to the rendering of the Psalms as sung by him. How I shall watch the faces of those Scotch Psalm singers then.

LOVE FOR GOD'S KINGDOM.

I love thy kingdom, Lord,
The house of thine abode,
The Church our blest Redeemer saved
With his own precious blood.

I love thy Church, O God!
Her walls before thee stand,
Dear as the apple of thine eye,
And graven on thy hand.

For her my tears shall fall,
For her my prayers ascend;
To her my cares and toils be given,
Till toils and cares shall end.

Beyond my highest joy
I prize her heavenly ways,
Her sweet communion, solemn vows,
Her hymns of love and praise.

PROVERB—"*Love not sleep, lest thou come to poverty: open thine eyes, and thou shalt be satisfied with bread.*"—xxi. 13.

Theme 68.

PSALMS.

Psalms is the Book of Experience.
The key-words are Prayer and Praise.
They begin with "Blessed is the man."
They end with "Praise ye the Lord."
When the stars have gone out the Psalms will live.
How many Psalms can you repeat from memory?
Who can repeat the Shepherd's Psalm as theirs?

⟶Gems of Thought.⟵

The Gospel of the Grace of God is no organized theory for the reconstruction of society; it is no utopian dream for the elevation of the human race; it comes before the world with no high-sounding phrases or elaborate schemes for the bettering of man's earthly condition. It is no philanthropic, humanitarian association for the elevation of the masses. It deals with man as a ruined, fallen, dead creature, and seeks to bring each individual one by one under the energy and power of the Holy Spirit.

It does not elevate, but it transforms; it seeks not to repair, but to renew. It has

Redemption by Substitution as its fundamental groundwork, and this substitution is the action and work of the Holy One, entirely apart from man in every form and shape.

Since God loved you (John iii. 16)—since Christ died for you (Rom. v. 8)—since the blood that cleanseth from all sin *has been shed* (1 John i. 7) God offers now (2 Cor. vi. 2) a free, full, and eternal salvation from the guilt and power of sin to whosoever will (Rom. vi. 23; Heb. v. 9; Heb. vii. 25; Rev. xxii. 17).

THE SHEPHERD'S PSALM—Psalm xxiii.

QUESTION—*Who can forgive sins?* —Mark ii. 7.

God only.—Mark ii. 7. No preacher or priest, none but God. We may and must forgive each other, but our sins are against the divine Sovereign, and from the throne alone can come the word of remission, and then only when we kneel humbly at the cross.

⟶Sayings about Songs.⟵

"The Psalms are the flower garden of the Bible, and some plant may be found there for the healing of every wound." It is a strange experience which can't find balm in the Gospel of David for help. Search closely, and you will get the remedy for bruised hearts.

GOD MY SALVATION.

God is my strong salvation;
  What foe have I to fear?
In darkness and temptation,
  My light, my help, is near:
Though hosts encamp around me,
  Firm in the fight I stand;
What terror can confound me,
  With God at my right hand?

Place on the Lord reliance;
  My soul, with courage wait;
His truth be thine affiance,
  When faint and desolate;
His might thy heart shall strengthen,
  His love thy joy increase;
Mercy thy days shall lengthen;
  The Lord will give thee peace.

PROVERB—"*There is that scattereth, and yet increaseth; and there is that withholdeth more than is meet, but it tendeth to poverty.*"—xi. 24.

71

PETER, THE PREACHER OF PENTECOST.

Peter of Pilate's hall—was weak.
Peter of Pentecost—was strong.
A fisherman chosen to fish for men.
His work was to feed the sheep and lambs.
His Epistles are milk for babes and meat for men.
Have you been converted?
Do you follow Christ afar off or near by?

✥Gems of Thought.✥

He (Peter) who before had taught me by his good life how I should stand, so as not to fall, hath now taught me by his repentance how, in case of my falling, I should rise again.—*St. Jerome.*

If it be necessary to *receive* Christ in order to salvation, it is equally necessary to *walk* with him in order to growth.—*Pulsford.*

I do not blame you so severely, because you have been so badly brought up. You have been studying catechisms and creeds so that you have had no time to study conduct. You have been so busy thinking about church machinery that you have not had much time to think about Christian spirit and life. You have studied the body until you have forgotten that there is such a thing as the soul.—*Beecher.*

PENTECOST CHAPTER—Acts ii.

QUESTION—*How shall we escape, if we neglect so great salvation?* —Heb. ii. 3.

Ye that neglect him, ye that turn from the cup of salvation to the waters of death, how answer you this mighty question? Some of you refuse to answer, but the Bible answers it for you: "For if they escaped not who refused him that spake on earth, much more shall not we escape, if we turn away from him that speaketh from heaven."—Heb. xii. 25.

✥Sayings about Songs.✥

"No discords" up there; no colds to clog one's voice; no quick medicines to get ready for the service; no sore throat to keep one from their place in the throng of singers; no staying in because it rains; no wintry days to chill both heart and voice. Hallelujah!

MISSIONARY HYMN.

From Greenland's icy mountains,
From India's coral strand;
Where Afric's sunny fountains
Roll down their golden sand;
From many an ancient river,
From many a palmy plain,
They call us to deliver
Their land from error's chain.

Shall we, whose souls are lighted
With wisdom from on high,
Shall we to men benighted
The lamp of life deny?

Salvation! O salvation!
The joyful sound proclaim,
Till earth's remotest nation
Has learned Messiah's name.

Waft, waft, ye winds, his story,
And you, ye waters, roll,
Till, like a sea of glory,
It spreads from pole to pole:
Till o'er our ransomed nature
The Lamb for sinners slain,
Redeemer, King, Creator,
In bliss returns to reign.

PROVERB—"*The wicked is snared by the transgression of his lips: but the just shall come out of trouble.*"—xii. 13.

MOSES, THE LAWGIVER.

The law came by Moses.
Grace and truth came by Jesus Christ.
Obedience is the key-word of both law and gospel.
Moses wrote of Christ, and the Pentateuch has hundreds of gospel
promises.
Do you keep the golden rule?
Will you obey the God of Moses?

Gems of Thought.

There must be the preaching of the law, and a law-work in the conscience, before men are likely ever to set out resolutely for heaven; and without this law-work, they do almost invariably turn back.—*Dr. Cheever.*

One of the finest sights in the world is a Christian at the end of a long course with an unsullied reputation; his hair may be white, but his leaf is green.—*Jay.*

The church is not obligatory any more than Fulton Ferry is. I can refuse to cross the river on the ferryboat, and say, "I won't pay the cent or two cents. I am going to swim." I should have a right to swim if I preferred, but I should be a fool if I did. And if you say, "I do not want to join the church," you are under no obligation to join it.—*Beecher.*

THE LAW CHAPTER—Romans vii.

QUESTION—*How can ye escape the damnation of hell?*
—Matt. xxiii. 33.

In no other way than by the blood of Jesus; that was shed that we might be sprinkled by it, and thus the destroying angel pass over. If we are not "under the blood" there can be no escaping the justice of God, and the punishment of the wicked.

Sayings about Songs.

Let there be much singing in the school room, for the memory of the songs will brighten life when the knowledge is set in motion like the wheels of some great factory. Many a fragment of college song has strengthened the merchant and manufacturer and lawyer when in great perplexity.

THE DIVINE LAW.

That blessed law of thine,
Jesus, to me impart;
The Spirit's law of life divine,
Oh, write it on my heart!

Implant it deep within,
Whence it may ne'er remove,
The law of liberty from sin,
The perfect law of love.

Thy nature be my law,
Thy spotless sanctity;
And sweetly every moment draw
My happy soul to thee.

Soul of my soul, remain!
Who didst for all fulfil,
In me, O Lord, fulfil again
Thy heavenly Father's will.

PROVERB—*"He that rebuketh a man, afterwards shall find more favor than he that flattereth with the tongue."*—xxviii. 23.

DANIEL, THE · MAN · OF CHARACTER.

Job xxix. is the Character Chapter.
Daniel had a purpose, and held to it.
More men like Daniel are needed now.
His was a life of prayer and power.
Though a captive he yet was a Christian.
Who, like Daniel, have been delivered?
Who will trust in Daniel's God?

—Gems of Thought.—

Remark that the two most devotional men in the Old Testament, David and Daniel, were men constantly engaged in the business and cares of this world.—*Ford.*

There are men who own a thousand acres of land,—in their soul,—and have but a quarter of an acre of it under cultivation.—*Beecher.*

Enthusiasm is the element of success in everything, it is the light that leads, and the strength that lifts men in and up in the great struggles of scientific pursuits and of professional labor. It robs endurance of difficulty, and makes a pleasure of duty.

If one limb is shorter than the other, we can splice out the shoe; but if a man is born without common sense, I do not know of any crutch or splice that will supply the lack. He must wiggle on the best way he can.—*Beecher.*

LION'S DEN CHAPTER—Daniel vi.

QUESTION—*Hast thou faith?* —Rom. xiv. 22.

A pointed question, and happy they who can say," Yea, Lord, I believe " Is thy faith a dead or living force? "Faith cometh by hearing, and hearing by the word of God." hence the Bible should be well read and often read.

Sinner, hast thou saving faith in Jesus the Christ?

—Sayings about Songs.—

God will build no mansion and leave it unfurnished. There will be such instruments of music in the homes of saved sinners on high as will delight the soul for eternity. I wait to press the key spring of some music box made by God's artizans.

JESUS OF BETHANY.

Jesus wept! those tears are over,
  But his heart is still the same:
Kinsman, Friend, and elder Brother,
  Is his everlasting name,
    Saviour, who can love like thee,
    Gracious One of Bethany?

When the pangs of trial seize us,
  When the waves of sorrow roll,
I will lay my head on Jesus,
  Pillow of the troubled soul.
    Surely, none can feel like thee,
    Weeping One of Bethany!

Jesus wept! and still in glory,
  He can mark each mourner's tear,
Living to retrace the story
  Of the hearts he solaced here.
    Lord, when I am called to die,
    Let me think of Bethany.

Jesus wept! that tear of sorrow
  Is a legacy of love;
Yesterday, to-day, to-morrow,
  He the same doth ever prove.
    Thou art all in all to me,
    Living One of Bethany!

PROVERB—"*The wicked flee when no man pursueth: but the righteous are bold as a lion.*"—xxviii. 1.

Theme 72.

WARNINGS TO·THE WICKED.

Flee from the wrath to come.
Escape for thy life.
Turn ye, turn ye, for why will ye die.
The wicked shall be turned into hell.
There shall be weeping and wailing and woe.
Who will turn from sin to Christ?
Who will escape by the way of the cross?

Gems of Thought.

Men shall be turned inside out; and amongst all sinners that shall then be brought before that judgment-seat, the most deformed sight shall be an unmasked hypocrite, and the heaviest sentence shall be his portion.—*Leighton.*

A deliberate purpose to practise things which one's conscience clearly condemns is a knife that cuts the tie of discipleship and separates one from Christ. It is spiritual suicide.

Hell is a barren place. You carry your lusts there, but find not food for them.—*Gurnall.*

God spared one thief, that no man might despair; but one, that none should presume. —*Baily.*

He who pardons the sinner that *repents,* will *grant no repentance* to the sinner that presumes.

Matt. xxv. 41. Behold in four words what hell is: *separated* from God, *accursed* of God, condemned to *fire,* and that *forever.* Does not our Lord speak as if there were real fire in hell? Is it possible then to suppose that the God of truth would speak in this manner if it were not so? Impute no such folly to the Most High.—*Wesley.*

HYPOCRITES' CHAPTER—Matt. xxiii.

QUESTION—*What is the destiny of the wicked?*

Everlasting punishment in the lake that burneth with fire and brimstone. Their portion, says God, shall be his hatred, and upon them shall he rain snares, fire and brimstone, and a horrible tempest.—Ps. xi.

The description of hell in the New Testament, as well as in the Old, should make all men flee from the wrath to come. Read carefully Rev. xxi. 8.

Sayings about Songs.

The world may sing its glees. The bacchanalian songs will do for those who have no Christ,—no Saviour,—but for me, give me the songs of Zion. Let the refrain of truth be mine. Let the words of the Book be set to music, and these be my consolation.

SINNER, COME.

Oh, do not let the word depart,
And close thine eyes against the light;
Poor sinner, harden not thy heart,
Thou wouldst be saved—why not to-night?

To-morrow's sun may never rise
To bless thy long-deluded sight;
This is the time. Oh, then, be wise!
Thou wouldst be saved—why not to-night?

Our God in pity lingers still,
And wilt thou thus his love requite?
Renounce, at length, thy stubborn will;
Thou wouldst be saved—why not to-night?

The world has nothing left to give—
It has no new, no pure delight;
Oh, try the life which Christians live;
Thou wouldst be saved—why not to-night?

PROVERB—*"Poverty and shame shall be to him that refuseth instruction: but he that regardeth reproof shall be honoured."*—xiii. 18.

75

TRUE REPENTANCE.

Repent, believe, be saved.
No repentance—no salvation.
Read Isaiah lv. 6, 7.
Repentance includes restitution.
The world needs more of John the Baptist.
Who will turn from sin?
Who will serve Christ?

Gems of Thought.

Repentance hath two parts—mourning and mending, or humiliation and reformation; the more God hath abated thee in the former, out of his gentleness, the more must thou increase in the latter, out of thy gratitude. Well may he expect more work to be done by thy hands, who hath laid less weight to be borne on thy shoulders.

Nothing shall be of greater confusion to sinners, than to behold greater sinners than themselves raised to glory; because the latter made use of the time for repentance, which they despised and rejected.—*Taylor.*

Faith without repentance is not faith, but presumption; like a ship all sail and no ballast, that tippeth over with every blast. And repentance without faith is not repentance, but despair; like a ship all ballast and no sail, which sinketh of her own weight.—*Sanderson.*

The murderer and adulterer are sometimes saved; the *virtuous* man rarely, because he disdains to descend. "*Remember me,*" saved a dying malefactor! '*God, I thank thee,*" condemned a proud Pharisee. When a man uncovers his sin, God covers it.—*St. Augustine.*

God sometimes fills the heart of the newly penitent with special inward consolations, until they become established. They are cordials and allurements, sometimes withholden from the more perfect.—*Cetanus.*

REPENTANCE CHAPTER—Luke xiii.

QUESTION—*Which way shall we go?* —2 Kings iii. 8.

Let the Word of God give the answer to this question: "Enter not into the path of the wicked, and go not in the way of evil men. Avoid it, pass not by it, turn from it and pass away."—Prov. iv. 14. 15. Jesus says, "Follow me."—Luke xviii. 22.

Sayings about Songs.

It is the testimony of an old farmer that he never knew a whistling laborer to find fault with either his food, his bed, or his work, and such men were invariably kind to both animals and the children.

THE SHEPHERD'S VOICE.

I was a wandering sheep,
    I did not love the fold;
I did not love my Shepherd's voice,
    I would not be controlled;
I was a wayward child,
    I did not love my home,
I did not love my Father's voice,
    I loved afar to roam.

The Shepherd sought his sheep,
    The Father sought his child;
They followed me o'er vale and hill,
    O'er deserts waste and wild;
They found me nigh to death,
    Famished, and faint, and lone;
They bound me with the bands of love,
    They saved the wandering one.

PROVERB—"*He that covereth his sins shall not prosper: but whoso confesseth and forsaketh them shall have mercy.*"—xxviii. 13.

GLAD TIDINGS.

Glad tidings from the City of Gold.
Sent to the vilest of men.
To tell them they all may be saved.
No other tidings so good as these.
It came from heaven, that we might go to heaven.
Who will hear the gospel story?
Who will love the Prince of Glory?

❧Gems of Thought.☙

This world would be a great groaning machine if God had not sent humor to make its wheels run smooth, and sparkling wit by which to light a torch that should guide a thousand weary feet in right ways.—*Beecher.*

There is no religion in making yourself miserable; God loves to make poor sinners happy: in the Old Testament, he bids you delight yourself in the Lord; and promises the desires of your heart. In the New, he says, " Rejoice in the Lord alway."

God did not call you to be canary-birds in a little cage, and to hop up and down on three sticks, within a space no larger than the size of the cage. God calls you to be eagles, and to fly from sun to sun, over continents.—*Beecher.*

If you know what torch to light,
Guiding others through the night,
Light it.

If you've any debt to pay,
Rest you neither night nor day—
Pay it.

REVIVAL CHAPTER—Joel ii.

QUESTION—*Watchman, what of the night?*   —Isa. xxi. 11.

The night is far spent, the day is at hand: let us therefore cast off the works of darkness, and let us put on the armour of light.—Rom. xiii. 12.

The world is waking up as the morning now breaks. Never was there such a gospel cry. See the printing presses night and day printing Bibles alone.

❧Sayings about Songs.☙

Earth has nothing so much like heaven as sacred song and music. Let me hear a thousand voices pealing forth " I will sing of my Redeemer," and with closed eyes I can imagine myself just outside the open gate of the city which hath foundations, whose builder and maker is God.

GRACE.

Grace! tis a charming sound,
Harmonious to the ear;
Heaven with the echo shall resound,
And all the earth shall hear.

Grace first contrived a way
To save rebellious man;
And all the steps that grace display,
Which drew the wondrous plan.

Grace taught my roving feet
To tread the heavenly road;
And new supplies each hour I meet,
While pressing on to God.

Grace all the work shall crown
Through everlasting days;
It lays in heaven the topmost stone,
And well deserves our praise.

PROVERB—*"Deceit is in the heart of them that imagine evil: but to the counsellors of peace is joy."*—xii. 20.

77

VICTORY, THE CHRISTIAN'S WATCHWORD.

Victory in the name of the Lord Jesus.
Victory by the power of the Holy Ghost.
Victory over the world, the flesh, and the devil.
Triumph both in temptation and trial.
Victory here and reward hereafter.
Who will enlist for Christ's service?
Who has had the victory in their lives to-day?

Gems of Thought.

Just in proportion as you gain a victory over the evil which you have become aware of in yourself, will your spiritual eyes be purged for a brighter perception of the Holy One.—*Channing.*

He that in the horrors of the tempest can say with the psalmist, "Bless the Lord, O my soul!" hath a sublime foretaste of his triumph on the great and terrible day of the Lord.—*Wilberforce.*

Success is a seven-fold good when God's blessing specially rests upon it.—*Dr. Davies.*

The measure of our success is in proportion as we satisfy our God. The man that pleases God is always successful.—*Krummacher.*

Hast thou not learned what thou art often told,
A truth still sacred, and believed of old,
That no success attends our spears and swords
Unblest, and that the battle is the Lord's?—*Cowper.*

VICTORY CHAPTER—Romans viii.

QUESTION—*Why art thou cast down, O my soul?*—Ps. xlii. 11.

Look up! look up! Look to Jesus; at the cross is light. O Israel, thou shalt not be forgotten of me. I have blotted out, as a thick cloud, thy sins: return unto me; for

I have redeemed thee.—Isa. xliv. 21, 22. In returning and rest shall ye be saved; in quietness and in confidence shall be your strength.—Isa. xxx. 15.

Sayings about Songs.

My friend, your harp of song has been hung on the willows long enough. Just take it down to-day and join us in our praises of the Prince of Peace. Don't sing in the minor key either. Pull out the great diapason of your soul and vie with the rest.

THE VICTORIOUS CHRIST.

Hark! ten thousand harps and voices
Sound the notes of praise above;
Jesus reigns, and heaven rejoices;
Jesus reigns, the God of love:
See, he sits on yonder throne;
Jesus rules the world alone.

Jesus, hail! whose glory brightens
All above, and gives it worth;
Lord of life, thy smile enlightens,
Cheers and charms thy saints on earth:
When we think of love like thine,
Lord, we own it love divine.

PROVERB—"*Pride goeth before destruction, and a haughty spirit before a fall.*
—xvi. 18.

78

TRÄINING CLÄSS LESSONS

CHARLES H. YATMAN.

OBJECT:

To train Christian men and women in the knowledge and use of Scripture, that they may LOVE the Bible; to fit them for active service in leading others successfully, wisely, and intelligently to Christ; also to profitably take part in religious meetings, as well as conduct the same when called upon.

TOPICS:

How to study the Bible by chapters, 1	Scripture for inquirers, . . . 15
The office and work of the Holy Spirit, 2	How to deal with inquirers, . . 16
How to mark your Bible, . . . 3	How to approach the unsaved about
The use of promises, ... 4	salvation, ... 17
Work every one can do, . . . 5	What consecration and sanctification
How to study the Bible by topics, . 6	mean, ... 18
The worker and his God, . . . 7	Hints on how to lead a meeting, . 19
The power of faith and prayer, . 8	How to give the gospel invitation to
How to raise money for christian	the unconverted, ... 20
work, ... 9	Illustrations—how to make and use
How to determine one's field of work, 10	them, ... 21
How to love your Bible, . . . 11	The worker and himself, . . . 22
Things to know, ... 12	A clear idea of conversion, . . 23
How to locate scripture texts. . . 13	Aids to soul winning, ... 24
Scripture for christian workers, . 14	Incentives to soul winning, . . 25

79

CHAPTERS OF PURE GOLD.

IT'S a grand thing to really love to read and search the dear old Bible. I want to help you to this experience. It is such a big book, we can only take it in bits (and that's the way to feed, anyway). Now, if you are hungry at heart, just read the Bread Chapter; or, if your feet are slipping, read the Rock Chapter; or, do you find yourself getting a little cross, read the Charity Chapter. Have you had lots of defeats with Satan, read the Victory Chapter. Have you no faith, then read Hebrews xi.

To tell a young convert or some inquiring soul to "read the Bible" is like sending a patient into a drug store with the injunction to help himself. That won't do. Well put prescriptions are needed. You will find some here, and others may be had by just a little study. May they do you good.

Abiding Chapter,	John 15	Fiery Furnace Chapter, Dan.3	Prodigal's P alm,	Ps. 51
Admonition Chapter, Heb. 13		Fisherman's Chapter, Luke 5	Professor's Chapter, Luke 12
Agrippa's Chapter,	Acts 26	Fool's Chapter,	Prov. 26	Purification Chapter, Num. 19
Anointing Chapter,	Ex. 30	Gift Chapter,	I Cor. 12	Question Chapter, Luke 20
Ascension Chapter,	Acts 1	Great Psalm,	Ps. 119	Redemption Chapter, Luke 23
Atonement Chapter,	Heb. 9	Harlot's Chapter,	Prov. 7	Repentance Chapter, Luke 13
Backslider's Chapter,	Jer. 3	Heaven Chapter,	Rev. 21	Rest Chapter,	Heb. 4
Baptism Chapter,	Matt. 3	Herod's Chapter,	Acts 12	Restoration Chapter, Micah 4
Beautiful Chapter,	Matt. 5	Household Chapter,	Col. 3	Revival Chapter,	Joel 2
Blessing Chapter,	Deut. 28	Humility Chapter,	Luke 18	Rich Man's Chapter, Luke 16
Bottomless Chapter,	Eph. 3	Hypocrite Chapter,	Matt. 23	Rock Chapter,	Deut. 32
Bread Chapter,	John 6	Intemperance Chap., Prov. 23	Sad Chapter,	Luke 22
Business Men's Chap., Prov. 8		I Will Chapter,	Hosea 2	Safety Psalm,	Ps. 91
Chapter of Contrasts, Luke 17		John and Peter's Chap.,Acts 4	Saul of Tarsus Chapter, Acts 9
Character Chapter,	Job 29	John the Baptist's Chap.,Lu. 3	Scorner's Chapter,	Prov. 1
Charity Chapter,	I Cor. 13	Judgment Chapter, Rom. 14	Seeking Chapter,	Amos 5
Chastening Chapter, Heb. 12		Knowledge Chapter, Luke 11	Separation Chapter, 2 Cor. 6
Christian's Chapter, I Pet. 2		Lame Man's Chapter, Acts 3	Service Chapter,	Luke 10
Circumcision Chapter,Acts 15		Law Chapter,	Rom. 7	Shepherd's Chapter, John 10
Come Chapter,	Isa. 55	Life Chapter,	Luke 7	Sinner's Chapter,	Luke 19
Commandment Chap., Ex. 20		Lost and Found Chap., Lu. 15	Soldier's Chapter,	Eph. 6
Conqueror's Chapter, Luke 4		Macedonian Chapter, Acts 16	Song Chapter,	Luke 1
Consecration Chap., Rom. 12		Marriage Chapter,	Eph. 5	Sower's Chapter,	Luke 8
Convert's Chapter,	Isa. 12	Marvelous Chapter, Luke 9	Stephen's Chapter,	Acts 7
Corinthian Chapter, Acts 18		Mercy Psalm,	Ps. 136	Sufferer's Chapter,	Isa. 53
Cornelius' Chapter, Acts 10		Millennium Chapter, Rev. 20	Teacher's Chapter,	Luke 6
Courage Chapter,	Joshua 1	Minister's Chapter, Ezek. 34	Tithing Chapter,	Mal. 3
Creation Chapter,	Gen. 1	Moralist's Psalm,	Ps. 14	To-day Chapter,	Heb. 3
Deacon's Chapter,	Acts 6	Mother's Chapter, Judges 13	Tonic Psalm,	Ps. 27
Duty Chapter,	Ezek. 33	Nativity Chapter,	Luke 2	Traveler's Psalm,	Ps. 121
Ephesian Chapter,	Acts 19	Passover Chapter, Exodus 12	Victorious Chapter, Luke 24
Faith Chapter,	Heb. 11	Peace and Promise C.,John 14	Victory Chapter,	Rom. 8
Fast Chapter,	Isa. 58	Pentecost Chapter,	Acts 2	Vow Chapter,	Num. 30
Fear Not Chapter,	Isa. 41	Philip's Chapter,	Acts 8	Watcher's Chapter,	Luke 21
Feast Chapter,	Deut. 16	Poor Man's Chapter, Luke 14	Wife's Chapter,	Prov. 31
Felix's Chapter,	Acts 24	Prayer Chapter,	John 17	Wisdom Chapter,	Prov. 3
Festus' Chapter,	Acts 25	Preacher's Chapter,	Isa. 61	Work Chapter,	James 2

CHRISTIAN WORKERS'

TRAINING CLASS LESSONS.

Lesson 1.

HOW TO STUDY THE BIBLE BY CHARACTERS.

First—Know Jesus, everything points to him from Genesis to Revelations. Know him as Redeemer and Friend.

Second—Know all the Bible says about the Holy Spirit, then know him as Comforter and Guide.

These two will lead to the knowledge of God the Father and his attributes. "He that hath seen Jesus hath seen the Father." Now begin the following:

Moses—As starting points take Hebrews xi. 24 and 25, then following him from Nile to Nebo. When you spend a month with him and his God your face like his will shine.

Paul—Next acquaint yourself with him. Put three "greats" to his name, then begin. "Great Sinner," "Great Apostle," "Great Writer." Begin with the "Saul of Tarsus" chapter, Acts ix., then follow him till from Rome "he climbs the marble stairs to the Palace of the King." One hour a day for four weeks on this name and 'twill take a ton weight to keep you from leaping for joy.

John—This character will take you from where he leaned his head on Jesus' breast to the glories of Revelation where the city of gold is seen from Patmos' hills. To study John you begin with the gospel by him, chapter xx., verse 31. Keep in mind three things, love, believe, and Jesus the Son of God. It is safe to say that never pen wrote like his, never. That matchless chapter is beyond comparison,—John xiv.

David—To study him you go from sheep pastures through battle fields to music halls and earthly thrones. David takes you from depths of sin to summits of glory where you behold in type the Lord.

Epaphroditus—The man who nearly killed himself working for Christ. Philippians, chapter ii.

Bartimeus—The man who got up a mighty Praise meeting in Jericho, and only a blind beggar. Luke xviii.

Daniel—The man of character, begin

Temple Themes—F

with a study of his converts, his friends, his purposes and his trials. Mark chapter xi. 32 and xii. 3.

Elijah—The mighty prophet.

Mary—The one who anointed Christ.

Joshua—The soldier.

The women of the Bible.

The writers of the Bible.

The converts of the Bible.

The lost people of the Bible. Rich man, Jezebel, etc.

The preachers of the Bible. Noah, Jonah, etc.

The prophets of the Bible. Isaiah, Malachi, etc.

The angels of the Bible.

The eight characters—Lost—Revelations xxi. 8.

The four characters who first saw Christ in Luke ii.

The converts of Paul in Acts.

The apostates and backsliders of the Bible, etc., etc.

Lesson 2.

THE OFFICE AND WORK OF THE HOLY SPIRIT.

The One Triune God—He the Third Person. Speak, think, and teach of him as a person and not "it" or an "influence."

Jesus and the Holy Spirit—Christ now in heaven as advocate. The Spirit here.

He convinces the world of sin, righteousness and judgment. This we cannot do. It is his work.

He is the author of the new birth, only by which we can enter the kingdom of heaven.

He is the Comforter—"Another" like Jesus, knowing us and our surroundings, both past, present, and future. He can comfort us as no one else can.

He gives wisdom—1 Corinthians xii. 8. This needed for Christian work. "We need more brains." Many have knowledge but are not wise. Wisdom priceless. Note what the Bible says about wisdom.

He sheds abroad the love of God in our hearts. This the only kind of love that will "love your enemies" and begets a desire for the salvation of the lost.

81

He guides into all truth—John xvi. 13. Truth is God's instrument for salvation. He wrote the Scriptures, hence can best open them to us. What Jesus did for the two disciples walking to Emmaus and to the eleven just before his ascension, the Spirit will do for us.

He helps mightily in prayer—Romans viii. 26. Unction and power in public or private prayer comes by the Holy Ghost.

He makes us "abound in hope"—Romans xv. 13. Not a little hope, but boundless hope. Hope in our work. Hope in death.

He gives great strength to the inner man—Ephesians iii. 16. This is the foundation of courage and perseverance.

He gives Liberty—2 Corinthians iii. 17. Tongues united and lips unsealed. Thoughts flow freely and with power.

He gives assurance of salvation—Romans viii. 16. This needed to one joyful in service.

He gives power to witness for Christ—Acts i. 8. Not only at home but over the whole world.

He reveals Christ in his fulness, administers redemption, sanctifies the heart, and dwells in our bodies.

NOTES TO BE REMEMBERED.

We should pray more for the Holy Ghost.

He is given to us by God.

We should be filled with the Spirit.

We should honor the Holy Ghost.

Don't work till we get his power.

THE GREAT QUESTION.

"Have ye received the Holy Ghost since ye believed?"

Lesson 3.

HOW TO MARK YOUR BIBLE.

Have one to mark, one of your own, one with good print, marginal references, well bound in silk, printed on rice paper that will stand ink. One with a text book bound in the back is the best.

Might as well use other people's hats or shoes as to use other people's Bibles. I'd sell my clothes any day to buy a good one if I had none.

Mark the first page with your name and your life text and then add your year text as the years come and go.

Make a memoranda of your conversion, and the dates of great spiritual blessings. If some earnest prayer gets a mighty answer, make a note of it, with a reference to the promise which brought the blessing.

Make the promises stand out by underlining them with ink. When you find a promise for gold mark that. There are hundreds of Bible verses that centre around Hag. ii. 8. I always go to them when in need of money, and it always comes. Take a promise like Matt. vii. 7, and you should mark it so you could find it almost in the dark, Take the prayer verses, mark them in red. Know just where they are to be found.

Every great event in your life ought to be marked in your Bible. That's the place to put it; for God by his promises and providences is working out your eternal welfare, all for good if you will let him.

Mark the books and the chapters, for instance, at the beginning of Exodus write "Book of Redemption;" over Jeremiah write "The Backsliders' Book;" over James write "Work;" over the eleventh chapter of Hebrews write "Faith Chapter;" and Proverbs xxxiii. "Wife's Chapter," and so on till each chapter and book is well marked up. When a preacher takes a text and gives you some good thoughts mark by its side date of sermon and preacher with the seed thoughts. when you turn to that it will all come back as fresh as when delivered. Don't mark your Bible up with poor sermons, and there are a mighty lot of them that we preachers give.

Take the promises for grace and mark them. Why, 2 Cor. 1-8 is as powerful as an army. One promise like that is better to trust in than forty centurian bands.

You want the passages marked that will help you in dealing with inquiries of every kind. Then, too, you want the texts that will help you to help weak and discouraged Christians. When souls come into the light put their names in your book, then when you see them, pray for them.

Now and then a stanza of some hymn will be so blessed to you that you will want to copy it on the blank pages. Have some blank pages put in with rubber; when full you can take it out. Also have a place where you can make a note of good illustrations. Lastly, have your own plan; but have one. If you don't make a note of the good things they will go from you. Put your own name alongside of the best promises; mine is written many times all through my Bible; this makes them more personal to me, and thus the Bible becomes a very precious book. I'd not take a thousand dollars cash for my own Bible. It's priceless.

Lesson 4.

THE USE OF PROMISES.

God's word is God's will.
The meaning of 2 Pet. i. 4.
Thirty thousand promises that cover every condition of life.
Some promises good only for twenty-four hours, like Deut. xxxiii. 25.
Others good for time. Matt. vi. 33.
Others good for time and eternity. Rom. viii. 32.
Two classes of promises—for saint and sinner.
Temporal promises.
Spiritual promises. 1 Tim. 4-8.
To love the Bible—prove the promises.
Trusting God's word is trusting God.
The conditions of fulfilment.
Meet the conditions—Obedience and faith.
A five dollar bill is as good in the hands of a beggar as in the hands of a prince.
Now—all promises are for the "Whosoever."
None to fail, Joshua xxiii. 14, and 1 Kings viii. 55.
Time when fulfilled, not always at once.

EXAMPLES.

The Spirit's power—800 years in answering, as in Joel ii. 28, and Pentecost.
It took 4000 years to have Gen. iii. 15 fulfiled.
God not slack concerning his promises as some men count slackness.
The promise in Joshua i. 5.
The promise in Ps. xxxii. 8 put me in the ministry.
The promise in Ex. iv. 12 and its fulfilment.
One thousand dollars on Phil. iv. 19.

Lesson 5.

WORK EVERY ONE CAN DO.

God doesn't want any idle or lazy Christians either here or in heaven. Every saved sinner can be a soul winner, and ought to be. Men, women, children, the sick and well, weak or strong, can do a little. Don't talk louder than you live. Hypocrites are poor witnesses. The first person you want to help is—YOURSELF. The next one to help is the nearest and most needy. Keep in mind the two classes—the saved and the lost. Help the lost sinner first. Invite them to service; do it by word or letter, or any good way. Pray for them in private. The power of prayer, illustrate. Speak of the meetings; attract them there by your praises. Give a timely tract or a good clipping.

Work with your scissors and pen. Get apt scripture passages and quote them. Scatter them like wheat over the field. Harvest is sure to follow. Introduce the unsaved to some one who will better tell them the way of salvation. If you can't run the engine you can serve as brakeman. Go with the inquirer to the anxious seat, altar, or inquiry room. Ask them to your home and talk and pray with them there. Help make every meeting you attend a good one. In public services always be brief, both in remarks and prayer. Watch for those who in any way manifest a desire for salvation, and lead them to Jesus or to some one else who will. Live for Christ in your home. This is the great need of to-day. Wash dishes, mold beds, broil steaks, sell calico or silk like a Christian. Keep sweet, happy, and hopeful. Be a walking sermon; don't growl with your looks. Work as follows:—wives at home, mothers with children, friends with friends. If you are sick show what grace can do. If you are tried bear as only a heaven-helped man can. If you are in trouble let the world see in you the peace of God and the comfort of the Holy Ghost. Let employers pay as they pray. Let employees give good service and work like Christians. Let love to God and man flow out in every act and word. Lead the children to Christ. This all can do. Keep away from doubtful things and thus help your weak brother. Ask God to direct you to work, and he will do it inside of forty-eight hours. Don't quit work till the breath quits the body. Then begin service on the other side—in heaven.

FOUR GREAT PROMISES.

Ex. iv. 12; Is. xli. 10; Josh. i. 5-9, and 2 Chron. xv. 7.

Lesson 6.

HOW TO STUDY THE BIBLE BY TOPICS.

Just study SALVATION. That's the first thing a man wants to know about. Who gives it? To whom it is given. How it is gotten. What it is when we get it. What it does for a sinner. A study of David's life will give it; also that of Peter. Begin with Is. xii. 3, and end with Judges xxiv. See what it saves from and what it saves to. Look at the things that represent it, like rock, tower, helmet, lamp, etc. Close by taking a heavy portion for your heavy heart.
Then look up all the Bible says about PRAISE. This will set the dumb man singing. Samuel and Psalms are food

books for this. Follow this with the study of THE BLOOD. Begin with the Passover and end with Calvary. Get God's estimate of it. Then apply it to your sin-burdened heart. John xix. 34, and Eph. i. 7.

LITTLE THINGS. — Go through the Book and find all the little things that God speaks about, and how he used them. As, for instance, the rod in Moses' hand, a cup of cold water, the napkin in Christ's grave, etc. Then take the WEAK THINGS, and see what mighty works have been wrought by them. Begin with 1 Cor. i. 27-30, and look both back and forward.

THE DOCTRINES. — Take the seven great doctrines of the Bible—God, man, sin, redemption, justification, regeneration, and sanctification. Give these all a full and complete research, and you will come out a regular theologian and strong Christian.

The way to study the Bible by topics is to study it so. Take any one great theme and STUDY IT. I like the following: Love, joy, grace, light, prayer, obedience, faith, power, Holy Spirit, truth, wisdom, able, punishment, heaven, reward, mercy, humility, angels, and a hundred more.

Take a great topic like ASSURANCE, and search what the Book teaches on that subject, find the "We knows" of Romans and 1 John. See who in the Bible knew they had passed from death unto life. Yet what is written on it from Genesis all the way down. Don't close the study till in prayer both the Bible and the Spirit witness to the fact that you are "born again from above."

Lesson 7.
THE WORKER AND HIS GOD.

We must never forget the following all-important truths. They are the rock upon which we build our hopes. They underlie all other themes. They are the pillars of our temple.

First, we are co-laborers with God. Second, his omnipotent power is ours for service. Third, we do the work, he gives the increase. Fourth, God is our Father, Jesus is our Advocate, and the Holy Spirit is always with us. Fifth, with God we can never fail. Sixth, his Word stands for himself. Seventh, the final result—the world for Christ. God and man co-laborers.—Matt. xi. 28-30, Christ's yoke; Acts xv. 4, all things that God had done with them; 1 Cor. iii. 9, laborers together with God. The dreamers. The wishers. "Do much and say

little" family. "Do little and say much" family. "Four pints to a quart." Omnipotent power—Acts i. 8, witnesses to the world. Begin at home. As much power will be given us as we can use. The character of this power—Can save by few or many, 1 Sam. xiv. 6. Is the source of all strength, 1 Chron. xxix. 12. All things are possible, Matt. xix. 26. "Shoes or no shoes—hallelujah!" Work and increase: 1 Cor. iii. 6. All the increase is of God. This will help to keep us humble. None can say, "I did it," hence boasting is in vain. Note—that if we want any increase one must plant and another water, or else God will not give the increase. The Triune God: "Our" Father makes Jesus our brother. The fatherhood of God — we children. Jesus our advocate in heaven. "Moody and his brother George." Let him in. The Holy Ghost, now here, administrator of redemption. His power our power. His wisdom our wisdom. He reveals Christ. He guides into all truth. Makes our tongues "tongues of fire." "Hump-back—black girl." No failures: We are afraid of making mistakes and failures. Mistakes keep us humble. No man ever failed whom God sent. See Moses in Egypt. Gideon and the Midianites. Feeding the hungry, Matt. xix. 15-21. God's word and himself: No Bible—no God. See Matt. iv. 4 and Deut. viii. 3. The more Bible—the more God. Study the Bible as often as you eat. God is never absent from his Word. The final result: Dan. ii. 44 and vii. 13, 14, "All people and nations shall serve Christ," "of his kingdom there shall be no end." Luke i. 33.

Lesson 8.
THE POWER OF FAITH AND PRAYER.

In these two the worker will find the mightiest human forces. They are the double steam engines of all Christian workshops. Prevailing prayer, or the prayer of faith, makes one in part omnipotent. James v 16. Faith is taking God at his word and asking no questions. Faith always rests upon the imperishable Word of God. The more simple faith is the more powerful it is. All things are possible to the man of mighty faith and persistent prayer. What faith and prayer have done is an evidence of what they will do. Examples: Elijah shut up the heavens for three years and a half. The walls of Jericho fell down for Joshua. Daniel's three friends delivered in the fire. Moses and the Hebrews saved from Egypt.

Brought an angel and delivered Peter; Acts xii. Saved Jehoshaphat and his people; 2 Chron. xx. Slew 185,000 Assyrians for Hezekiah; 2 Kings xix. These from the Bible—We also get help from each other's victories. For your help in studying these two great subjects let me append an outline.

PRAYER.—Look up in the Bible (and elsewhere) all about earnest prayer, persistent prayer, prevailing prayer, importunate prayer. The prayer of faith. The prayers of the righteous. The prayers of the wicked. The publican's prayer. Our Lord's prayer. The Prayer Chapter, John xvii. Prayers answered and not answered in the Bible. How prayer is to be offered. What to pray for. Bible rules for praying by precept and example. Repetition and ostentation in prayer. Keep in mind that prayer is based on the fatherhood of God.

FAITH.—To study this find in the Bible its definition. How it comes. Who had it. What are its possibilities. Its relation to God and his Word. What it has done. What is promised by God that it will do. Who can have it. Note specially what faith receives. Search every written word Christ said of it. Faith, trust, and belief are blood relations. No Christian can either live or work without faith and prayer.

Lesson 9.

HOW TO RAISE MONEY FOR CHRISTIAN WORK.

Every one has as much right to pray for gold as for grace. Two things at least are needed to carry on Christian work, grace and gold, and God will give both if you ask him in the right way. To get grace you go direct to God, and it is given to us by Jesus Christ through faith by the Holy Ghost. That's the way to get grace. With gold it's different. You go to God for it, and he gives it by his providences and his people. A great many people never pray for gold in their Christian work. This is wrong. Men think they own the purse and hold its strings, but Hag. ii. 8 of the Bible says not so. A spiritual church will never lack for funds. Now, to raise money for any needed work you

First. Find what the Bible says about temporal blessings. Search out the promises that bear that way. Mark the words of the book that teach about giving, like Prov. xi. 24, 25, Ex. xxv. and xxxv., 2 Cor. ix. 6, 7, Luke vi. 38, and many more. See what stress God lays

on the provisions for carrying on his work here. Paul's great Resurrection Chapter is followed immediately by these words, "Now concerning the collection."

Second. Give yourselves; don't ask others to give 'till you have gone down in your own pocket, and it is better to put in your share before prayers. One of the biggest collections in the Scriptures is told of in 1 Chron. xxix. There you get the order of giving.

Third. Get people to have a conscience on the matter. Touch a man's conscience and you have his open purse. People need education on this line.

Fourth. When you have asked God for money, go to his people and get it. Use tact in going, as follows: A—Ask for and expect big things. B—Don't be afraid; you are on the King's business. C—Have a good cause to present or don't go. D—Size up your man. E—Better see him when he has had a good dinner. F—See him alone and when he can give you a hearing. G—Don't think that "no" always means a refusal. H—State your case tersely and tenderly. I—Don't use undue haste; a day may double the amount. J—Don't get tired. K—Don't get discouraged.

Fifth. Put great trust in Ps. lxxxi. 10. Write your needs alongside of promises, as in Ps. xxxvii. 3-5.

Sixth. Don't lean on the rich. Mites can make millions, and poor people, as a rule, are the best givers.

Seventh. Note the plans used by different men—George Muller, of Bristol, England, Mr. Kimball, and others.

Eighth. Suggestions: Let preachers beg less and preach the gospel of giving more; don't scold, but reason and persuade folks who give little or nothing; teach systematic giving, like "Thanksgivings Ann;" doubt the conversion of the church members who don't give; don't touch blood-money or unholy gains; see the evil of church fairs, festivals, or the like for money-making; it educates the young in the wrong way. Note the difference between "wants" and "needs" in Phil. iv. 19.

Lesson 10.

HOW TO DETERMINE ONE'S FIELD OF WORK.

God leaves no Christian without some definite work. Our work here determines our reward hereafter. In each field faithfulness is required, not success. Our work should be determined by God's will and not our choice alone. How his will may be known:

First—By his specific and direct call of the Holy Spirit.

Second — By his call through the Church.

Third—By his Word, which is his will.

Fourth—By his special providences.

Fifth—By his gift of talents.

Sixth—By his birthright of sex and blood.

Seventh—By his gift to us of reason and judgment.

All work of a Christian should be Christian work. Ability often determines,—no blockheads for preachers or teachers. Birth and blood often fixes position. Hodcarriers and philosophers both wanted. Faithfulness and fruit in one place may bring promotion. A wife's "call" is to love and help husband and home. A mother's field is her children and home. "To every one his work" means

a—Some for preachers.

b—Others for missionary fields.

c—Some to make money.

d—Others to spend it.

e—Some to be masters.

f—Others to serve.

g—Some as teachers.

h—Others as scholars.

i—Some for the pulpit.

j—Many for the pew.

"Opportunity" is God's mighty voice saying, "I want you." Take a view of the whole world, see where you can fit in —there work, win, and die. Be guided by these three—the Holy Spirit, promises, and providences. God never wants any one in two places at the same time. Patient waiting is often one's work. Time and prayer and providences make the field we are to fill very plain. The following may mislead us: 1. Love of money. 2. Desire for honor and praise. 3. Popularity. 4. Ease, pleasure, and power. 5. Egotism. 6. Success of others. 7. A lack of knowledge of self.

Suggestions: Finish the work in hand. Do the things right about you. Some are sowers and some are reapers. Read 1 Cor. xii. Finally, get all the light you can from every source; then you settle your life-work with prayer and your own heart.

Lesson 11.

HOW TO LOVE YOUR BIBLE.

FIRST, KNOW IT. You can't love anything you don't know. Like good people, the better you know them the better you love them. It is the VOICE OF GOD to his people, "Lost men, this way to

safety!" Boy lost in fog; his father's voice, "Steer this way!" The whole book was written for YOU. Mark carefully 2 Tim. iii. 16. It is either the Bible or nothing, for God is only known in love, mercy, and justice by revelation either in his Word or Jesus, his Incarnate Son or by his Spirit's presence. Simply reading it will not give its sweetness any more than looking at a man will reveal his character. It must be searched and studied to be loved.

SECOND, USE IT. We love the things that serve us well. That which is of the greatest service is of the greatest value. The Bible is eyes to the blind, ears to the deaf, sword to the soldier, water to the thirsty, chart to the mariner, etc. It is ever ready, ever faithful, ever powerful. None can appeal to it in vain for truth.

THIRD, PROVE IT. "A friend in need is a friend indeed." The "Proven promises" of the Bible. Little faith people, prove Mark xi. 23. Stingy people, prove Luke vi. 38. Business men, prove Matt. vi. 33. Sinful men, prove Isa. i. 18, 19. Troubled people, prove Ps. xxxiv. 17. Let judges prove Deut. i. 17. Let backsliders prove Deut. iv. 29-31. Hungry and homeless, prove Deut. viii. 7-9. Young people, prove Ps. lxxxiv. 11. Storm driven men, prove Isa. xxv. 4. Mr. Great Desire, prove Isa. lxiv. 4. Poor and needy, prove Isa. xli. 17. Mrs. Very Anxious, prove Ezek. xxxiv. 25. Mr. Bad Heart, prove Ezek. xxxvi. 25-28. Mr. Many Wants, prove Mal. iii 10. If afraid of death prove 1 Cor. xv. 55-57. Everybody prove Heb. vii. 25. Every sinner prove 1 Pet. ii. 24.

Love the old Testament because of its promises and telling of Jesus. Its the only book that explains the grave and immortality. Should the bride love the letters of her absent bridegroom?— "Christ in heaven." Does one love the will which bequeaths to them fortune upon fortune. Shall the one who is pursued by the avenger have no thought or love or care for the sign posts that point the way to the City of Refuge? Shall we not love the only writing that tells where our jewels are hid.—"Baby in Heaven." Shall we carefully guard the medicine the Great Physician has left for souls sick unto death with sin.—2 Pet. i. 4. Shall "Mother's Bible" have none of our love? It is more to us than was the Ark of the Covenant to the Israelites of old. The Bible is all to us that the pillar of cloud and fire was to the pilgrims to Canaan.

Lesson 12.
THINGS TO KNOW.

Your own mind and heart must fully grasp the following facts, all of which are clearly taught in the Bible :—That outside of Christ there is no salvation.—Acts. iv. 12. That all have sinned and come short of the glory of God.—Isa. liii. 6. That God commands men at all times and everywhere to repent and turn unto him —Acts xvii. 30. That the Holy Ghost convinces the world of sin.—John xvi.8,9. That To-DAY is the day of salvation.— Heb. iii. 15. That none ever come unto Christ and are cast out.—John vi 37. That none can enter the kingdom of heaven unless *born again* of the Holy Spirit by the word of God.—John iii. 5-8. That saving faith is when the heart clings to the object of its trust — Christ.—Isa. xii. 2. That faith and not feeling is the condition of salvation.—Eph. ii 8,9. That repentance means turning from sin and making restitution when necessary.—Prov. xxviii.13. That the blood of Christ makes atonement and not good works.—Lev. xvii 11; Eph. i. 7. That he that believeth is not condemned, but he that believeth not is condemned already.—John iii. 18. That it is faith in Christ, not in a creed, that saves.—Acts. xvi. 31. That assurance of salvation is by God's Word and his Spirit and the fruit thereof.—John xx. 31; Rom. viii. 16; Matt. vii. 20. That obedience and blessing always go together.— Isa. i. 14. That the Bible is man's only guide for rule and practice.—Joshua i. 8,9. That we are hastening to the judgment day when the redeemed shall pass to their eternal reward, and the impenitent to their eternal punishment.—Matt. xxv. 46. That there is no escape from death and no salvation in hell.—Rev. xx. 14, 15. "That all who repent of their sins and believe in the Lord Jesus Christ receive the forgiveness of sin, which is *Justification.* And that all who receive the forgiveness of sin are immediately made by the Spirit new creatures in Christ Jesus, which is *Regeneration.* That all who are thus born again are called the children of God, which is *A-doption;* and all who are adopted may have the witness of the Holy Spirit. That all who truly and earnestly desire and seek it may love God with all their heart and soul and mind and strength, and their neighbors as themselves, which is *Sanctification.*

Lesson 13.
HOW TO LOCATE SCRIPTURE TEXTS.
The Bible is God's storehouse. It is a big one; has numberless rooms, all filled with bins that are heaped to the full with good seed. It is not all the same kind, but it is all good. Where to find what you want is the question When a farmer wants to plant corn, he does not go to the bin of wheat, nor to the barley sack when he would sow rye. So with the promises, if you want to reap joy you get that kind of seed verses. If you want grace you go to the Scriptures that promise just that, like 2 Cor. ix. 8. I find it very helpful to lay my finger right on the verse that will cover the need. A five dollar bill will stand one in hand right well if he is hungry and near a restaurant, but though he has it yet can't lay his hands on it because it is lost on his person or in his room, of what value is it to him? Now thousands of souls go hungry because these promises, which are exchangable for bread, are lost, —lost here in the Book. How shall we find them? How locate them so that when we are in need they can be used at a moment's notice? I tell. you, friends, if you dont use the promises of God you will never know their value. You will never love the Bible. Gold as gold, is worth but little, it is only when it is exchanged for our necessities that we get to see how good it is. So with the Word of God.

Some say they can't locate these promises; now that is not so, they can. Put them in as salesmen and they will soon find where the goods are kept in the store. Just the way a clerk locates the wares of a shop, so locate scripture passages. Here comes a customer, he wants "encouragement in christian work." You take him over to the Psalm room, first bin, third shelf, "And he shall be like a tree planted by the rivers of water, that bringeth forth his fruit in his season, his leaf also shall not wither, and whatsoever he doeth shall prosper." Now you send him away with plenty of goods like that and he will soon set up business for himself. Take a good wife and she knows just where every thing is kept in the house. She doesn't go looking for linen in the refrigerator or searching for china in the clothes closet. Why, bless your heart, she can find the sheets and pillow cases in the dark. Now, in the same way a good Christian ought to know where to find the promises. What is the use of looking in Jeremiah, the book of backslidings, for the promise, "Peace I leave with you, my peace I give unto you—let not your heart be troubled, neither let it be afraid." It is not there,

John xiv. 27 has that. Often I see Christians searching in the Old Testament for Hebrews, or looking towards the end of the Bible for Leviticus,—might as well look for New York on the Pacific coast. Have one Bible that you use and mark, that will help a great deal. I feel lost in work without this Bible I've used for ten years; why, some promises I could find in the dark, almost,—I know just where they lay, (take Joshua i. 5, 8, 9,) and they are as clear to me at midnight as midday. Others I mark in blue and red, that makes them stand out on the page, so I know where to find them. Another way is to locate the verses that are alike, as in Isaiah. The eleventh verses, that is, the eleventh verses of certain chapters, begin with chapter xxi. then go to the fortieth and forty-first, by the time you get to the forty-second you too will shout. Then read the forty-third, with the fifty-first, fifty-fifth and fifty-eighth, and the chances are you will rejoice like a Methodist. Take the three 3-16ths of the Bible, it is easy to remember that, Malachi iii. 16, John iii. 16, Ephesians iii. 16, and you have what every Christian ought to do, first, to speak often, second, what to speak about, and third, strength to speak. The great trouble will be in wanting to do too much at once. Build Rome in a day? it can't be done. It is one at a time; you can't win in this race with a spurt; slow and sure is the only way of winning. Get in your mind the great chapters of the Bible, that will help you. Take that last chapter I just named which is the bottomless chapter of the Bible, once get the twentieth verse in your mind and it will never leave you. The Holy Spirit has brought that to me I suppose a thousand times in prayer and work. Dig out the promises in the eighth of Romans; who that has proved and marked them can ever forget verses 18, 28, 31 and 32. You might as well try to blot out Jupiter from the sky as to erase Psalm xxxii. 8 from my memory. Glorious things of that promise I could tell. When I want money, I go to the money promises of the Book, and never yet have I been disappointed. Oh, you that must raise funds for God's work, why dont you pray more and prove the promises? You would have both less of worry and work. You will find that Christ knew where to find the Scripture he wanted. That is proven in Luke iv. 17. So did Peter on the day of Pentecost. In fact every one that God has used to any great degree, knew his Word, knew it well. Oh, may

the Spirit of wisdom be given us as promised in James i. 5, till hundreds, yes, even thousands of the mighty promises of our God shall be known by us, both in location, in mind, and better than all, in "fulfilment."

Lesson 14.

SCRIPTURE FOR CHRISTIAN WORKERS.

Begin with the last half of Zech iv. 6. There is but little power in you, but omnipotent power in God. Then take Isa. lviii. 11. That will guide you as well as give strength. So as not to grow lukewarm or cold, mark the "Duty or Blood" verse in Ezek. xxxiii. 8. John xv. 16 assures one of his position and work. With this study Mark xvi. 15, which is the Master's parting commission. When the day of battle comes have ready 1 Cor. xv. 57 and Zech. x. 5. For courage and help be sure to read Isa. xli. 10. The following verses need a month's meditation, Deut. vi. 6, 7. In the same book, chapter eight, mark verses 7 to 9. All theology centres around Lev. xvii. 11. The following "twentieth" chapters are especially for you — Exodus, Deuteronomy, 2 Chronicles, Psalms, Jeremiah, John, and Revelation. No worker should miss the second chapter of Joel.

The following texts, often named, should be marked in red: Ps. xxxii. 8 and lxxxi. 10; Dan. xii. 3 and xi. 32; 2 Cor. ix. 8 with Jude xxiv.; Joshua i. 5, 8, 9 with Jer. xxxii. 17; Dan xv. 7 with Matt. vii. 7; Eph. iii. 20 with Isa. lxiv. 4; John v. 24 with Ps. xxxvii. 3-5; Luke xix. 10 with Rev. xxii. 17; Rom. viii. 28, 32, 37 with 2 Cor. v. 1, and last and best of all, Heb. ix. 14 with Rev. xxi. 7.

These but give an inkling of what God has in his Word for you. There are marked in my Bible fully two thousand passages that at one time or another I have profited by personally.

Prov. xiii. 22 lets in a stream of light on the reason why so many bad men get rich, and what shall become of their money. I reckon it's a mighty good thing to let them make the fortune and we to spend it.—That's a new thought to me, but as God says it's so I just take him at his word. So you, young men, that propose to lie, and cheat, and steal, and plan with Satan to make shekels by fair or foul, go on, wade in, push and pull till widows cry and the poor grow hungry because of the wages you pay, but on the margin of your bank book write, "the wealth of the sinner is laid up for the just." We shall walk in with our empty baskets and some day come from your store full. There are thousands of young men who to-day will find it to their advantage to take a step backward and make the first half of this prophetic verse true rather than the last. Remember heaven and earth will pass away before a jot or a tittle of what is there written.

Lesson 15.

SCRIPTURE FOR INQUIRERS.

A *few* well chosen passages are much better than many. For those who anxiously ask,

WHAT MUST I DO TO BE SAVED?
John iii. 16, x. 9 with John iii. 36 and v. 24. If others are needed, have ready Eph. i. 7; Isa. liii. 6; Rom. x. 9, 10; John i. 12, 29.

FOR THE BACKSLIDER,
And, alas, there are too many, but God in his infinite mercy has gracious words for them. Search the prophecy of Jeremiah for the words to this class, especially mark chapter ii. 19 and iii. 13, 14; also Hosea xiv. 4 with Isa. i. 16-18.

FOR THE "GOOD ENOUGHS."
For there are many who feel no need of a Saviour, or say they feel no need. These must be shown their lost condition and sinfulness before God. The fourteenth Psalm is most helpful, with the following passages: Rom. iii. 10, 23; 1 John i. 10; Isa. liii. 6. If you want others, take Eccles. vii. 20; Ps. cxliii. 2.

FOR THE "CAN'T HOLD OUTS."
Oh, how people stumble at this, just as though Christ can save but cannot keep. It is ours to *hold on*, not *hold out*. Why will they climb mountains before they reach them, or cross ditches before they are even in sight? Is the God of Daniel dead? Has the "Mighty to Save" and "Strong to Deliver" been shorn of his strength? Nay, nay; he is yet able to make Heb. vii. 25 true, and the one hundred and twenty-first Psalm a verity to millions. Give them the following: Jude 24; John x. 28, 29; Rom. viii. 38, 39; Deut. xxxi. 6; and Isa. xli. 10, xliii. 1, 2.

FOR THE "NOT NOWS."
Sad indeed is it to see men and women live on in open rebellion against God the giver of every good and perfect gift; sadder yet to have them say, "Not now," when in Christ's stead men beseech them to become reconciled. Awful is the thought that possibly he may say, "Thou fool, this night thy soul shall be required

of thee." Read to them Prov. xxvii. 1; James iv. 13, 14; 2 Cor. vi. 2; Prov. xxix. 1; Heb. iii. 13.

FOR THE "I CAN'T GIVE UPS,"
Which means they *don't want* to give up. For anybody, who wants to, *can*, with the mighty grace of God ever ready to help. Let them choose between the sin of earth with attending woe in hell, and the cross of Christ with the joys of heaven. There is no habit so strong but what the will,` with the power of God, can overcome. There is no sin so full of pleasure but what is completely swallowed up in the joy and peace of Christian service and salvation. Joshua xxiv. 15; Mark viii. 36, 37; Luke xiv. 24; Philip. iii. 7, 8.

FOR THE "I WILL TRYS."
Try what? To trust God? Absurd! Suppose you told your wife or mother or friend you *would try* to trust them. How ridiculous. The very words imply doubt or unbelief, which is sin. Tell them to change the "I will try" to "I will trust," and have them read Isa. xxvi. 3, 4; John x. 9; and Isa. lxiii. 1.

FOR THE "I'M AS GOOD AS OTHERS."
To be sure they are, may be better, and yet both may be lost. Hypocrites have no part with Christ. Why even stumble at the inconsistencies of Christians? "Every one of us shall give an account of himself to God."—Rom. xiv. 12. At the day of final reckoning it will not serve any to plead his neighbor's faults. He will stand or fall by the light and living of his own life. Rom. ii. 1; xiv. 3, 4; Matt. vii. 1-5.

FOR THE "I DON'T KNOW HOWS."
These words might come with truth from Pagan lips, but surely not from those who dwell beneath the shadow of God's house, or in hearing of the church bells. But tell them the simple story of the cross, and slip in their hand the Gospel by John, or turn with them to your own Bible and let them read John i. 12. 29, then Rev. xxii. 17, after which that matchless promise in Ezek. xxxvi. 25. 28.

FOR THE "I'VE TRIED BEFORES."
Tried and failed! Whose fault was it that they did not succeed? Surely not God's, for he says, "Ye shall seek me and find me, when ye shall search for me with all your heart, and I will be found of you."—Jer. xxix. 13, 14. In matters of time if we fail once we try again. Shall we do less with those interests that concern our welfare throughout eternity? Give them Prov. iii. 5; Deut. iv. 29 with Rom. iv. 5 and Eph. ii. 8.

Lesson 16.

HOW TO DEAL WITH INQUIRERS.

Be perfectly natural and courteous in your approach, and when talking with them. Have your own Bible so marked that you can find the passages given for different classes; also try and be able to quote them correctly, giving chapter and verse. It is always best to deal with inquirers alone. Before giving the word of God ascertain the condition of mind, that you may rightly divide the word of truth unto them. Pray inwardly, and depend wholly upon the Holy Spirit to guide both worker and seeker; expect and work for immediate results; show that you are in dead earnest, but avoid excitement. Explain all objections by the Word of God, but do not enter into argument, it only does harm. Avoid giving your own experience, as this may lead them to expect conversions in like manner as yours, which is not likely to be the case. If your work is in the revival service or inquiry room, or at the altar or anxious seat, so far as you can, select persons of your own sex and age, and talk with them. Offer Christ as the immediate remedy for every shade of want or doubt or sin. After having done your best, and there seems to be no result, leave, prayerfully, the sinner and the seed you have sown to God, the Judge of all. It is good to have just a word of prayer (very informal) before your conversation, and always after. When the sinner has found Christ, let the fact be doubly assured to both mind and heart by Isa. xii. 1, 2. You can often lead a sinking heart into the kingdom as they pray with you. Urge an immediate confession of their conversion, both at home and to the pastor or church of which they will unite at the next communion. Take the full name and address, with their church affiliations, and hand to the leader of the meeting or pastor of the church. When parting with them give a promise of prayer, and then three passages from the Word of God, which they should find and mark in their Bible, and make constant use of: 1 Cor. x. 13, 2 Cor. ix. 8, Isa xii. 10.

Lesson 17.

HOW TO APPROACH THE UNSAVED ABOUT SALVATION.

Keep in mind the three classes:

1. Those who want to be saved.
2. Those who are indifferent.
3. Those who don't want to be saved.

To all of these three go earnestly, wisely, naturally, and with the gospel of Jesus Christ. Keep in mind that "love never fails." Approach them frankly and plainly. Show no spirit of "I am above you."

To those who are anxious for salvation: 1. Go with the message of reconciliation. 2. Approach them as one that can help. 3 Have ready God's word to them. 4. Lead them away from self to Christ. 5. If at all possible pray together. 6. Don't leave them till they are saved. 7. Urge an immediate confession of Christ.

To those who are in part or totally indifferent to the matter of their soul's welfare: 1. Go to them when they are alone. 2. Select an opportune moment. 3. Especially approach them when serious. 4. Take no sides with them against God. 5. Show them their awful condition. 6. Plead with them; don't scold. 7 Present both the justice and mercy of God.

To those who don't want to be saved or have anything to do with God, religion, the church, or prayer, go as follows: 1. Pray much before you approach them at all. 2. Try and get them under gospel influences. 3. Quote to them scripture upon scripture. 4. Remind them of death and judgment. 5. Show the conditions of saved and lost. 6. Get them to take some first step. 7. Give them a promise of help and prayer.

SUGGESTIONS:

If you are not the best person, get someone else to approach them. Pray much that the Holy Spirit will convict of sin. Don't let modesty or fear of giving offence deter you from approaching those whom God has given you to "reprove, rebuke, exhort with all long suffering and doctrine." To keep your minds and hearts alive to the work of seeking to save men by the cross, think of the brevity of life, the length of eternity, the mighty happiness of the saved, and the awful woe of the lost.

Lesson 18.

WHAT CONSECRATION AND SANCTIFICATION MEAN.

Consecration is our part; sanctification is God's part, and both mean "The setting apart for service." Sanctification is the perfecting of the work wrought at conversion, and is an act of God's free grace by the Holy Spirit, making us love God with all our heart, and ready for his work. It is instantaneous, like conversion. There is progressive sanctification, like afflictions being sanctified unto us. Christ made perfect through suffering. The many names given to it by sects and individuals. Must be wrought on us to be understood, like conversion. Justification is not sanctification. Read and study the following texts: 1 Thes. v. 23; Rom xv. 16; 1 Cor. i. 30; John xvii. 17, 19; Col. i. 12, 21, 22; 2 Cor. iii. 5. The character of consecrated or sanctified persons may be found in the following two chapters, Rom. xii. and 2 Cor. vi. This to be prayed for and expected. Read what John Wesley, C. G. Finney, and Alfred Cookman have to say about it. Mr. Moody says it is "being filled with the Spirit." Sanctification and service always go together. How shall our sanctification he known? *a*—By an holy life. *b*—By abundance of good works. *c*—By communion with God. Sanctification makes us more like Christ, giving us these three: first, a perfect Saviour; second, a perfect love; third, a perfect obedience in desire; and one who is sanctified will, like him, seek to save the lost.

CONSECRATION — Its meaning. The giving ourselves fully to God to do his will, whatever it may be. It includes: 1. The giving of our hearts. 2. The giving of our minds. 3. The giving of our bodies. 4. The giving of our possessions.—All a consecrated man has belongs by the act of consecration to God: he is steward.—Progressive consecration, what it is.—The Consecration Chapter, Rom. xii.—The blessing of God given at consecration.—The divine side of consecration.—All doubtful things go at consecration.—Consecration to God's service is the fuller meaning of, a physician's consecration to his profession; a merchant's consecration to his business; a lawyer's consecration to his practice; a wife's consecration to her husband and home.—Partly consecrated people, or degrees of consecration.—How the depth of one's consecration may be determined: 1st. As a missionary, where would you go for Christ? 2d. Your money and possessions, how much would you willingly give to God's cause? 3d. Your bodies, are they constantly kept as temples of the Holy Ghost? 4th. In service, what and how much are you willing to do?—Francis Ridley Havergal's consecration hymn.—Experiences of consecration.

Lesson 19.

HINTS ON HOW TO LEAD A MEETING.
Come filled to the brim with your sub-

ject. Let your words be on fire. Be tremendously in earnest. Be on time in opening and closing. Be perfectly natural. See that the air, light, and seats are in good condition. Keep out of the old ruts. Speak so all can hear. Don't take others' time. Have something to say as leader. Say it. Don't let persons speak or pray too long. Don't sing funeral hymns at a praise service. Have plenty of scripture, and give its meaning. Don't mind critics. Don't wear squeaky shoes. Adapt yourself to circumstances. Be guided by the Holy Spirit. Keep to the theme, and make others do so. Always give the best you have. Put soul power into the service. Never lose your grip. Select both hymns and scripture beforehand. Keep your voice right to the size of the room. Sit out where the people can see you. Don't let cranks take part. Be master of the situation, by the grace of God. Strike for results when the iron is hot. Be wise in giving the invitation to the unsaved. Keep in mind the fifteen minutes after service. Use your own Bible and get others to use theirs. Don't let organist or pianist give a concert, with preludes, interludes, etc. Urge brevity and brightness. Help the weak and timid ones to take part. Have great variety in all services. Make the stranger welcome. If your plans don't work try others. Don't imagine you are the meeting: you are only leader under God. Pray much before you come, while there, and after. Depend on God for help more than on the people. Don't be afraid—mistakes, wrong plans, etc. God will make true Rom. viii. 28. Let your face and manner be blessed to the people's good. Get in a devotional spirit. Have both solemnity and joyousness in the meetings. Have faith in God. Have an aim and object in every service you lead. Don't sing too slow or too fast. Get the people's mind off you and on Christ. Try and build up Christians, and get sinners converted. Services that don't honor God, and help people to live better and brighter had better never be held. All people are not leaders. The way to learn how to lead meetings is to lead them. Don't try for what can't be had in the service.

Lesson 20.

HOW TO GIVE THE GOSPEL INVITATION TO THE UNCONVERTED.

TEXT.—"He that winneth souls is wise." To understand the theme, first know what it means to be "fishers of men."

a—Must go where the fish are.

b—Can't catch fresh-water fish in the sea.

c—The difference between a whale and a mackerel.

d—Some caught with hooks, others with nets.

e—Use bait the fish like.

f—Cast the net on the "right side."

THE TWO INVITATIONS.

First, the personal—Given to the individual.

Second, the general—Given to a company.

THE THREE CONSTRAINING ELEMENTS.

1. Love — "The goodness of God should lead to repentance."

2. Fear — "Flee from the wrath to come."

3. Duty—"Give me thy heart."

With these may be added: The immortality of the soul. The unsatisfying nature of worldly things. The satisfying nature of Christian religion. The final judgment day of all men. The evil or good influence of a life. Personal responsibility to God. The call of conscience.

Always remember that the *final* invitation should be such as to reach both the conscience and the will.

Keep in mind the three classes of sinners: The *careless*, without desire for salvation; the *awakened*, conscious of needing a Saviour; the *convicted*, calling for a Saviour.

Get the spirit and words of Moses in Deut. xxx. 15-20.

In the majority of cases *in the general invitation*, it is best to so give it as to have the sinner take a bold stand on the side of Christ. The exceptions are where the sinner will in a quiet way take a first step, and thereby get confidence both in himself and Christ for a bolder stand. Make sure of all this in all invitations, that the sinner understands there is salvation in nothing, or nowhere but in Christ. Every invitation must mean at the bottom, "The full surrender of all to God. The complete giving of all we have and are to the service of Christ, and trusting him."

SPECIAL KINDS OF INVITATION.

Who will come to the altar or anxious seat to seek Christ? Who will come to the inquiry room? Will you come and be one of the class to be instructed "how to be saved?" Will you rise up in your seat? While all Christians are standing or bowed in prayer, get them to rise or lift a hand for prayer; this is a first step. Ask all who have decided to become Christians to rise and say, "I have," or "I will." Have them repeat "Christ for me." Make the seat an altar of prayer. Get them first to rise for prayer, then to come forward as seekers for salvation. Get them to lift the hand or rise for prayer or as seekers, then invite them to an after service. Have them remain in their seat, and some Christian worker will talk with them. "Who will meet with the others and hear the plan of salvation?" Who will sign an "I will" card? Then get a book like "Good news for you." Have all who want Christ, or will seek him, to walk out of their seat to the inquiry room. Give the plans of salvation, and then get them to say, "I will trust,' "I will take," or "I will choose." While heads are bowed in prayer, get them to rise and say, "I take Christ." Ask, "Who will receive Jesus?" Give full plan of salvation, then get Christians and all who will give themselves to God to stand and sing "My God is reconciled." Ask those who have or will give themselves to God to come forward and shake hands with the leader or minister. Get the Christians and the sinners to the altar. Ask all who will seriously listen to the truth to stand. Get them to ask for prayer by written request. Invite them to meet you in your own room. Sing "Who will go," and ask who will. Who will promise to meet me in heaven? Who will meet loved ones in heaven? Ask the older Christians to stand, then "who will take their keeping Saviour?" Who will accept the King's invitation to be present at the marriage supper of the Lamb? Who will pray, "God be merciful to me a sinner?" Who will call on the name of the Lord? Who will meet the pastor of the church? Go from seat to seat seeking sinners. While preaching, stop and urge an immediate giving of themselves to God. Between the verses of song or solo get them to decide. While singing an invitation hymn, get them to decide and come. Ask, "Will you be a Christian now?" and get them to decide then and there. Let unsaved seekers come forward and seek till they find that light. Ask, "Who will give up all sin and serve God?" Who will write their names after "fear not" in Isa. xliii. 1. Who will receive and who will reject Christ? Get those who have the most influence with the individual to invite them. Get them to come to the unconverted people's meeting.

Lesson 21.

ILLUSTRATIONS—HOW TO MAKE AND USE THEM.

First note their power: A child will always listen to a story. We never grow beyond liking them. Crowds will hang upon their narration. Jesus always used them. Every successful preacher uses them. This kind of truth is remembered longest. See how the world uses this power, in theatres—a tale acted out; newspapers—"The cry for something new in story;" platform—lectures illustrated, etc. A soul winner must be able to illustrate truth: 1. It will secure him a hearing. 2. It will gain the attention. 3. It will enable him to reach the conscience, the feelings and the will. Illustrations, like bread, can both be made or bought. To *buy* them we must pay the price of, first, close attention; second, a retentive mind; third, a quick discernment; fourth, a ready application. They are to be had from sermons, addresses, newspapers, magazines, books, conversations, and every like source. "Use the scissors." Pencil and paper are necessary to their being stored up for use. To *make* them we must have the faculty of construction. An eye that can detect good material. An ear that catches meaning as well as sound. Ability to read between the lines, and some knowledge of cause and effect. There must be a study of human nature and mental philosophy, either with or without books, or both.

BIBLE ILLUSTRATIONS.

These are the most powerful, because of the most truth in them. Joseph in prison — God's watch care. Daniel's prayer meetings — illustrate prayer. Saul going to Tarsus—religion at home. Shunamite woman—good guests. Feeding the five thousand—much in a little. Lot's visit to his sons—warn the wicked. Four men at one time—earnestness. Valley of dry bones—what God can do. The ten lepers—ungratefulness; and a thousand more. Bible illustrations usually carry or make their own points. Never let an illustration cover up the truth, but make it clear. Illustrations from your own experience are the best for you, as a rule. Keep them fresh. Clothe your illustrations in words that all will understand—language of common life. Leave out technical terms, and never use Greek or Latin. Men don't carry Webster's unabridged. Illustrations may be either real or supposed, like a parable, as is that of the Prodigal Son.

Use your imagination. An illustration is simply a medium by which truth is conveyed to the mind. The barbed arrow is the instrument of carrying the poison to the enemy's heart. Be careful of too much illustration; it can be overdone. My plan of getting and using them: First, incidents in my work; second, incidents in my past life; third, happenings around me; fourth, keep everything good I hear; fifth, make them in my walks and rides; sixth, use them the first chance I get; seventh, keep all that's good and no more; the rest throw away.

Lesson 22.

THE WORKER AND HIMSELF.

Before going to war, count the cost. Let every one who would toil in the Master's vineyard carefully examine himself or herself. When a lack is found, supply it at once.

The following are some of the "musts" of one who would work for Jesus: Have salvation; and know it. Look away from your weakness to God's strength. Choose lines of work fitted for you. Recognize the constant inward warfare. Constantly labor with yourself. Have an aim, and make it by the grace of God. Have plans, and work them. Be yourself—sanctified individuality is a mighty power. God never uses fools for his work. Be like men only as they are like Christ. Blaze and burn with zeal for souls. Take all discouragements to God in prayer. Feed yourself before giving to others. Study the Bible first for your own heart. Don't be a preacher when you ought to be a ploughman. God will guide you if you will let him. Many die from overwork in business, but mighty few from overwork in religion. Be sure and have a fresh personal experience. Keep your hands clean and heart pure. Think much on John xv. 7 and Jer. xxxii. 17. Dress neatly and be clean in every way. Don't use tobacco, liquors, or over eat. Get plenty of sleep, but don't forget Prov. xxiv. 33, 34. Think while on your feet, and cultivate memory. Learn by others' mistakes rather than your own. Keep humble, or God won't use you. Read good books, and keep good company. Don't be so modest as to miss your opportunity. Know yourself and men about you. Let your purposes be founded on the Rock. Don't be idle, but take rest, and eat well. Live ever ready for Christ's coming. Make a covenant with your eyes and ears. Die rather than sin. Be as much like Christ as grace and God can make you.

Lesson 23.

A CLEAR IDEA OF CONVERSION.

" I have been converted " means, in full, a change of service from Satan to God, and the heart regenerated by the Word of God through the power of the Holy Spirit. John iii. 7, " Ye must be born again "—" Ye are his whom ye obey." At conversion there is :

REPENTANCE—toward God. A change of will. Giving up all sin. Making restitution. Leaving the world. It is our part in conversion. It is the prodigal coming to himself, and not only resolving, *but going* to his Father. Luke xiii. 3; Isa. lx. 6, 7; Prov. xxxvii. 13.

FAITH—saving faith is a personal trust in Jesus Christ for salvation. It is believing he died *for me.* It is taking God at his word and resting thereon for the forgiveness of sins. Faith that by the blood of Christ we have redemption. Faith that God receives us in reconciliation. It has knowledge, assent, and, greatest of all, appropriating power or laying hold. It is our part in conversion, assisted by the free grace of God. Acts xiii. 38, 39; viii. 37; xvi. 30, 31; Isa. xii. 2.

REGENERATION—a work wrought on the heart by the Holy Ghost, whereby a new nature is given us, which is the germ or principle of divine life. It is not the old nature fixed up. Being dead in trespasses and sin, by regeneration we get the gift of eternal life. It is God's work in conversion. Sometimes the soul is conscious of the moment when this is done ; sometimes not. Regeneration gives life.

ADOPTION—We are made Sons of God by adoption the moment we are converted, so that we belong to God as a child belongs to its father. We are of the household of faith. Christ is the great Shepherd and we are one of his flock. We are not our own, but belong to God, who will keep both us and our trust if we will let him.

JUSTIFICATION — At conversion we stand justified before God, because having faith in Christ and his atonement for sin we have his righteousness imputed unto us. We drop our own righteousness as filthy rags and trust alone in the merit of the Son of God, for Christ is the end of the law for righteousness to every one that believeth. We are justified not by good works or deeds of the law, but only by faith in him who alone is righteous. Justification gives peace.

CONFESSION—This is always a part of conversion, and means the declaration given by us to the world that we are followers of Christ. Practically, it is both by word of mouth and a godly walk, life, and conversation. It should always embody the taking of the sacrament, and uniting with the visible church of Christ. Rom. x 8, 9; Ps. xcii. 13.

The evidences of conversion are of three kinds :

First, the inner consciousness of it by the Spirit of God, which is usually known by the love of God shed abroad in our heart. " The Spirit himself beareth witness with our spirit that we are the children of God."—Rom. viii. 16. There is a consciousness of love for God, his people, his service, and his holiness.

Second, the Word of God, which becomes life to us, and we have hope in it. The promises become unto us the title deeds of our everlasting inheritance. 1 John v. 13; John v. 24.

Third, by the fruit bearing of our lives. "Ye shall know them by their fruit." We do good for Christ's sake. The motive is changed from that which we had before conversion, wherein we did good from various motives, but never for Christ's sake and to glorify God. This is the difference between the good works of the righteous and the wicked, or the saved and the unsaved.

At conversion the mind is changed toward God ; we hate sin and love righteousness. " There is no peace, saith my God, to the wicked." At conversion the kingdom of God is put within us, which is righteousness, peace, and joy in the Holy Ghost. Reformation is not regeneration. At conversion the old nature is not destroyed, but a new nature added, and this struggle of the new nature with the old nature is called the christian warfare. It is the will fighting against the sensibilities. A new convert is a babe in Christ, and must grow in grace and knowledge. Children may be so taught that neither they or their parents can tell when they were converted. It ought to be so in all possible cases. Temptations and trials are no proof we are not converted; it is rather a proof of it. Having doubts, or falling into sin, is no proof that we are not or never have been converted. Notice the great contrasts in the conversions of the Bible. Paul, Lydia, the jailor, the thief on the cross, the woman at the well, the publican, and others.

FEELING.

There is a godly sorrow for sin, sometimes before, sometimes after conversion. There is conviction of sin, more or less.

deep; the deeper it is before conversion the better. Joy over conversion never comes till we have completely submitted and surrendered to God and received Jesus as Saviour. Sometimes it does not come then. Sooner or later it will come. Never depend on feelings.

Lesson 24.
AIDS TO SOUL WINNING.

There are two sides to soul winning work, the human and the divine, God will always do his part if we do ours. To be a soul winner, either in a broad or narrow sphere the worker must have— Deep piety and constant communion with God   Ability to set others to work. Ability to illustrate truth—make it plain. Sympathy that opens the fountain of tears. Knowledge of the surroundings of men. Humanity that exalts God. A knowledge of God and his power. Ability to cover successfully critical points. A pure motive to glorify God. Good common and uncommon sense. Ability to rightly divide the word of truth. A knowledge of the plans of the soul winners. Willingness to do little things and look after details. Power to discern the workings of Satan. A conscience as tender as the apple of your eye. The courage of your convictions. A joy from heaven in soul and countenance. An intense love for souls. Ability to look at men as God sees them. Unction in public and private prayer. Liberty in address by the Spirit. Power and love to deal with the individual. Power to quicken cold churches. A living personal testimony. Command of your voice. To live as though this were your last day. A reliance on God for temporal care. Perfect unconcern about yourself. Ability to discern the signs of the times. Power to be hopeful under all circumstances. Willingness to preach to one or ten thousand. Aim for immediate results. Reach the feelings, the conscience, and the will. Aim for conviction of sin. Preach a full and free gospel. Be filled with joy and the Holy Ghost—Power and strength. Have boldness and great courage—Better than an army. Have zeal with knowledge—This insures success. Perseverance and earnestness set on fire — Burn through difficulties. Get a knowledge of human nature—This is power. Have the power to comprehend situations — This is mighty. Have tact and common sense —The more of this the more success. A knowledge of sin and its consequences —Must be had. Aptness in putting

truth—Strike in the right place. Big faith, mountain moving kind —Omnipotent power. Love that not only constrains, but wins — Highest power. Plain preaching, well illustrated—The need of the hour. Great and wise use of Scripture—No fools. A thorough knowledge of sound doctrine—Must have it. An intense hatred of sin—How to get it. A burning love for souls—Born of God. Knowledge of opportunities—Once last, lost forever. Prayer—Prevailing and persistent, public and private. Untiring work—"Stick at-it-ive ness." Ability to create measures and use them. Power to adapt others' measures to your manners. Wisdom from above, as in James i. 5. A right putting of the invitation. Felt knowledge of eternal punishment. Power to get out of ruts. Fearlessness before all men, especially the rich and educated. Perfect obedience to God's word and will.

Lesson 25.
INCENTIVES TO SOUL SAVING WORK.

First. The command of our Lord. Second. The reward for the service. Third. The good that comes to those saved. Fourth. The greater praise that comes to God. Fifth. The blessing that comes to society. Sixth. The joy in three worlds. Seventh. The defeat of Satan.

THE COMMAND.

This is explicit and direct. Mark xvi. 15; John xv. 16; 2 Cor. v. 12-20; Ezek. xxxiii. 8. Have we been saved if we deny the cup of salvation to others? Can we be saved if we fail in this command? See that awful warning in Ezek. xxxiii. 12. To neglect to give the patient the medicine and he die thereby, are we not responsible for the death? Consider the result of a Levite who refused to tell the serpent-bitten Israelites that Moses had lifted the brazen remedy,. and he that would look should live.. Read John iii. 14, 15. Christ said, " If ye love me keep my commandments." " If I be lifted up I will draw all men unto me." It's ours to lift him up that the whole world may see him. See John xvii. 20, 21.

THE REWARD.

James v. 20; here is the promise of a double reward. Dan. xii. 3 gives the eternal reward. John xii. 26 has a depth of meaning in it which only heaven can reveal. Think of meeting those you have led to Christ, in heaven.   1. There is no joy like that of soul saving.   2. We grow mightily in grace thereby. 3. We make friendships that are eternal. 4. It brings gladness next to our own conversion. 5. We gain the love and esteem of the Church. 6. It helps to answer prayer. 7. It sets all heaven singing for joy.—Luke xv.

THE GOOD THAT COMES.

A soul saved from hell. A wicked life changed to one of righteousness. The fires of a burning conscience put out, and peace, like a river, put in. A soul set free from the service of Satan. Good influences let loose, bad influences changed. A soul reconciled to God. "Harmony once more." Hope restored, manhood regained, life found. Condemnation gone; victory over death. Companionship of Jesus. The indwelling God and power of the Holy Ghost. Love the controlling motive, and not self or selfishness.

THE GREATER PRAISE OF GOD.

A soul saved will sing forever. God will never hear the last of "saving a sinner like me." Everlasting praise for everlasting salvation.

BLESSING TO SOCIETY.

Hatred, malice, strife lessened, and love, joy, and peace increased. There is no Christianity without morality. Convert the race and prisons close, two-thirds of all asylums and hospitals will not be needed. One judge will do for every fifty we now have. War will be known only in memory, and every soldier can beat his gun into pruning hooks and go to work. The cry of the poor will be stopped with mouthfuls of meat, and the destitute will sing for joy of plenty.

JOY IN THREE WORLDS.

Heaven will rejoice. Earth will rejoice. Some mother will weep tears of joy over her boy saved at last. Wife will have the glad knowledge that she and her husband will not part forever at the grave. Brother and sisters will sing the same songs of salvation. Hell will rejoice. Yes, strange as it may seem, lost brothers, like the one in Luke xvi. 27-30, will be glad to know that others of the same household have escaped the torments of the wicked.

THE DEFEAT OF SATAN.

The enemy of Christ foiled at last. Seeking whom he may devour, he has lost his prey. Christ and the angels victorious. Satan and the devils defeated. The glory of triumph in battle. One more in heaven—one less in hell.

TRAINING CLASS THEMES FOR CONSIDERATION.

A Church Member's Duty.
Assurance—its Privileges and Power.
Bible Revivals.
Christ—his Divinity.
"   his Humanity.
"   his Miracles.
"   his Parables.
"   his Sacrifice.
Evangelistic Work.
Following Up Your Work.
Getting People to Come.
Helps to Bible Study.
How the Pew may help the Pulpit.
How to do Personal Work.
How to Get Converts.
Modern Revivals.
Music—its Use and Power.
Organizing Training Classes.
Praying in Public and in Private.
Preparation and Adaptation.
Profitable Prayer Meetings.
Ripe Fields for Christian Workers.
Special Thoughts for Leaders.
Successful Christian Workers.
The Doctrine of the Resurrection.
The Kind of Christian Workers needed.
The Law of Christian Giving.
The Use of Tact and Common Sense.
The Worker and his Bible.
What is it to be a Christian?
What is Saving Faith?
What to do in a Revival.
Young Converts and Their Needs.

TEMPLE SONGS

SELECTED BY

CHARLES H. YATMAN.

MUSICAL EDITORS:

JNO. R. SWENEY AND WM. J. KIRKPATRICK.

PHILADELPHIA:

Published by JOHN J. HOOD, 1018 Arch St.

TEMPLE · SONGS

Hide Thou Me.

FANNY J. CROSBY.   "Thou art my hiding place."—Ps. xxxii. 7.   ROBERT LOWRY. By per.

1. In thy cleft, O Rock of a-ges, Hide thou me; When the fitful tempest
2. From the snare of sinful pleasure, Hide thou me; Thou, my soul's eternal
3. In the lonely night of sorrow, Hide thou me; Till in glory dawns the

ra-ges, Hide thou me; Where no mortal arm can sev-er From my
trea-sure, Hide thou me; When the world its power is wielding, And my
mor-row, Hide thou me;   In the sight of Jordan's bil-low, Let thy

heart thy love forev-er, Hide me, O thou Rock of a-ges, Safe in thee.
heart is almost yielding, Hide me, O thou Rock of a-ges, Safe in thee.
bo-som be my pillow; Hide me, O thou Rock of a-ges, Safe in thee.

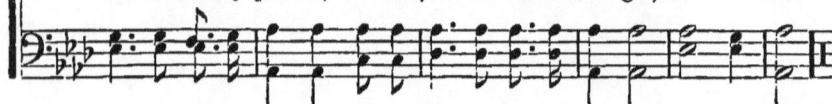

3

4   Jesus is Good to Me.

Rev. E. H. Stokes. D. D.

Jno. R. Sweney.

1. I love my Saviour, his heart is good, He has loved me o'er and o'er;
2. He calls, I rise, and he maketh me whole,—How fond his tender embrace!
3. I want to love him with all my heart, Tho' all its powers are small;
4. He's good to me in my sorrow's night, He's good in the tempest's roll;

He sought me wand'ring, I'm saved by his blood, And I love him more and more.
He cleanses and keeps me and blesses my soul'—My day the smile of his face.
I will not keep from him any part, For he is worthy of all.
He bringeth from darkness into light,—With joy he filleth my soul.

CHORUS.

Je - sus is good to me, . . . Je - sus is good to me; . . .
to me,   to me;

So good! so good! Je - sus is good to my soul.

Abiding.

Rev. E. H. Stokes, D.D.   Jno. R. Sweney.

1. My soul for light and love had earnest longings, Oh, how it longed for
2. Oh, how en - riching is this sacred treasure! En - riching to this
3. Oh, yes, I rest, how blessed is the rest - ing! I rest to- day, I'm

fellowship di-vine! I sought it here and there, I sought it ev'rywhere, At
soul, this soul of mine; There's nothing any where Can with this love compare, And
resting all the time; "Come," echoes thro' the air, "Come," and the resting share, And

CHORUS.

last, thro' faith, the holy boon was mine. I'm a - bid - ing, gracious
I henceforth, for-ev- er, Lord, am thine.
Je- sus will be yours as he is mine.

Sav - iour, I'm a - bid- ing in thy precious love to - day; I'm a-

bid - ing, yes, a - bid - ing In thy love, thy precious love, to - day.

DO RE MI FA SO LA SI

Behold the Bridegroom.

"And at midnight there was a cry made, Behold, the bridegroom cometh : go ye out to meet him."—Matt. xxv. 6.

R. E. H.   R. E. Hudson.

1.   Are you ready for the Bridegroom When he comes, when he comes? Are you
2. Have your lamps trimm'd and burning When he comes, when he comes; Have your
3.   We will   all go out to meet him When he comes, when he comes; We will
4.   We will   chant   al - le - lu - ias When he comes, when he comes; We will

ready for the Bridegroom When he comes, when he comes, Behold! he cometh!
lamps trimm'd and burning When he comes, when he comes, He quickly cometh!
all go out to meet him When he comes, when he comes; He surely cometh!
chant   al - le - lu - ias When he comes, when he comes; Lo! now he cometh!

D.S.—Behold ! he cometh !

Fine.

be-hold! he cometh! Be robed and read - y, for the Bridegroom comes.
he quick - ly cometh, O soul, be read - y when the Bridegroom comes.
he sure - ly cometh! We'll go   to meet him when the Bridegroom comes.
lo! now he cometh! Sing al - le - lu - ia! for the Bridegroom comes.

be - hold! he cometh! Be robed and read - y, for the Bridegroom comes.

CHORUS.   D. S.

Behold the Bridegroom, for he comes, for he comes!
Behold the Bridegroom, for he comes, for he comes

DO RE MI FA SO LA SI

Say, are You Ready?

A. S. KIEFFER. "Therefore be ye also ready."—Matt. xxiv. 44. T. C. O'KANE.

1. Should the death an - gel knock at thy cham - ber, In the still
2. Ma - ny sad spir - its now are de - part - ing In - to the
3. Ma - ny redeemed ones now are as - cend - ing In - to the

watch of to - night, Say, will your spir - it pass in - to torment,
world of des - pair; Ev - 'ry brief moment brings your doom nearer;
mansions of light; Je - sus is pleading, pa - tiently pleading,

CHORUS.

Or to the land of de - light? Say, are you read - y?
Sin - ner, O sin - ner, be - ware!
O let him save you to - night.

Oh, are you read - y If the death an - gel should call?
should call?

Say, are you read-y? Oh, are you read-y? Mercy stands waiting for all.

DO RE MI FA SO LA SI

Always Abounding.

"Always abounding in the work of the Lord."—1 Cor. xv. 58.

E. A. BARNES. WM. J. KIRKPATRICK.

1. Be earnest, my brothers, in word and in deed, Be active in reaping and
2. Be ready, my brothers, his call to o-bey, In seeking the erring and
3. Be zealous, my brothers, the light to extend, And unto all nations the

sow- ing the seed; And thus in the vineyard, with Je-sus to lead, Be
show-ing the way; And thus as his servants, remem - ber, we pray, Be
gos - pel to send; And thus, till the harvest in glo - ry shall end, Be

REFRAIN.

always abounding in the work of the Lord. Be always abounding in the

work of the Lord, Be always abounding in the work of the Lord; Be earnest, be

active, re- lying on his word, Be always abounding in the work of the Lord.

DO RE MI FA SO LA SI

One more Day. 9

FRANK GOULD.   JNO R. SWENEY.

1. One more day   its twilight brings,   One more day   its shadow
2. One more day   of conflict passed,   One more vic - t'ry gained at
3. One more day   of reaping o'er,   One more sheaf   to crown our
4. Saviour, when   as now we rest,   Leaning, trust - ing on thy

flings;   One sweet hour   of grate-ful prayer,   Calling to
last;   One sweet hour   in praise to spend,   While at a
store;   One sweet hour   to bathe the soul   Here in the
breast,   We shall cross   the nar-row sea   Still may we

CHORUS.

rest . . . from toil and care. One day near - - er the land of
throne . . . of grace we bend.
streams . . of joy that roll.
sing, . . . inspired by thee :—

song, One day near - - er the white-robed throng; There at the

gate they watch and wait For a meeting that shall last forever.

they watch and wait,

Copyright, 1884, by JOHN J. HOOD.

DO   RE   MI   FA   SO   LA   SI

Over There.

T. C. O'Kane.

1. O, think of a home over there, By the side of the river of light,
2. O, think of the friends over there, Who before us the journey have trod,
3. My Saviour is now over there, There my kindred and friends are at rest;
4. I'll soon be at home over there, For the end of my journey I see;

Over there,

Where the saints all immortal and fair, Are robed in their garments of white.
Of the songs that they breathe on the air, In their home in the palace of God.
Then away from my sorrow and care, Let me fly to the land of the blest.
Many dear to my heart, over there, Are watching and waiting for me.

Over there.

REFRAIN.

O- ver there,   o- ver there,   O, think of a home over there,
O- ver there,   o- ver there,   O, think of the friends over there,
O- ver there,   o- ver there,   My Saviour is now o- ver there,
O- ver there,   o- ver there,   I'll soon be at home over there,

Over there,   over there,   over there,

O- ver there,   over there, over there, O, think of a home over there.
O- ver there,   over there, over there, O, think of the friends over there.
O- ver there,   over there, over there, My Saviour is now over there.
O- ver there,   over there, over there, I'll soon be at home over there.

over there,

P. P. B.   *"Behold, the half was not told."—Kings x. 7.*   P. P. BLISS.

1. Re - peat the sto - ry o'er and o'er, Of grace so full and free;
2. Of peace I on - ly knew the name, Nor found my soul its rest
3. My high - est place is ly - ing low At my Redeem - er's feet;
4. And oh, what rapture will it be With all the host a - bove,

I love to hear it more and more, Since grace has res - cued me.
Un - til the sweet-voiced angel came To sooth my wea - ry breast.
No re - al joy in life I know, But in his ser - vice sweet.
To sing through all e - ter - ni - ty The won - ders of his love!

CHORUS.

The half was never told, The half was never told,
nev - er told,   nev - er told,

1. Of grace divine, so wonder-ful, The half was never told.
2. Of peace, etc.
3. Of joy, etc.
4. Of love, etc.

nev - er told.

DO RE MI FA SO LA SI

1. Cast thy bread up-on the wa-ters, Ye who have but scant supply,
2. Cast thy bread up-on the wa-ters, Poor and weary, worn with care,—
3. Cast thy bread up-on the wa-ters, Ye who have a-bundant store;
4. Cast thy bread up-on the wa-ters, Far and wide your treasures strew,
5. Cast thy bread up-on the wa-ters, Waft it on with praying breath,

An-gel eyes will watch above it;— You shall find it by and by!
Oft-en sitting in the shadow, Have you not a crumb to spare?
It may float on man-y-a bil-low, It may strand on many-a shore;
Scat-ter it with willing fin-gers, Shout for joy to see it go!
In some distant, doubtful moment It may save a soul from death;

He who in his righteous balance Doth each human ac-tion weigh
Can you not to those around you Sing some lit-tle song of hope,
You may think it lost for-ev-er, But, as sure as God is true,
For if you do close-ly keep it, It will on-ly drag you down;
When you sleep in solemn silence, 'Neath the morn and evening dew,

Will your sac-ri-fice remem-ber, Will your loving deeds re-pay.
As you look with longing vision Thro' faith's mighty tel-e-scope?
In this life or in the oth-er, It will yet return to you.
If you love it more than Je-sus, It will keep you from your crown.
Stranger hands, which you have strengthened, May strew lilies over you.

Praise ye the Lord.

FANNY J. CROSBY.   WM. J. KIRKPATRICK.

1. Praise ye the Lord, the hope of our sal-va-tion; Praise ye the Lord, our
2 Praise ye the Lord, whose throne is everlasting; Praise ye the Lord, whose

.CHO.—Praise ye the Lord, for good it is to praise him; O let the earth his

soul's a - bid- ing trust; Great are his works and wonderful his counsels;
gifts are ev - er new; Praise ye the Lord, whose tender mercy falleth

ma - jest - y proclaim; Shout, shout for joy and bow the knee before him;

Fine.

Praise ye the Lord, the only wise and just. Praise ye the Lord, our strength and our Re-
Pure as the rain and gentle as the dew. Praise ye the Lord, oh, glory! hal- le-

Sing to the harp and magnify his name.

deemer, Praise ye the Lord, his mighty love recall,—Tell how he came from
lujah! Praise ye the Lord, whose kingdom has no end; Praise ye the Lord, who

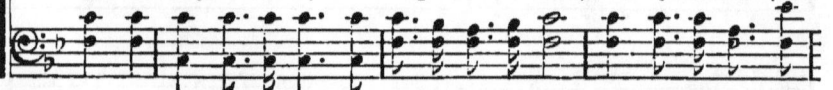

Chorus. D. C.

bondage to de - liv - er, Tell how he came to purchase life for   all.
watcheth o'er the faithful, Praise ye the Lord, our never changing Friend.

14 **Oh, the Joy that Awaits Me.**

Geo. R. Clarke.   E. F. Miller.

1. Beyond   the silent river,   In the glo - ry summer lands, In the
2. And when I cross that river,   The first   I will a - dore;   The
3. The next one who will greet me, In the mansions fair and bright, Will
4. Then cur - ly headed brother   And lit - tle ba - by dear,   And

beautiful forever, Where the jeweled city stands, Where the ever blooming
first to bid me welcome, Up - on that golden shore, Will be   my loving
be my sainted mother Arrayed in garments white, And then that gray-haired
bright eyed little sister,   With merry laugh and cheer, They all will gather

flowers Send forth their sweet perfume, My heart's most loved and cherished
Saviour,   The one who died for me,   That in   that long for - ev - er,
father,   Close pressing by her side,   Will grasp my hand with fervor
round me,   To   bid me welcome home, And watch with me the gath'ring

CHORUS.

In heavenly beauty bloom. Oh, the joy that there awaits me, When I
From sin   I might be free.
Just o'er   the swelling tide.
Of loved ones yet to come.

[no more!
reach that golden shore, When I grasp the hands of loved ones, To part with them

At the Golden Landing.

15

EDGAR PAGE.

JNO. R. SWENEY.

1. Friends of yore have flown to heaven, Springing from the house of clay;
2. Oft- en at the shades of evening, When I sit me down to rest,
3. And I seem to see their fac - es, Beaming with ce - les- tial love,
4. And I think I hear them speaking, As they oft - en spake to me,
5. Broth- er, sis - ter, faithful sol - dier, If our mingling here so sweet,

Glad to gain their joy - ful free- dom, Borne by an - gel bands a- way.
One by one I count them o - ver, They who are in glo - ry blest.
Shin- ing as their blessed Mas- ter, White-robed, with the saints above.
While I seem to hear them say - ing, " Pil- grim, heaven is waiting thee."
What shall be our joy- ous rap- ture When we at the landing meet!

CHORUS.

While on Pisgah's mount I'm standing, Looking t'ward the vernal shore,

There I seem to see them banding, Just beside the Golden Landing,

Wait - ing to receive me o'er, Precious ones who went before!

16   In the Morning.

LIZZIE EDWARDS.   JNO. R. SWENEY.

1. We are pilgrims looking home, Sad and wea- ry oft we roam, But we
2. O these tender broken ties, How they dim our aching eyes, But like
3. When our fettered souls are free, Far beyond the narrow sea, And we
4. Thro' our pilgrim journey here, Tho' the night is sometimes drear, Let us

know 'twill all be well in the morning; When, our anchor firmly cast, Ev'ry
jewels they will shine in the morning; When our victor palms we bear, And our
hear the Saviour's voice in the morning; When our golden sheaves we bring To the
watch and persevere till the morning; Then our highest tribute raise For the

Fine.

storm- y wave is past, And we gather safe at last in the morn- ing.
robes immor- tal wear, We shall know each other there, in the morn- ing.
feet of Christ our King, What a chorus we shall sing in the morn- ing.
love that crowns our days, And to Jesus give the praise in the morn- ing.

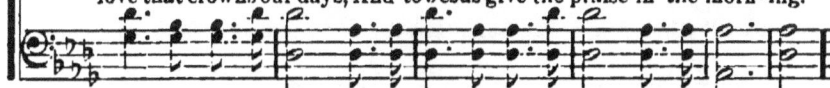

D. S.—sun - ny region bright, When we hail the blessed light of the morn- ing.

CHORUS.

When we all meet a-gain in the morn- ing, On the sweet blooming

D. S.

hills in the morn - ing; Nev - ermore to say good night In that

Cast thy Burden on the Lord.

"Casting all your care upon him, for he careth for you."
1 Peter v. 7.

W. J. K.

Wm. J. Kirkpatrick.

1. Wea-ry pil - grim on life's pathway, Struggling on beneath thy load,
2. Are thy tir - ed feet unstead - y? Does thy lamp no light af - ford?
3. Are the ties of friendship severed? Hushed the voices fond- ly heard?

Hear these words of con- so - la-tion,—"Cast thy bur - den on the Lord."
Is thy cross too great and hea- vy? Cast thy bur - den on the Lord.
Breaks thy heart with weight of anguish, Cast thy bur - den on the Lord.

CHORUS.

Cast thy bur- den on the Lord, Cast thy bur-den on the Lord, And he will

ad lib.

strengthen thee, sustain and comfort thee; Cast thy bur- den on the Lord.

4 Does thy heart with faintness falter?
Does thy mind forget his word?
Does thy strength succumb to weak-
Cast thy burden on the Lord. [ness?

5 He will hold thee up from falling,
He will guide thy steps aright;
He will strengthen each endeavor;
He will keep thee by his might.

Temple Songs–B

18   **Wonderful Love of Jesus.**

"The love of Christ, which passeth knowledge."
Eph. iii. 19.

E. D. MUND.   E. S. LORENZ.

1. In vain in high and ho-ly lays My soul her grateful voice would raise; For
2. A joy by day, a peace by night, In storms a calm, in darkness light; In
3. My hope for pardon when I call, My trust for lift-ing when I fall; In

who can sing the worthy praise Of the won-derful love of Je-sus?
pain a balm, in weakness might, Is the won-derful love of Je-sus.
life, in death, my all in all, Is the won-derful love of Je-sus.

CHORUS.

Won-derful love! won-derful love! Won-der-ful love of Je-sus!

Wonder-ful love! won-derful love! Wonder-ful love of Je-sus!

From "Holy Voices," by per.

Mary D. James.   Jno. R. Sweney.

1. Should the summons, quickly fly - ing, On the slumb'ring nations fall,—
2. What if now the startling man - date Should the sleeping virgins hear,—
3. Is there oil in all your ves - sels? Are your garments pure and white?
4. Rise! ye vir-gins,—sleep no long - er,—Lest the call your souls surprise!

Lo! the heavenly Bridegroom com-eth, Would the sound your souls appal?
Are your lamps all trimm'd and burning? Should the Bridegroom now appear?
Are they wash'd in the cleansing fountain, Fit to stand in Je - sus' sight?
Lest ye fail to meet the Bridegroom, When he cometh from the skies.

CHORUS.

Are you read - y? Are you read - y? Should you hear the midnight call?
Are you read - y? Are you read - y? Now to see your Lord ap - pear!
Are you read - y? Are you read - y? Are your lamps all clear and bright?
Oh, be read - y! Oh, be read - y! When he cometh from the skies;

Are you read - y? Are you read - y? Should you hear the midnight call?
Are you ready? Are you ready? Should you hear the midnight call? Should you hear the midnight call?
Are you read - y? Are you read - y? Now to see your Lord appear?
Are you ready? Are you ready? Now to see your Lord appear? Now to see your Lord ap - pear!
Are you read - y? Are you read - y? Are your lamps all clear and bright?
Are you ready? Are you ready? Are your lamps all clear and bright? Are your lamps all clear and bright?
Oh, be read - y! Oh, be read - y! Hasten, from your slumbers rise!
Oh, be ready! Oh, be ready! Hasten, from your slumbers rise! Hasten, from your slumbers rise!

DO RE MI FA SU LA SI

20   I Want to be a Worker.

I. B.   "The laborers are few."—Matt. ix. 27.   I. BALTZELL.

1. I want to be a worker for the Lord, I want to love and trust his holy
2. I want to be a worker ev -'ry day, I want to lead the erring in the
3. I want to be a worker strong and brave, I want to trust in Jesus' pow'r to
4. I want to be a worker; help me, Lord, To lead the lost and erring to thy

word; I want to sing and pray, and be bu - sy ev -'ry day In the
way That leads to heav'n above, where all is peace and love In the
save; All who will tru - ly come, shall find a hap-py home In the
word That points to joy on high, where pleasures never die In the

CHORUS.

1. vineyard of the Lord.   I will work,   I will pray,   In the
2, 3, 4. kingdom of the Lord.   I will work and pray, I will work and pray,

vineyard, in the vineyard of the Lord; of the Lord; I will work, I will

pray, I will la - bor ev -'ry day In the vineyard of the Lord.

By permission.   ● ♦ ● ♮ ● ● ♦
                 DO RE MI FA SO LA SI

Help Just a Little.

Music from " The Wells of Salvation,"
new words by Rev. W. A. Spencer.

Wm. J. Kirkpatrick.

1. Brother for Christ's kingdom sighing, Help a lit- tle, help a lit- tle;
2. Is thy cup made sad by tri - al? Help a lit- tle, help a lit- tle;
3. Though no wealth to thee is giv- en, Help a lit- tle, help a lit- tle;

Help to save the mil - lions dy - ing, Help just a lit- tle.
Sweet- en it with self - de - ni - al, Help just a lit- tle.
Sac - ri - fice is gold in heav - en, Help just a lit- tle.

CHORUS.

Oh, the wrongs that we may righten! Oh, the hearts that we may lighten!

Oh, the skies that we may brighten! Helping just a lit- tle.

4 Let us live for one another,
   Help a little, help a little;
   Help to lift each fallen brother,
   Help just a little.

5 Tho' thy life is pressed with sorrow,
   Help a little, help a little;
   Bravely look t'ward God's to-morrow,
   Help just a little.

Sound the Battle Cry.

W. F. S.   WM. F. SHERWIN. By per.

Vigorously, in march time.

1. Sound the bat - tle cry, See! the foe is nigh; Raise the standard high
2. Strong to meet the foe, March-ing on we go, While our cause we know
3. Oh! thou God of all, Hear us when we call, Help us, one and all,

For the Lord; Gird your ar - mor on, Stand firm ev - 'ry one.
Must pre - vail; Shield and ban- ner bright, Gleam- ing in the light,
By thy grace; When the bat - tle's done, And the vic - t'ry won,

CHORUS.

Rest your cause up - on his ho - ly word. Rouse, then, sol- diers!
Bat - tling for the right, we ne'er can fail.
May we wear the crown be - fore thy face.

2d CHO.—*Rouse, then, freemen,*

ral - ly round the banner! Ready, stead-y, pass the word a-long; Onward,

come from hill and valley; Fathers, brothers, earnest, brave, and strong! Onward,

forward, shout a-loud, Ho-san- na! Christ is Captain of the migh- ty throng.

forward, all u- nit - ed ral - ly, " Death to Alchohol !" your bat -tle song.

Ye Must be Born Again.

23

"Verily, verily, I say unto thee, except a man be born again, he cannot see the kingdom of God."—John iii. 3.

W. T. SLEEPER.   GEO. C. STEBBINS. By per.

1. A rul-er once came to Jesus by night, To ask him the
2. Ye children of men, at-tend to the word So sol-emn-ly
3. O ye who would enter that glo-ri-ous rest, And sing with the
4. A dear one in heaven thy heart yearns to see, At the beauti-ful

way to salvation and light; The Master made answer in words true and plain, "Ye
uttered by Jesus the Lord, And let not this message to you be in vain, "Ye
ransomed the song of the blest; The life everlasting if ye would obtain, "Ye
gate may be watching for thee; Then list to the note of this solemn refrain, "Ye

CHORUS.

must be born again."   Ye must be born again,   Ye must be born again,
again.   again.   again.

I ver-i-ly, ver-i-ly, say unto thee, Ye must be born again, again.

The New Song.

Flora L. Best.
Jno. R. Sweney.

Moderato.

1. There are songs of joy that I loved to sing, When my heart was as blithe as a
2. There are strains of home that are dear as life, And I list to them oft 'mid the

bird . . in spring; But the song I have learned is so full of cheer, That the
din . . of strife; But I know of a home that is wondrous fair, And I

dawn shines out in the darkness drear. O, the new, new song! O, the
sing the psalm they are singing there.

CHORUS. *Vivace.*

O, the new, new song!

new, new song, I can sing it now With the
O, the new, new song, I can sing Just now With the

ran - som'd throng: . . Pow-er and do - min-ion to him that shall
ransom'd, the ransom'd throng: . .

reign;
that shall reign;

Glo - ry and praise to the Lamb that was slain.

3 Can my lips be mute, or my heart be sad,
When the gracious Master hath made me
glad ? [be,
When he points where the many mansions
And sweetly says, ' There is one for thee ' ? |

4 I shall catch the gleam of its jasper wall
When I come to the gloom of the evenfall,
For I know that the shadows, dreary and
dim,
Have a path of light that will lead to him.

From "Gems of Praise," by per.

Fill Me Now.

Rev. E. H. Stokes, D.D.

Jno. R. Sweney.

1. Hov- er o'er me, Ho - ly Spir - it; Bathe my trembling heart and brow;
2. Thou can'st fill me, gracious Spir - it, Tho' I can - not tell thee how;
3. I am weakness, full of weakness; At thy sa - cred feet I bow;
4. Cleanse and comfort; bless and save me; Bathe, oh, bathe my heart and brow!

:S: Fine.

Fill me with thy hal - low'd presence, Come, oh, come and fill me now.
But I need thee, great- ly need thee, Come, oh, come and fill me now.
Blest, di- vine, e - ter - nal Spir- it, Fill with power, and fill me now.
Thou art comfort - ing and sav - ing, Thou art sweet - ly fill - ing now.

D.S. Fill me with thy hal-low'd presence,—Come, oh, come and fill me now.

CHORUS. D.S.

Fill me now, fill me now; Je - sus, come, and fill me now;

Some Sweet Day.

ARTHUR W. FRENCH.　　　"The hour is coming."—John v. 28.　　　D. B. TOWNER. By per.

Moderato.

1. We shall reach the riv - er side　Some sweet day, some sweet day;
2. We shall pass in - side the gate　Some sweet day, some sweet day;
3. We shall meet our loved and own　Some sweet day, some sweet day;

We shall cross the storm - y tide　Some sweet day, some sweet day;
Peace and plen - ty for us wait　Some sweet day, some sweet day;
Gath'ring round the great white throne　Some sweet day, some sweet day;

We shall press the sands of gold,　While be - fore our eyes un - fold
We shall hear the wondrous strain,　Glo - ry to the Lamb that's slain,
By the tree of life so fair,　Joy and rap - ture ev - 'rywhere,

Heav-en's splendors, yet un - told,　Some sweet day, some sweet day.
Christ was dead, but lives a - gain,　Some sweet day, some sweet day.
O the bliss of o - ver there!　Some sweet day, some sweet day.

E. F. M.   Isa. ix. 6.   E. F. MILLER.

1. I have heard a most wonderful sto - ry, Of Je-sus the Saviour and King,
2. With the poor and the lowly he mingled, Yes, even the vil- est of men,
3. A poor woman was brought to him, helpless, To be stoned for her sins in the past;
4. See him weep at a grave in the hour When tears of anguish are shed;
5. Yes, he came to give life to the dying, To heal all the broken in heart;

How he came from the bright realms of glory Glad news of salvation to bring.
Showing mercy and love as they lingered To hear his blest words unto them.
He re-plied to them, "He that is sinless, By him let the first stone be cast."
See him bursting the tomb by his power, Saying, " Laz'rus, come forth from the dead!
And he promised a home where's no sighing, And loved ones shall ne'er again part.

CHORUS.

O wonderful, wonderful Sav-iour, Thy praises with joy we will sing;

For coming to earth to redeem us, We crown thee forev - er our King.

By permission of E. F. Miller.

Tell it to Jesus.

J. E. RANKIN, D. D.   Matt. xiv. 12.   E. S. LORENZ.

1. Are you wea - ry, are you heavy-heart - ed? Tell it to Je - sus,
2. Do the tears flow down your cheeks unbidden? Tell it to Je - sus,
3. Do you fear the gath'ring clouds of sor- row? Tell it to Je - sus,
4. Are you trou- bled at the thought of dy- ing? Tell it to Je - sus,

Tell it to Je - sus; Are you griev-ing o - ver joys de-part - ed?
Tell it to Je - sus; Have you sins that to man's eye are hid - den?
Tell it to Je - sus; Are you anx- ious what shall be to - mor- row?
Tell it to Je - sus; For Christ's coming Kingdom are you sigh - ing?

CHORUS.

Tell it to Je-sus a-lone. Tell it to Je-sus, Tell it to Je-sus,

He is a friend that's well known; You have no oth - er

such a friend or broth- er, Tell it to Je - sus a lone.

By permission.

DO RE MI FA SO LA SI

He Saves.

FRANK M. DAVIS. John iii. 17. E. C. AVIS.

1. Sing glo-ry to God in the highest, For wonderful things he hath done;
2. Oh! perfect redemption to sinners, The purchase of Jesus' own blood,
3. Rejoice, then, rejoice, all ye peo-ple, The wondrous transaction is done!

He so loved the world that he gave us His on-ly be-gotten dear Son.
The vil-est offend-er is pardoned, Is saved thro' the promise of God.
The life-gate is o-pen, come, ent-er, Thro' Jesus, the Cru-cified One.

CHORUS.

Hal-le-lu-jah! hal-le-lu-jah! He saves thro' the death of his Son;

Hal-le-lu-jah! hal-le-lu-jah!

Hal-le-lu-jah! hal-le-lu-jah! He saves thro' the Crucified One.

Hal-le-lu-jah! hal-le-lu-jah!

Blessed Assurance.

F. J. Crosby.   " He is faithful that hath promised."—Heb. x. 23.   Mrs Jos. F. Knapp.

1. Blessed as - surance, Jesus is mine! Oh, what a foretaste of
2. Perfect sub-mis-sion, perfect de - light, Visions of rap - ture
3. Perfect sub-mis-sion, all is at rest, I in my Saviour am

glory di - vine! Heir of sal - va - tion, purchase of God, Born of his
burst on my sight, Angels descend- ing, bring from a - bove Echoes of
happy and blest, Watching and waiting, looking a - bove, Filled with his

CHORUS.

Spir - it, washed in his blood. This is my sto - ry, this is my
mer - cy, whispers of love.
goodness, lost in his love.

song, Praising my Sav - iour all the day long; This is my

sto - ry, this is my song, Praising my Saviour all the day long.

ANON.   ARRANGED.

1. I am dwell-ing on the mountain, Where the gold-en sunlight gleams
2. I can see far down the mountain, Where I wandered wea-ry years,
3. I am drink-ing at the fountain, Where I ev-er would a-bide;

O'er a land whose wondrous beauty Far ex-ceeds my fondest dreams;
Oft-en hin-dered in my jour-ney By the ghosts of doubts and fears,
For I've tast-ed life's pure riv-er, And my soul is sat-is-fied;

Where the air is pure, e-the-real, Laden with the breath of flowers,
Brok-en vows and dis-appointments Thickly sprinkled all the way,
There's no thirst-ing for life's pleasures, Nor a-dorn-ing, rich and gay,

CHO.—Is not this the land of Beu-lah, Blessed, bles-sed land of light,

D. S. Chorus.

They are blooming by the fountain, 'Neath the am-a-ranthine bowers.
But the Spir-it led, un-er-ring, To the land I hold to-day.
For I've found a rich-er treasure, One that fad-eth not a-way.

Where the flow-ers bloom for-ev-er, And the sun is always bright.

4 Tell me not of heavy crosses,
  Nor the burdens hard to bear,
  For I've found this great salvation
  Makes each burden light appear;
  And I love to follow Jesus,
  Gladly counting all but dross,
  Worldly honors all forsaking
  For the glory of the Cross.

5 Oh, the Cross has wondrous glory!
  Oft I've proved this to be true;
  When I'm in the way so narrow
  I can see a pathway through;
  And how sweetly Jesus whispers:
  Take the Cross, thou need'st not fear,
  For I've tried this way before thee,
  And the glory lingers near.

Is my Name Written There?

M. A. K.

Frank M. Davis.

1. Lord, I care not for riches, Neither silver nor gold; I would make sure of
2. Lord, my sins they are many, Like the sands of the sea, But thy blood, O my
3. Oh! that beauti - ful cit - y, With its mansions of light, With its glorified

heaven, I would en-ter the fold; In the book of thy kingdom, With its
Saviour! is suf - fi-cient for me; For thy promise is written, In bright
be-ings, In pure garments of white; Where no evil thing cometh, To de-

pag- es so fair, Tell me, Jesus, my Saviour, Is my name written there?
let- ters that glow, "Tho' your sins be as scarlet, I will make them like snow."
spoil what is fair; Where the angels are watching,—Is my name written there?

REFRAIN.

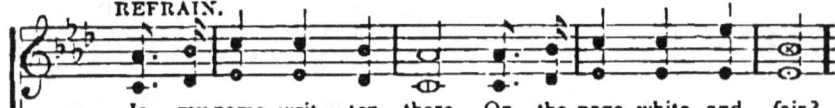

Is my name writ - ten there, On the page white and fair?

In the book of thy king- dom, Is my name written there?

DO RE MI FA SO LA SI

Is Your Lamp Burning.

33

"Let your light so shine before men, that they may see your good works, and glorify your
Father which is in heaven."—Matt. v. 16.

Mrs. E. M. H. GATES.   C. C. WILLIAMS.

1. Say, is your lamp burning, my brother? I pray you look quickly and see;
2. Upon the dark mountains they stumble, They are bruised on the rocks as they lie
3. If once all the lamps that are lighted Should steadily blaze in a   line,

For if it were burning, then surely, Some beam would fall brightly on me.
With white, pleading faces turned upward, To the clouds and the pitiful sky.
Wide o - ver the land and the o - cean, What a girdle of glory would shine!

There are many and many around you,   Who follow wherever you go,
There is many a lamp that is lighted—We behold them a-near and a-far;
How all the dark places would brighten! How the mists would turn up and away!

D.S. Say, is your lamp burning, my brother? I pray you look quickly and see;

D.S. for Chorus.

If you tho't that they walked in the shadow, Your lamp would burn brighter, I know
But not many among them, my brother, Shine steadily on like a   star.
How the earth would laugh out in her gladness, To hail the millennial day!

For if it were burning, then surely, Some beam would fall brightly on me!

Temple Songs–C

W. A. OGDEN.

1. They have reach'd the sunny shore, And will never hunger more, All their
2. Now they feel no chilling blast, For their winter time is past, And their
3. They have fought the weary fight, Jesus sav'd them by his might, Now they

grief and pains are o'er, Over there; And they need no lamp by night, For their
summers always last, O-ver there; They can never know a fear, For the
dwell with him in light, Over there; Soon we'll reach the shining strand, But we'll

D. S.—All their streets are shining gold, And their

Fine. CHORUS.

day is always bright, And their Saviour is their light, Over there. O-ver
Saviour's always near, And with them is endless cheer, Over there.
wait our Lord's command, 'Till we see his beck'ning hand, Over there.

glo-ry is untold, 'Tis the Saviour's blissful fold, O-ver there.

D. S.

there, over there, They can never know a fear, Over there;
over there, over there, over there;

From " New Silver Song," by per.

I Hope to Meet You All in Glory.

EMMA PITT.

WM. J. KIRKPATRICK.

1. I hope to meet you all in glo - ry, When the storms of life are o'er;
2. I hope to meet you all in glo - ry, By the tree of life so fair;
3. I hope to meet you all in glo - ry, Round the Saviour's throne above;
4. I hope to meet you all in glo - ry, When my work on earth is o'er;

I hope to tell the dear old sto - ry, On the bles- sed shin-ing shore.
I hope to praise our dear Redeem- er For the grace that brought me there.
I hope to join the ransomed arm - y Singing now redeem-ing love.
I hope to clasp your hands rejoic- ing On the bright e - ter- nal shore.

CHORUS.

On the shin - ing shore, On the gold - en strand, In our

Father's home, In the hap - py land: I hope to meet you there, I

hope to meet you there,—A crown of vict-'ry wear,—In glo - ry.

36 Blessed be the Fountain.

E. R. LATTA. H. S. PERKINS.

1. Blessed be the fountain of blood, To a world of sinners revealed;
2. Thorny was the crown that he wore, And the cross his bod- y o'ercame;
3. Father, I have wandered from thee; Of-ten has my heart gone astray;

Bless- ed be the dear Son of God, On - ly by his stripes we are healed;
Grievous were the sorrows he bore, But he suffered not thus in vain;
Crimson do my sins seem to me, Wa- ter cannot wash them a - way;

Tho' I've wandered far from his fold, Bringing to my heart pain and woe;
May I to that fountain be led, Made to cleanse my sins here below;
Je- sus to that fountain of thine, Leaning on thy promise I'll go;

Wash me in the blood of the Lamb, And I shall be whiter than snow.
Wash me in the blood that was shed, And I shall be whiter than snow.
Cleanse me with thy washing divine, And I shall be whiter than snow.

CHORUS.

Whit - - - er than snow; Whit - - - er than snow.

Whiter than the snow; Whiter than the snow; Whiter than the snow; Whiter than the snow, the snow:

From " River of Life," by per.

Wash me in the blood of the Lamb, And I shall be whiter than snow.
of the Lamb,   the snow.

Give me Jesus.

Arr. by W. J. K.

1. When I'm hap-py, hear me sing, When I'm happy, hear me sing, When I'm
2. When in sor-row, hear me pray, When in sorrow, hear me pray, When in
3. When I'm dy-ing, hear me cry, When I'm dying, hear me cry, When I'm
4. When I'm ris-ing, hear me shout, When I'm rising, hear me shout, When I'm
5. When in heav-en, we will sing, When in heav-en, we will sing, When in

CHORUS.

hap-py, hear me sing, Give me Je - sus, Give me Je - sus, Give me
sorrow, hear me pray, Give me Je - sus,
dying, hear me cry, Give me Je - sus,
rising, hear me shout. Give me Je - sus,
heaven, we will sing, Blessed Je - sus, Bles-sed Je - sus, Bles-sed

Je - sus; You may have all the world: Give me Je - sus.
Je - sus, By thy grace we are saved, Bles-sed Je - sus.

38 We are More than Conquerors.

"Stand ye still, and see the salvation of the Lord."
2 Chron. xx. 17.

Mrs. Flora B. Harris.　　　　　　　　　　　　Jno. R. Sweney.

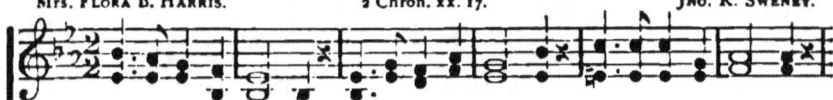

1. What shall separate us From the love that bought us? Shall the pangs of anguish
2. Things to come or present, Whatso'er betide us,—Life nor death shall ever
3. Depths that are beneath us, Heights that are above us, Have no power to sunder,

Which the cross hath wrought us? Doubtings and distresses, Fier-y tri-als
From our Lord divide us; Angels, powers, do-min-ions, These shall fall be-
Since he stooped to love us. Prince of our Redemp-tion, Sons to glo-ry

prove us; Yet am I per-suad-ed, None of these shall move us.
fore us; Clothed in his sal-va-tion, With his banner o'er us.
bring-ing, Thou hast made from sin-ners Victors, crowned and singing.

CHORUS.

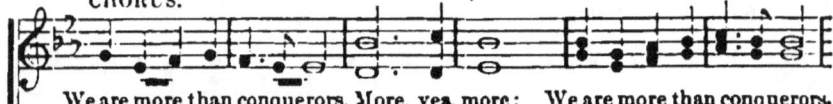

We are more than conquerors, More, yea, more; We are more than conquerors,
More, yea, more, more, yea, more;

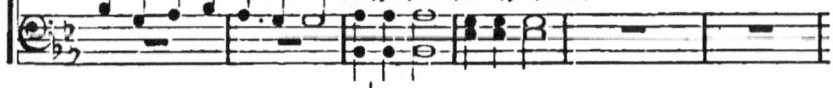

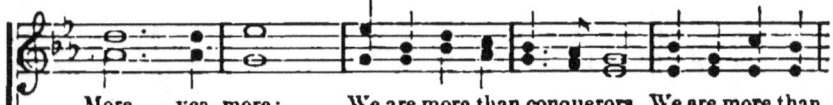

More, yea, more; We are more than conquerors, We are more than
More, yea, more, more, yea, more;

conquer-ors, We are more than conquerors Thro' him that loved us.

More Faith in Jesus.

HENRIETTA E. BLAIR.   WM. J. KIRKPATRICK.

1. While struggling thro' this vale of tears I want more faith in Je-sus; A-
2. To war against the foes with-in I want more faith in Je-sus; To
3. To brave the storms that here I meet I want more faith in Je-sus; To
4. I want a faith that works by love, A constant faith in Je-sus; A

D. S.—And

Fine. CHORUS.

mid tempta-tions, cares, and fears, I want more faith in Je - sus. I
rise a-bove the powers of sin I want more faith in Je - sus.
rest con-fid-ing at his feet I want more faith in Je - sus.
faith that mountains can remove, A liv-ing faith in Je - sus.

this my cry, as time rolls by, I want more faith in Je - sus.

D. S.

want more faith, I want more faith, A clearer, brighter, stronger faith in Jesus;

Are You Drifting?

MARY D. JAMES.   WM. J. KIRKPATRICK.

1. Are you drifting down life's current, Drift- ing on a dang'rous tide?
2. Down the stream of worldly pleasure Drift- ing, drifting ev - er- more
3. Heed, oh, heed the kind moni - tion! Give your aimless wand'rings o'er;

Near the rapids' fearful   per - il   All unconscious do ye glide?
T'ward the great unfathomed o - cean, Bound for yon e - ter- nal shore?
Cease to seek in earth your pleasure, Head your bark for heav'n's bright shore,

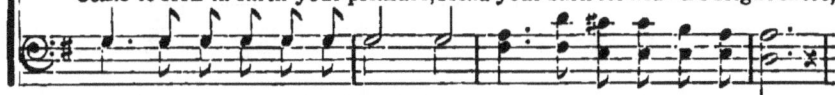

Down the stream of sin and   fol - ly,—Heed- ing not the danger near,
Drift - ing, drifting,—going,—whither? Aim - less, purposeless;— how vain!
Take on board the skillful   pi - lot, Use the oars of faith and prayer;

Drift - ing on in self-com- pla - cence, Feel - ing no remorse or fear?
To the dark and dread forev - er! What, oh, what have ye to gain?
Then you'll make the port of glo - ry, God will guide you safely there.

CHORUS.

Hark the voice . . of yonder pilot: Cease your drifting, seize the oar;

Hark the voice, the warning voice of yonder pilot :   seize the oar;

Make the blest, celestial harbor, Steer your bark for Canaan's shore.
Make the blest, celestial harbor, make the harbor,

Light after Darkness.

JNO. R. SWENEY.

DUET.

1. Light af-ter dark-ness, Gain af-ter loss, Strength af-ter
2. Sheaves af-ter sow-ing, Sun af-ter rain, Sight af-ter
3. Near af-ter dis-tant, Gleam af-ter gloom, Love af-ter

weak-ness, Crown af-ter cross, Sweet af-ter bit-ter,
mys-tery, Peace af-ter pain, Joy af-ter sor-row,
loneliness, Life af-ter tomb; Af-ter long a-go-ny,

Song af-ter fears, Home af-ter wan-der-ing, Praise af-ter tears.
Calm af-ter blast, Rest af-ter wea-riness,—Sweet rest at last.
Rap-ture of bliss; Right was the path-way Leading to this!

From "Goodly Pearls," by per.

42 God so Loved the World.

FANNY J. CROSBY. John iii. 16. WM. J. KIRKPATRICK.

Solo ad lib.

1. God loved the world so tenderly His only Son he gave, That all who on his
2. Oh, love that only God can feel, And only he can show! Its height and depth, its
3. Why perish, then, ye ransom'd ones? Why slight the gracious call? Why turn from him
4. O Saviour, melt these hearts of ours, And teach us to believe That whosoever [whose

name believe Its wondrous pow'r will save.
length and breadth Nor heav'n nor earth can know!
words proclaim E-ter-nal life to all?
comes to thee Shall endless life receive.

CHORUS.

For God so loved the world that he gave his on-ly Son, That who-so-ev-er be-lieveth in him Should not per-ish, should not per-ish; That who-so-ev-er be-lieveth in him Should not per-ish, but have ev-er-last-ing life.

DO RE MI FA SO LA SI

Leading Souls to Jesus.

J. E. Rankin, D. D.   Jno. R. Sweney.

1. Leading souls to Jesus who are sad and lost, Who upon life's waters have been
2. Leading souls to Jesus, telling them the way Out of nature's darkness into
3. Leading souls to Jesus from their want and sin, Setting up his kingdom with its
4. Leading souls to Jesus, as the stars to shine, In some humbly station, Master,

tempest-tossed; All the heavy-laden, burdened with their load, Whisp'ring of sal-
God's own day; Kneeling with the sinner at the Saviour's feet, Even angels
peace within; Till the Spirit witness in them o'er and o'er, Cleans'd are thy trans-
be   it mine; With forgiven sin-ners, not alone, to stand When I rise to

CHORUS.

vation thro' the Lamb of God. Leading souls to Jesus! oh, may this be mine,
can not know of work more sweet.
gressions: go, and sin no more.
glo-ry in the bet - ter land.

Till I cross the riv - er to that home divine; Sowing by all wa - ters,

till the great day come, When with joy the reapers shout the harvest home.

DO RE MI FA SO LA SI

O Prodigal, Don't Stay Away.

J. E. RANKIN, D. D.   "I will arise and go unto my Father."—Luke xv. 18.   J. W. BISCHOFF.

1. O prod-i-gal, don't stay away! The Fa-ther is waiting to-day; There's
2. O prodigal brother, come home! Why longer in wretchedness roam? You're
3. O prodigal, what will you do? Love's ta-ble is wait-ing for you; For-
4. O prod-i-gal brother, a-rise! For pardon, look up to the skies; No

room and to spare, There is raiment to wear, O prod-igal, don't stay a-way.
lone-ly and lost, You are driven and toss'd, O prod-igal brother, come home.
giveness so sweet, Sure, your coming will greet, O prodigal, what will you do?
longer then stray From thy Father away, O prod-i-gal brother, a-rise.

CHORUS.

Will you come? Will you come? Will you come, come home to-day? There is

Will you come?   Will you come?   Will you come?

welcome for you, There's a kiss, kind and true, Then, O prodigal, don't stay away.

Marching On.

JENNIE GARNETT.   WM. J. KIRKPATRICK.

1. With our col-ors waving bright in the blaze of gos-pel light We are
2. Oft the tempter we shall meet, but we will not fear de-feat, Though his
3. We have gird-ed on the sword and the ar-mor of the Lord, We have
4. Soon we'll reach the pearly gate, where the blessed army wait, Soon their

marshall'd on the world's great field; great field; We are ready for the strife and the
arrows at our ranks may fly; may fly; Thro' a Saviour's mighty love more than
ta-ken up the cross he bore; he bore; Oh, the trophies we shall win, oh, the
welcome, welcome song may ring; may ring; When we lay our armor down and re-

bat-tle work of life, Ev-er trusting in the Lord our shield.
conquerors we shall prove, Shouting, Glo-ry be to God on high.
vic-tory o-ver sin, When the bat-tle and the strife are o'er!
ceive a star-ry crown, Shouting, Glo-ry be to God our King.

CHORUS.

Glo-ry to God! we are marching, marching on, Marching to a home above;

Glo-ry to God! we are marching, marching on, Happy in a Saviour's love.

Copyright, 1884, by JOHN J. HOOD.

Glory to Jesus, He Saves.

P. B.

P. BILHORN.

1. Glo - ry to Je - sus who died on the tree, Paid the great price that my
2. Once in my heart there was sin and despair, Now the dear Saviour him-
3. Come, then, ye wea- ry, who long to be free, Come to the Saviour, he

soul might be free; Now I can sing hal - le - lu - jah to God,
self dwelleth there, And from his pres - ence comes peace to my soul,
wait - eth for thee; Then with the ransomed this song you can sing,

CHORUS.

Glo - ry! he saves, he saves. Glo - ry! he saves, glo - ry! he saves,

Saves a poor sin - ner like me; Glo - ry! he saves,

glo - ry! he saves, Saves a poor sin - ner like me. like me.

'Tis the Blessed Hour of Prayer. 47

"—— went into the temple at the hour of prayer."
Acts iii. 1

FANNY J. CROSBY.

W. H. DOANE. By per.

1. 'Tis the bless-ed hour of prayer, when our hearts lowly bend, And we
2. 'Tis the bless-ed hour of prayer, when the Saviour draws near, With a
3. 'Tis the bless-ed hour of prayer, when the tempted and tried To the
4. At the bless-ed hour of prayer, trusting him we be-lieve That the

gath-er to Je-sus, our Sav-iour and Friend: If we come to him in
ten-der com-pas-sion his chil-dren to hear; When he tells us we may
Saviour who loves them their sorrow con-fide; With a sym-pathiz-ing
blessing we're needing we'll sure-ly re-ceive, In the ful-ness of this

faith, his protec-tion to share, What a balm for the wea-ry! oh, how
cast at his feet ev-'ry care, What a balm for the wea-ry! oh, how
heart he removes ev-'ry care; What a balm for the wea-ry! oh, how
trust we shall lose ev-'ry care; What a balm for the wea-ry! oh, how

Fine. CHORUS. *D.S.*

sweet to be there! Blessed hour of prayer, Blessed hour of prayer;

The Promises.

L. E Hewitt.   Jno. R. Sweney.

1. The prom - is - es, how precious! The words of God's own book! They
2. They fall up - on waste plac-es Like gen - tle drops of rain, Re-
3. Yes, they shall stand forev - er! God's word shall still endure, A-

shine amid our darkness Like stars on some lone brook; Or, like the joy-ous
fresh-ing and uplifting The soul that's faint with pain. They speak a Father's
mid time's devas-tations E - ter - nal-ly secure. He's faithful that hath

sunshine. They fill our path with light, The fore-gleams of that glory Where
blessing, They breathe a Saviour's love; Our comfort in life's sorrows, Our
promised, I trust his words divine; Oh, show me all their fulness, Blest

CHORUS.

com - eth no more night.
pledge of joys a - bove. The prom - is - es, how pre - cious! I
Spir - it, make them mine.

love to call them mine. Sealed by my Saviour's dying blood, In covenant divine.

Oh, Sing of His Mighty Love.

"Mighty to save."—Isa. xliii. 1.

Rev. Frank Bottome, D. D.

Wm. B. Bradbury. By per.

1. Oh, bliss of the pu- ri-fied, bliss of the free, I plunge in the crimson tide
2. Oh, bliss of the pu- ri-fied, Je - sus is mine, No long- er in dread condem
3. Oh, bliss of the purified, bliss of the pure! No wound hath the soul that his
4. O Je - sus the crucified! thee will I sing, My blessed Redeemer, my

opened for me; O'er sin and uncleanness ex - ult - ing I stand, And
na- tion I pine; In conscious sal- vation I sing of his grace, Who
blood cannot cure, No sor - row bowed head but may sweetly find rest, No
God and my King; My soul, filled with rapture, shall shout o'er the grave, And

CHORUS.

point to the print of the nails in his hand. Oh, sing of his mighty love,
lift - eth up- on me the light of his face.
tears but may dry them on Jesus' breast.
triumph in death in the "Mighty to save."

rit.

Sing of his mighty love, sing of his mighty love, Mighty to save.

Temple Songs–D

50   The Future.

MISS JENNIE STOUT.   A. A. ARMEN.

1. Oh, I oft-en sit and pon-der, When the sun is sink-ing low,
2. Shall I be at work for Je-sus, Whilst he leads me by the hand,
3. But perhaps my work for Je-sus Soon in fu-ture may be done,

Where shall yonder fu-ture find me: Does but God in heav-en know?
And to those a-round be say-ing, Come and join his hap-py band?
All my earthly tri-als end-ed, And my crown in heav-en won;

Shall I be a-mong the liv-ing? Shall I min-gle with the free?
Come, for all things now are rea-dy, Come, his faithful foll-'wer be;
Then for-ev-er with the ran-somed Thro' e-ter-ni-ty I'd be

Where-so-e'er my path be lead-ing, Saviour, keep my heart with thee.
Oh, where'er my path be lead-ing, Saviour, keep my heart with thee.
Chanting hymns to him who bought me With his blood shed on the tree.

CHORUS.

Oh, the fu - - - - ture lies be-fore me, And I
Oh, the fu-ture lies be-fore me, And I know not where I'll be, Oh, the

From "Our Sabbath Home," by per.

know . . not where I'll be, But where'er - - my path be
future lies before me, And I know not where I'll be, But where'er my path be leading, Saviour,

lead - - ing, Saviour, keep . . . my heart with thee.
keep my heart with thee, But where'er my path be leading, Saviour, keep my heart with thee.

I'll Live for Him.

C. R. DUNBAR.

1. My life, my love I give to thee, Thou Lamb of God, who died for me;
2. I now believe thou dost receive, For thou hast died that I might live;
3. Oh, thou who died on Cal - va- ry, To save my soul and make me free,

CHO.—I'll live for him who died for me, How happy then my life shall be!

D. C.

Oh, may I ev - er faith- ful be, My Saviour and my God!
And now henceforth I'll trust in thee, My Saviour and my God!
I con - secrate my life to thee, My Saviour and my God!

I'll live for him who died for me, My Saviour and my God!

52 At the Cross.

R. KELSO CARTER.   ARR. BY E. E. NICKERSON.

1. O Je - sus, Lord, thy dy - ing love Hath pierced my con-trite heart;
2. A - mid the night of   sin and death Thy light hath filled my   soul;
3. I   kiss thy feet, I   clasp thy hand, I   touch thy bleed-ing   side;
4. My Lord, my light, my strength, my all, I count my gain but   loss;

Now take my life, and let me prove How dear to me thou art.
To me thy lov - ing voice now saith, Thy faith hath made thee whole.
O   let me here for - ev - er stand, Where thou wast cru-ci - fied.
For - ev - er let thy love enthrall, And keep me at the   cross.

CHORUS.

At the cross, at the cross, where I first saw the light, And the

bur - den of my heart roll'd a - way, It was there by

faith I receiv'd my sight, And now I am hap - py night and day!

Follow On!

53

W. O. CUSHING.

ROBERT LOWRY. By per.

1. Down in the valley with my Saviour I would go, Where the flowers are
2. Down in the valley with my Saviour I would go, Where the storms are
3. Down in the valley, or up-on the mountain steep, Close beside my

blooming and the sweet wa-ters flow; Ev'rywhere he leads me I would
sweeping and the dark wa-ters flow; With his hand to lead me I will
Saviour would my soul ev-er keep; He will lead me safely, in the

fol-low, fol-low on, Walking in his footsteps till the crown be won.
nev-er, nev-er fear, Dangers cannot fright me if my Lord is near.
path that he has trod, Up to where they gather on the hills of God.

REFRAIN.

Follow! follow! I would follow Jesus! Anywhere, ev'rywhere, I would follow on!

Follow! follow! I would follow Jesus! Ev'rywhere he leads me I will follow on!

Copyright, 1880, by Bigelow & Main.

In the Shadow of His Wings.

Rev. J. B. ATCHINSON.   E. O. EXCELL.

1. In the shadow of his wings There is rest, sweet rest; There is rest from care and
2. In the shadow of his wings There is peace, sweet peace, Peace that passeth under-
3. In the shadow of his wings There is joy, glad joy, There is joy to tell the

la - bor, There is rest for friend and neighbor, In the shadow of his wings,
standing, Peace, sweet peace that knows no ending, In the shadow of his wings,
sto - ry, Joy ex - ceeding, full of - glo - ry; In the shadow of his wings,

There is rest, sweet rest, In the shadow of his wings There is rest, sweet rest,
There is peace, sweet peace, In the shadow of his wings There is peace, sweet peace,
There is joy, glad joy, In the shadow of his wings, There is joy, glad joy,

CHORUS.

There is rest,   There is peace,   There is joy   In the shadow of his wings;
sweet rest,   sweet peace,   glad joy,

There is rest,   there is peace,   There is joy   In the shadow of his wings.
sweet rest,   sweet peace,   glad joy,

Drinking at the Living Fountain. 55

The "Lanan."

P. BILHORN.

1. I have found a balm for all my woe, Jesus is the living fountain;
2. When I came to Je-sus in my sin, Bending at the living fountain;
3. As I heard his voice so kind and sweet, Sounding at the living fountain;
4. To the fountain come, O come to-day, Flowing is the living fountain;

I am full of joy, as Christ I know, Drinking at the fount of life.
Then he heard my prayer and made me clean, Cleansed me at the fount of life.
Then I wept and sang low at his feet, Drinking at the fount of life.
If you come he'll wash your sins a-way, Je-sus is the fount of life.

CHORUS.

O the fount is Christ, in him believe, Drinking at the living fountain;

All who come to him, the life received, Jesus is the fount of life.

Coming To=Day.

FANNY J. CROSBY.　　　　　　　　　　　　　　　JNO. R. SWENEY.

1. Out on the des-ert, looking, looking, Sinner, 'tis Je-sus looking for thee;
2. Still he is waiting, waiting, waiting, O, what compassion beams in his eye,
3. Lovingly pleading, pleading, pleading, Mercy, tho' slighted, bears with thee yet;
4. Spirits in glory, watching, watching, Long to behold thee safe in the fold;

Tender - ly calling, calling, calling, Hither, thou lost one, O, come unto me.
Hear him repeat-ing gent-ly, gently, Come to thy Saviour, O, why wilt thou die.
Thou canst be happy, hap-py, hap-py, Come, ere thy life-star forever shall set.
Angels are waiting, waiting, waiting, When shall thy story with rapture be told?

CHORUS.

Jesus is looking, Jesus is calling, Why dost thou linger, why tarry away?

Run to him quickly, say to him gladly, Lord, I am coming, coming to-day.

The Child of a King. 57

HATTIE E. BUELL.   Arr. from Melody by Rev. JOHN B. SUMNER.

1. My Fa-ther is rich in houses and lands, He holdeth the wealth of the
2. My Father's own Son, the Saviour of men, Once wander'd o'er earth as the
3. I once was an out-cast stranger on earth, A sin-ner by choice, an
4. A tent or a cot-tage, why should I care? They're building a palace for

world in his hands! Of ru-bies and diamonds, of silver and gold   His
poorest of men, But now he is reigning for-ev-er on high, And will
al-ien by birth! But I've been a-dopt-ed, my name's written down,—An
me o-ver there! Tho' exiled from home, yet, still I may sing: All

CHORUS.

cof-fers are full,—he has riches un-told. I'm the child of a King, The
give me a home in heaven by and by.
heir to a man-sion, a robe, and a crown.
glo-ry to God, I'm the child of a King.

ad lib.

child of a King; With Je-sus my Saviour I'm the child of a King.

DO RE MI FA SO LA SI

58 By the Grace of God we'll Meet.

FANNY J. CROSBY.   JNO. R. SWENEY.

1. Thro' the gates of pearl and jasper To the ci-ty paved with gold,When the
2. When the harvest work is ended, And the summer days are past, When the
3. Let us fol-low on with firmness, keeping ev - er in the way Where our

ransomed host shall en - ter, And their gracious Lord be- hold. When they
reap - ers go re- joic - ing To their bright re- ward at last; When the
bles - sed Lord has taught us, To be faith-ful, watch and pray; Then, in

meet in bliss - ful triumph By the tree of life so fair Shall we
white-robed an- gel leads them to the gates of joy so fair, Shall we
garments pure and spotless, By the tree of life so fair, We shall

join   the no - ble arm - y, And   re- ceive a wel - come there?
join   their hap - py num - ber? Will they bid us wel - come there?
sing through endless ag - es With the count- less mil - lions there.

CHORUS.

By the grace . . . . of God we'll meet . . . . In the
By the grace of God we'll meet, By the grace of God we'll meet In the

DO RE MI FA SO LA SI

ci - - ty's golden street, Shouting, glo - - - - ry! hal-le-

ci - ty's gold - en street, golden street, Shouting, glo-ry! hal-le-lu-jah! Shouting,

lu - - - - jah! At the dear - - - - - Redeem-er's feet.

glo - ry! hal - le - lu - jah! At our dear Re-deem-er's feet, Re-deem-er's feet.

C. J. B.

A Sinner like Me.

CHAS. J. BUTLER.

1. I was once far away from the Saviour, And as vile as a sinner could be,

I wondered if Christ the Redeemer, Could save a poor sinner like me.

2 I wandered on in the darkness,
Not a ray of light could I see, [ness,
And the thought filled my heart with sad-
There's no hope for a sinner like me.

3 I then fully trusted in Jesus,
And oh, what a joy came to me;
My heart was filled with his praises,
For saving a sinner like me.

4 No longer in darkness I'm walking,
For the light is now shining on me,
And now unto others I'm telling,
How he saved a poor sinner like me.

5 And when life's journey is over,
And I the dear Saviour shall see,
I'll praise him forever and ever,
For saving a sinner like me.

DO RE MI FA SO LA SI

60 Happy Tidings.

LIZZIE EDWARDS.   JNO. R. SWENEY.

1. Tidings, happy tidings, Hark! hark! the sound! Hear the joyful e - cho
2. Tidings, happy tidings, Hark! hark! they say, Do not slight the warning,
3. Tidings, happy tidings, Hark! hark! a - gain! Rushing o'er the mountain,

Thro' the world resound; Christ the Lord proclaims them, Hear and heed the call,
Come, oh, come to-day; Christ, our lov- ing Sav- iour, Still repeats the call,
Sweeping o'er the plain; Onward goes the message, 'Tis the Saviour's call,

REFRAIN.

Come, ye starving ones that perish, Room, room for all. Whoso- ev - er ask- eth,
Come, ye weary, hea- vy- laden, Room, room for all.
Come, for ev'rything is ready, Room, room for all.

Jesus will receive; Whosoever thirsteth, Jesus will relieve; See the living

waters, Flowing full and free; Oh, the blessed whosoever! That means me.

DO RE MI FA SO LA SI

Jesus of Nazareth Passeth By.

Miss Etta Campbell.   Mark x. 47.   Theo. E. Perkins. By per.

1. What means this eager, anxious throng, Which moves with busy haste along—
2. Who is this Jesus? Why should he The ci - ty move so might-i-ly?
3. Je-sus! 'tis he who once be-low Man's pathway trod, 'mid pain and woe;
4. Again he comes! From place to place His ho-ly footprints we can trace.

These wondrous gath'rings day by day? What means this strange commotion pray?
A pass-ing stranger, has he skill To move the mul-ti-tude at will?
And burdened ones, where'er he came, Brought out their sick, and deaf, and lame.
He paus-eth at our threshhold—nay, He en-ters—con-descends to stay.

In accents hushed the throng reply: "Je-sus of Naz-areth passeth by,"
A-gain the stirring notes re-ply: "Je-sus of Naz-areth passeth by,"
The blind rejoiced to hear the cry: "Je-sus of Naz-areth passeth by,"
Shall we not glad-ly raise the cry—"Je-sus of Naz-areth passeth by,"

In accents hushed the throng reply: "Je-sus of Naz-areth pass-eth by."
A-gain the stirring notes re-ply: "Je-sus of Naz-areth pass-eth by."
The blind rejoiced to hear the cry: "Je-sus of Naz-areth pass-eth by."
Shall we not gladly raise the cry—"Je-sus of Naz-areth pass-eth by."

5 Ho! all ye heavy-laden, come!
Here's pardon, comfort, rest, and home.
Ye wanderers from a Father's face,
Return, accept his proffered grace.
Ye tempted ones, there's refuge nigh:
"Jesus of Nazareth passeth by."

6 But if you still this call refuse,
And all his wondrous love abuse,
Soon will he sadly from you turn,
Your bitter prayer for pardon spurn.
"Too late! too late!" will be the cry—
"Jesus of Nazareth *has passed by.*"

62 The Saviour is My All in All.

P. B.   "Wherefore he is able to save them to the uttermost."—Heb. vii. 25.   P. Bilhorn.

1. The Saviour is my all in all, He is my constant theme!
2. His Spir-it gives sweet peace within, And bids all care de - part!
3. And whatso - ev - er I may ask, To glo - ri - fy his name,
4. Oh, praise the Lord, my soul, rejoice, Give thanks unto thy God!

rit.

By sim - ply trusting in his word He keeps me pure and clean.
He fills my soul with righteousness, And pu - ri - fies the heart.
The Fa - ther free - ly gives to me, Since Christ the Saviour came.
Who took thee in thy sin - fulness, And cleansed thee by his blood!

CHORUS.

Glo - ry! oh, glo - ry! Je - sus hath redeemed me;

rit.

Glo - ry! oh, glo - ry! He washed my sins a - way, a - way!

What's the News.

Words arranged by W. H. G.

Rev. W. H. Geistweit.

1. Whene'er we meet we always say, "What's the news? Pray what's the
2. God has pardoned all my sin, That's the news! I feel the
3. And now if a - ny one should say, What's the news? O tell him
4. Wea - ry pilgrim, hear the call, Bless - ed news! Christ Je - sus

or - der of the day, What's the news?" His work's re - viv - ing
wit - ness deep with - in, That's the news! And since he took my
you've be - gun to pray, That's the news! That you have joined the
came to save us all, That's the news! He died to set poor

all a - round, And sin - ners hear the gos - pel sound, Re-
sins a - way, And taught me how to watch and pray, I'm
conqu'ring band, And now with joy at God's command, You're
sin - ners free, That we from death might ran - somed be, And

joic - ing in a Saviour found, That's the news! That's the news!
hap - py now from day to day, That's the news! That's the news!
marching to the bet - ter land, That's the news! That's the news!
with him reign e - ter - nal - ly, That's the news! That's the news!

God be with You.

"The grace of our Lord Jesus Christ be with you."
Rom. xvi. 20.

J. E. RANKIN, D. D.   W. G. TOMER.

1. God be with you till we meet again, By his counsels guide, uphold you,
2. God be with you till we meet again, 'Neath his wings securely hide you;
3. God be with you till we meet again, When life's perils thick confound you;
4. God be with you till we meet again, Keep love's banner floating o'er you;

With his sheep securely fold you, God be with you till we meet again.
Dai - ly manna still provide you, God be with you till we meet again.
Put his arms unfailing round you, God be with you till we meet again.
Smite death's threat'ning wave before you, God be with you till we meet again.

CHORUS.

Till we meet, till we meet, Till we meet at Je - sus' feet;
Till we meet, till we meet, till we meet,   till we meet;

Till we meet, till we meet, God be with you till we meet again.
Till we meet, till we meet, till we meet,

From "Gospel Bells," by per.

Oh, Bless Me, Saviour.

Peter Stryker, D. D.　　　　　　　　　　　　　　Wm. H. Geistweit.

1. Oh, bless me, Saviour, bless me! I come to thee for grace; Life's
2. Oh, bless me, Saviour, bless me! I come to thee for rest; My
3. Oh, bless me, Saviour, bless me! I come to thee for joy; Not

bat - tle fiercely ra- ges, Help me my foes to chase. Like Gideon's band of
wea- ry head I'd pil- low Up- on thy lov-ing breast. By day, by night I'll
on - ly peace, but gladness, and bliss without alloy. I may not have this

he - roes, My onward way shall tend; And faint, yet still pursu - ing, I'll
trust thee, Awake, or when I sleep; Assured that thou wilt ev- er Thy
bless- ing In all its ful- ness here; 'Tis kept for me in heav - en, Where

CHORUS.

triumph in the end. Bless me now, Bless me now, Pre- cious Re-
vig - il o'er me keep.
nev- er falls a tear. *Faster.*

rit. *Repeat pp*

deem- er, Come and bless me now.

4 Bless me, I know thou'lt bless me
　In all my pilgrim way,
And bring me where the shadows
　Will never gloom the day.
My joy is now to journey
　Close to thy loving side,
And hope with thee in glory
　Forever to abide.

　　Temple Songs–E

The Lily of the Valley.

English Melody, arranged

1. I have found a friend in Jesus, he's ev'rything to me, He's the fairest of ten
2. He all my griefs has taken, and all my sorrows borne; In temptation he's my
3. He will never, never leave me, nor yet forsake me here, While I live by faith and

thousand to my soul; The Li-ly of the Valley, in him alone I see All I
strong and mighty tower; I have all for him forsaken, and all my idols torn From my
do his blessed will; A wall of fire about me, I've nothing now to fear; With his

D. S.—Lily of the Valley, the bright and Morning Star, He's the

Fine.

need to cleanse and make me fully whole; In sorrow he's my comfort, in
heart, and now he keeps me by his power; Tho' all the world forsake me, and
manna he my hungry soul shall fill; Then sweeping up to glo-ry to

fair-est of ten thousand to my soul. Cho.—In sorrow, etc. (*after each verse.*)

D. S.

trouble he's my stay, He tells me ev'ry care on him to roll.   He's the
Satan tempts me sore, Thro' Jesus I shall safely reach the goal.   He's the
see his blessed face, Where rivers of delight shall ever roll.   He's the

Rise Up and Hasten.

67

"Rise up, my love, my fair one, and come away."

J. DENHAM SMITH. Arr. Song of Sol. ii. 10. Arr. by JAMES McGRANAHAN.

1. Rise up, and hast-en! my soul, haste along! And speed on thy
2. Why should we linger when heaven lies before! While earth's fast re -
3. Loved ones in Je-sus they've passed on before, Now rest-ing in
4. No condem-nation! how blessed is the word, And no sep-a-

jour-ney with hope and with song; Home, home is near-ing, 'tis
ced-ing, and soon will be no more; Pleasures and treasures which
glo-ry, they weary are no more; Toils all are end-ed, and
ra-tion! for-ev-er with the Lord; He will be with us who

coming in-to view, A little more of toiling and then to earth adieu.
once here we knew, No more can they charm us with such a goal in view.
nothing now but joy, And prais-es ascending, their ev-er glad employ.
loved us long before, And Je-sus, our Je-sus, is ours for ev-ermore.

CHORUS.

1st.
Come then, come, and raise the joyful song! Ye children of the wilderness, our
Home, home, home, oh, why should we delay? The

2d.
time cannot be long. morn of heaven is dawning, we're near the break of day.

68 What a Gath'ring that will be.

J. H. K.   "Gather my saints together unto me."—Ps. l. 5.   J. H. KURZENKNABE.

1. At the sounding of the trumpet, when the saints are gather'd home, We will
2. When the angel of the Lord proclaims that time shall be no more, We shall
3. At the great and final judgement, when the hidden comes to light, When the
4. When the golden harps are sounding, and the angel bands proclaim, In tri-

greet each other by the crystal sea, With the friends and all the lov'd ones there a-
gather, and the saved and ransom'd see,   Then to meet again to-gether, on the
Lord in all his glo-ry we shall see;   At the bidding of our Saviour, "Come, ye
umphant strains the glorious jubilee;   Then to meet and join to sing the song of

crystal sea;

wait-ing us to come, What a gath'ring of the faith-ful that will be!
bright ce-lestial shore, What a gath'ring of the faith-ful that will be!
bless-ed, to my right, What a gath'ring of the faith-ful that will be!
Mos-es and the Lamb, What a gath'ring of the faith-ful that will be!

CHORUS.

What a gath - - - 'ring,   gath - - - 'ring,   At the
What a gath'ring of the loved ones when we'll meet with one an-oth-er,

sounding of the glorious ju-bi-lee!   What a gath - - 'ring,
ju-bi-lee! What a gath'ring when the friends and all the

DO ME MI FA SO LA SI

gath - - - 'ring, What a gath'ring of the faith-ful that will be!
dear ones meet each oth - er,

Oh! 'tis Glory in My Soul.

FLORA L. BEST.   JNO. R. SWENEY.

1. To thy cross, dear Christ I'm clinging, All my re - fuge and my plea;
2. Long my heart hath heard thee calling, But I thrust a- side thy grace;
3. Love e - ter - nal, light e - ter- nal, Close me safe - ly, sweetly in;

Matchless is thy lov- ing kindness, Else it had not stoop'd to me.
Yet, O boundless con - de-scension, Love is shin - ing from thy face.
Sav- iour, let thy balm of healing, Ev - er keep me free from sin.

CHORUS.

Oh, 'tis glo - ry! oh, 'tis glo - ry! Oh, 'tis glo - ry in my soul,

For I've touch'd the hem of his garment, And his pow'r doth make me whole.

DO RE MI FA SO LA SI

Calvary.

" The place which is called Calvary, there they crucified him."

Rev. W. M'K. Darwood.   Luke xxiii. 33.   Jno. R. Sweney.

1. On Calv'ry's brow   my Saviour died,   'Twas there my
2. 'Mid rending rocks   and dark'ning skies,   My Saviour
3. O Je-sus, Lord,   how can it be,   That thou shouldst

Lord   was cruci - fied: 'Twas on the cross   he bled for
bows   his head and dies;   The opening vail   reveals the
give   thy life for me,   To bear the cross   and ag-o-

me,   And purchased there   my par-don free.
way   To heaven's joys   and endless day.
ny,—   In that dread hour   on Cal - va - ry!—

mf CHORUS. *p*   *m*   *p*   *pp*

O Cal - va - ry! dark Calva - ry! Where Jesus shed his blood for me, for me;

mf   *ff*   *mf*   *rit. p*

O Cal - va - ry! blest Cal - va - ry! 'Twas there my Saviour died for me.

Over Jordan.

Mrs. M. B. C. Slade.   Deut. xi. 31; viii 7, 8.   J. R. Murray.

1. With his dear and loving care Will the Saviour lead us on, To the
2. Through the rocky wilderness Will the Saviour lead us on, To the
3. With his strong and mighty hand Will the Saviour lead us on, To that
4. In the Promised Land to be Will the Saviour lead us on, Till fair

hills and valleys fair, O - ver Jor - dan? Yes, we'll rest our weary feet
land we shall possess, O - ver Jor - dan? Yes, by night the wondrous ray,
good and pleasant land, O - ver Jor - dan? Yes, where vine and olive grow,
Canaan's shore we see, O - ver Jor - dan? Yes, to dwell with thee at last,

By the crystal waters sweet, When the peaceful shore we greet, O - ver
Cloudy pil - lar by the day, They shall guide us on our way, O - ver
And the brooks and fountains flow,Thirst nor hunger shall we know.O-ver
Guide and lead us, as thou hast, Till the parted wave be passed, O - ver

CHORUS.   1st.

Jor - dan.   O - ver Jor - dan! o - ver Jordan! Yes, we'll rest our weary feet

2d.

By the crystal waters sweet, When the peaceful shore we'll greet, Over Jordan.

From "Pure Diamonds," by per., Brainard & Sons.

72 Wilt thou be made whole?

W. J. K.   Wm. J. Kirkpatrick.

1. Hear the foot-steps of Je- sus, He is now passing by, Bearing balm for the
2. 'Tis the voice of that Saviour, Whose mer-ci - ful call Freely off- ers sal-
3. Are you halting and struggling, O'erpowered by your sin, While the waters are
4. Bless- ed Saviour, as- sist us   To   rest on thy word ; Let the soul-healing

wounded, Healing all who ap - ply; As he spake to the suff'rer Who
va - tion   To   one and to   all; He is now beck'ning to him Each
troubled Can you not en - ter   in ? Lo, the Saviour stands waiting To
pow - er On us now be out-poured: Wash away ev- 'ry sin-spot, Take

lay at the pool, He is say-ing this moment, "Wilt thou be made whole?"
sin tainted   soul, And lov- ing - ly asking, "Wilt thou be made whole?"
strengthen your soul, He is earnest- ly pleading, "Wilt thou be made whole?"
per-fect con - trol, Say to each trusting spirit, "Thy faith makes thee whole."

REFRAIN.

Wilt thou be made whole? Wilt thou be made whole? O come, wea-ry

suff'rer, O come, sin-sick soul; See, the life-stream is flow-ing, See, the cleansing waves roll, Step in-to the cur-rent and thou shalt be whole.

Glorious Fountain.

COWPER.   T. C. O'KANE.

1. { There is a fountain filled with blood, filled with blood, filled with blood, There
And sinners plung'd beneath that flood, beneath that flood, beneath that flood, And

2. { The dy-ing thief rejoiced to see, rejoiced to see, rejoiced to see, The
And there may I, tho' vile as he, tho' vile as he, tho' vile as he, And

is a fount-ain filled with bood, Drawn from Imman-uel's veins, }
sinners plunged beneath that flood, Lose all their guilt-y stains. }
dy-ing thief rejoiced to see That fount-ain in his day, }
there may I, tho' vile as he, Wash all my sins a-way. }

CHORUS.

Oh, glo-ri-ous fount-ain! Here will I stay, And in thee

ev-er Wash my sins a-way.

3 Thou dying Lamb, ‖: thy precious blood :‖
Shall never lose its power,
Till all the ransomed ‖:Church of God ‖
Are saved, to sin no more.

4 E'er since by faith ‖: I saw the stream ‖
Thy flowing wounds supply,
Redeeming love ‖: has been my theme,:‖
And shall be till I die.

DO RE MI FA SO LA SI

74 **Nothing but the Blood of Jesus.**

R. LOWRY.   R. LOWRY.

1. What can wash a-way my stain? Nothing but the blood of Je - sus;
2. For my cleansing this I see— Nothing but the blood of Je - sus;
3. Noth-ing can for sin a-tone— Nothing but the blood of Je - sus;
4. This is all my hope and peace— Nothing but the blood of Je - sus;

What can make me whole a-gain? Nothing but the blood of Je - sus.
For my par-don this my plea— Nothing but the blood of Je - sus.
Naught of good that I have done— Nothing but the blood of Je - sus.
This is all my righteous-ness— Nothing but the blood of Je - sus.

REFRAIN.

Oh, pre-cious is the flow That makes me white as snow;

No oth-er fount I know, Nothing but the blood of Je - sus.

5 Now by this I'll overcome—
  Nothing but the blood of Jesus;
  Now by this I'll reach my home —
  Nothing but the blood of Jesus.

6 Glory! glory! thus I sing—
  Nothing but the blood of Jesus;
  All my praise for this I bring—
  Nothing but the blood of Jesus.

Robert Morris, LL. D.   "Jesus walked in Galilee."—John vii. 1.   H. R. Palmer.

1. Each coo-ing dove   and sighing bough,   That makes the
2. Each flowery glen   and mossy dell,   Where hap-py
3. And when I read   the thrilling lore   Of him who

eve   so blest to me,   Has something far   divin - er
birds   in song a - gree,   Thro' sunny morn   the praises
walked   up-on the sea,   I long, oh, how   I long once

now,   It bears me back   to Gal - i - lee.
tell   Of sights and sounds   in Gal - i - lee.
more   To follow him   in Gal - i - lee.

CHORUS.

O Gal - i - lee! sweet Gal - i - lee! Where Jesus loved so much to be; O

Gal - i - lee! blue Gal - i - lee! Come, sing thy song again to me!

By permission.

DO RE MI FA SO LA SI

76

Until Ye Find.

Rev. E. H. Stokes, D. D.

Luke xv.

Jno. R. Sweney.

Andante con espress.

1. A - las! a - las! a wayward sheep Had wandered from the fold, Far
2. He sought with many-a footstep sore, From early morn till night; Thro'
3. How long, O Lord, must I still go? How long search for the sheep? They've

o'er the mountains rough and steep, Where howling tempests rolled; The
rock - y wastes, where torrents roar,—All pathways but the right; Then
wandered far a - way, I know,—Discouraged, lo, I weep: How

Shepherd, with a burdened mind, Went forth the missing one to find, The
cried, with sad and burdened mind, The missing I have failed to find, The
long thus go, with burdened mind? "Go;" Jesus saith, "until ye find;" The

miss - ing one, far, far a - way, The miss - ing one to find.
miss - ing one, far, far a - way, A - las! I've failed to find.
miss - ing one must not be lost,—Go, seek un - til ye find!

CHORUS.

Go, seek un - til ye find; Go, seek un - til ye find; The
Chorus to last verse :—
Joy! joy! the lost is found; Joy! joy! the lost is found; The

miss - ing one must not be lost,—Go, seek un - til ye find.
miss - ing one, no long - er lost, The miss-ing one is found.

4 I've sought my friends for many-a day,
Have prayed for many-a year;
Yet, still they wander far away,
O'er mountains dark and drear;
How long thus seek with burdened mind?
"Seek," Jesus saith, "until ye find;"
The missing one must not be lost,—
"Go, seek until ye find!"

5 Lord, at thy word I go again,
Believing I shall find:
I listened, and a low refrain
Came to me on the wind;
Led by the sadly joyful sound
I rushed, and, lo, the lost was found!
Joy! joy! O blessed joy divine!
The lost one I have found.

Trustingly.

H. Bonar.

Wm. J. Kirkpatrick.

1. Trust - ing - ly, trust - ing - ly, Je - sus, to thee Come I; Lord,
2. Peace - ful - ly, peace - ful - ly Walk I with thee; Je - sus, my
3. Hap - pi - ly, hap - pi - ly Pass I a - long, Ea - ger to

lov - ing - ly, Come thou to me! Then shall I lov - ing - ly,
Lord, thou art All, all to me; Peace thou hast left to us,
work for thee, Ear-nest and strong; Life is for ser - vice true,

rit.

Then shall I joy - ful - ly walk here with thee, Walk here with thee.
Thy peace hast giv - en us; So let it be, So let it be.
Life is for bat - tle, too, Life is for song, Life is for song.

78 Praise and Magnify our King.

LIZZIE EDWARDS.　　　　　　　　　　　　　　　　　　JNO. R. SWENEY.

1. Great is the Lord, who rul-eth o-ver all! Wake, wake and sing,
2. Great is the Lord, who spake and it was done; Wake, wake and sing,
3. Great is the Lord, oh, come with ho-ly mirth; Wake, wake and sing,
4. Great is the Lord, and ho-ly is his name! Wake, wake and sing.

wake, wake and sing; Down at his feet in ad-o-ra-tion fall,
wake, wake and sing; Hon-or and strength, dominion he has won,
wake, wake and sing, Come and re-joice, ye na-tions of the earth,
wake, wake and sing; An-gels and men, his wondrous works proclaim,

CHORUS.

Praise and mag-ni-fy our King. O ye redeemed above, Strike, strike your

harps of love, Hail the Blessed One, Hail the Mighty One, Sweetly his

wonders tell, Lond-ly his glo-ry swell, Praise and magni-fy our King.

Take me as I am.

Anon. Rev. J. H. Stockton.

1. Je-sus, my Lord, to thee   I cry, Unless thou help me I must die;
2. Helpless I   am, and full   of guilt, But yet for me thy blood was spilt,
3. I thirst, I   long to know thy love, Thy full sal-vation I would prove;
4. If thou hast work for me   to   do, Inspire my will, my heart renew,
5. And when at last the work is done, The bat-tle o'er, the vic-t'ry won,

Fine.

Oh, bring thy free sal - va - tion nigh, And take me as   I   am!
And thou can'st make me what thou wilt, But take me as   I   am!
But since to thee   I   can-not move, Oh, take me as   I   am!
And work both in and by me, too, But take me as   I   am!
Still, still my cry shall be   a - lone, Oh, take me as   I   am!

D. S.— bring thy free sal - va- tion nigh, And take me as   I   am!

REFRAIN.

D. S.

Take me as   I   am,   Take me as   I   am;   Oh,

Take me, take me as I am, Take me, take me as I am;

Copyright, 1878, by John J. Hood.

DO RE MI FA SO LA SI

Charlotte Elliott. **JUST AS I AM.** Tune and Chorus above.

1 JUST as I am, without one plea,
But that thy blood was shed for me,
And that thou bid'st me come to thee,
    O Lamb of God, I come!

2 Just as I am, and waiting not
To rid my soul of one dark blot,
To thee whose blood can cleanse each
    O Lamb of God, I come! [spot,

3 Just as I am, though tossed about
With many a conflict, many a doubt,
Fightings within, and fears without,
    O Lamb of God, I come!

4 Just as I am—poor, wretched, blind;
Sight, riches, healing of the mind,
Yea, all I need, in thee to find,
    O Lamb of God, I come!

5 Just as I am—thou wilt receive,
Wilt welcome, pardon, cleanse, relieve;
Because thy promise I believe,
    O Lamb of God, I come!

6 Just as I am—thy love unknown
Hath broken every barrier down,
Now, to be thine, yea, thine alone,
    O Lamb of God, I come!

Hiding in Thee.

"My strong rock, for a house of defense." Ps. xxxi. 2.

Rev. WILLIAM O. CUSHING.   IRA. D. SANKEY. By per.

1. O safe to the Rock that is high-er than I, My soul in its
2. In the calm of the noontide, in sorrow's lone hour, In times when temp-
3. How oft in the conflict, when pressed by the foe, I have fled to my

conflicts and sor-rows would fly; So sin-ful, so wea-ry, thine,
ta-tion casts o'er me its power; In the tempests of life, on its
Re-fuge and breathed out my woe; How oft-en,when tri-als like

thine would I be; Thou blest "Rock of A-ges," I'm hid-ing in thee.
wide, heaving sea, Thou blest "Rock of A-ges," I'm hid-ing in thee.
sea-billows roll, Have I hid-den in thee, O thou Rock of my soul.

REFRAIN.

Hiding in thee, Hiding in thee, Thou blest "Rock of Ages," I'm hiding in thee.

Sweet Peace, the Gift of God's Love. 81

P. H. ROBLIN.

P. BILHORN.

1. There comes to my heart one sweet strain, A glad and a joyous re - frain,
   sweet strain, refrain,
2. By Christ on the cross peace was made, My debt by his death was all paid,
   was made, all paid,
3. When Jesus as Lord I had crowned, My heart with this peace did abound,
   had crowned, abound,
4. In Jesus for peace I a- bide, abide, And as I keep close to his side, his side.

I sing it a-gain and a - gain, Sweet peace, the gift of God's love.
No oth - er founda- tion is laid For peace, the gift of God's love.
In him the rich blessing I found, Sweet peace, the gift of God's love.
There's nothing but peace doth betide, Sweet peace, the gift of God's love.

CHORUS.

Peace, peace, sweet peace! Won- der- ful gift from a - bove! a- bove! Oh,

won- derful, wonder- ful peace! Sweet peace, the gift of God's love!

Temple Songs–F

The Great Physician.

REV WM. H. HUNTER. D. D.   Arranged by J. H STOCKTON.

1. The Great Phy-si-cian now is here, The sym-pa-thiz-ing Je-sus:)
He speaks the drooping heart to cheer, Oh, hear the voice of Je-sus.)

CHORUS.

Sweet-est note in ser-aph song, Sweetest name on mor-tal tongue,

Sweet-est car-ol ev-er sung, Je-sus, bles-sed Je-sus.

2 Your many sins are all forgiven,
Oh, hear the voice of Jesus;
Go on your way in peace to heaven,
And wear a crown with Jesus.

3 All glory to the dying Lamb!
I now believe in Jesus;
I love the blessed Saviour's name,
I love the name of Jesus.

4 The children too, both great and small,
Who love the name of Jesus,
May now accept his gracious call
To work and live for Jesus.

5 Come, brethren, help me sing his praise,
Oh, praise the name of Jesus;
Come, sisters, all your voices raise,
Oh, bless the name of Jesus.

6 His name dispels my guilt and fear,
No other name but Jesus;
Oh, how my soul delights to hear
The precious name of Jesus.

7 And when to that bright world above,
We rise to see our Jesus,
We'll sing around the throne of love
His name, the name of Jesus.

MY SOUL, BE ON THY GUARD.—Laban, key D.

1 My soul, be on thy guard,
Ten thousand foes arise;
The hosts of sin are pressing hard
To draw thee from the skies.

2 Oh, watch, and fight, and pray;
The battle ne'er give o'er;
Renew it boldly every day,
And help divine implore.

3 Ne'er think the vict'ry won,
Nor lay thine armor down;
The work of faith will not be done
Till thou obtain the crown.

4 Then persevere till death
Shall bring thee to thy God;
He'll take thee, at thy parting breath,
To his divine abode.

E. E. Hewitt.   Wm. J. Kirkpatrick.

Matt. xi. 28. 1. Come unto me, the Saviour said, Come unto me, the Saviour said;
John xiv 6. 2. I am the way, the truth, the life, I am the way, the truth, the life;
Mark x. 21. 3. Take up the cross, and follow me, Take up the cross, and follow me;
Matt. vii. 7. 4. Ask and it shall be given you, Ask and it shall be given you;

Come unto me, the Saviour said, And I will give you rest.
I am the way, the truth, the life, I am the light of the world. John viii. 12.
Take up the cross, and fol - low me, And thou shalt have treasure in heaven.
Ask and it shall be giv - en you, Seek and ye shall find.

CHORUS.

Oh, the blessed words of Je - sus! Precious words! hallowed words!

Oh, the blessed words of Je - sus! Words of life to me.

John iii. 36.
5 He that believeth | on the Son, :||
Hath everlasting | life.

Is. xlv. 22.
6 Look unto me, and | be ye saved, :||
All the ends of the | earth.

Matt. v. 8.
7 Blessed are the | pure in heart, :||
For | they shall see | God.

Matt v. 12.
8 Re- | joice and be ex- | ceeding glad, :||
For | great is your reward in | heaven.

John xiv. 18.
9 I | will not leave you | comfortless, ||
I will come unto | you.

John vii. 37.
10 If | any man thirst let him | come unto
And drink of the water of | life. [me,:||

Mark. x. 14.
11 Suffer little children to | come unto
me, :|| [heaven.
For of | such is the kingdom of |

John xiv. 2.
12 I | go to prepare a | place for you, ||
In my Fathers' house.

84.

Take hold, hold on.

Advice of an aged colored man to young converts, "Take hold, hold on, hold fast
and never let go!"

PRISCILLA J. OWENS.   WM. J. KIRKPATRICK.

1. O, turn not back in the Christian race Till the prize is won we know;
2. O, turn not back on life's battle-field, Tho' the world's a mighty foe,
3. Truth's anchor firm-ly, sure-ly clasp, As the billows near thee flow,
4. Though danger threatens or death alarms, In each ris-ing flood of woe,

Reach up to Christ for abounding grace, Take hold and nev-er let go!
God's arms are round thee as a shield, Take hold and nev-er let go!
God's hand will close o'er thy feeble grasp, Take hold and nev-er let go!
Still cling to God's ev-er-last-ing arms, Take hold and nev-er let go!

CHORUS.

Take hold, hold on, Hold fast and nev-er let go! No
Take hold, hold on, hold on!

matter how the wind in the tempest may blow, Take hold and never let go!

Jesus Saves.

PRISCILLA J. OWENS. **WM. J. KIRKPATRICK.**

1. We have heard a joy - ful sound, Je - sus saves, Je - sus saves;
2. Waft it on the roll - ing tide, Je - sus saves, Je - sus saves,
3. Sing a - bove the bat - tle's strife, Je - sus saves, Je - sus saves;
4. Give the winds a might - y voice, Je - sus saves, Je - sus saves,

Spread the glad- ness all a - round, Je - sus saves, Je - sus saves;
Tell to sin - ners, far and wide, Je - sus saves, Je - sus saves;
By his death and end- less life, Je - sus saves, Je - sus saves;
Let the na - tions now re - joice, Je - sus saves, Je - sus saves;

Bear the news to ev - 'ry land, Climb the steeps and cross the waves,
Sing, ye is - lands of the sea, E - cho back, ye o - cean caves,
Sing it soft - ly thro' the gloom, When the heart for mer - cy craves,
Shout sal - va - tion full and free, High- est hills and deep- est caves,

Onward, 'tis our Lord's command, Je - sus saves, Je - sus saves.
Earth shall keep her ju - bi - lee, Je - sus saves, Je - sus saves.
Sing in tri - umph o'er the tomb, Je - sus saves, Je - sus saves.
This our song of vic - to - ry, Je - sus saves, Je - sus saves.

Copyright, 1882, by JOHN J. HOOD.

DO RE MI FA SO LA SI

When my Saviour I shall See.

"I shall be satisfied when I awake with thy likeness"

Arr. by P. H. Roblin.

P. Bilhorn.

1. When my Sav-iour I shall see, In his glo-rious likeness be,
2. When I'm whol-ly freed from sin, Spot-less, clean, and pure within,
3. When my feet shall press the shore Trod by an-gels' feet be-fore,
4. Oh, till then be this my care, More his im-age blest to wear;

Clad in robes by love supplied, Then shall I be sat-is-fied.
Meet to stand by Je-sus' side, Then shall I be sat-is-fied.
Near to liv-ing streams that glide, Then shall I be sat-is-fied.
More to con-quer self and pride, So shall I be sat-is-fied.

CHORUS.

Sat-is-fied with love divine, Sat-is-fied since Christ is mine,

Ev-'ry need in him supplied, Then shall I be sat-is-fied.

Seeking to Save.

"For the Son of Man is come to seek and to save that which was lost."
Luke xix. 10.

P. P. B.

P. P. BLISS.

1. Ten-der-ly the Shepherd, O'er the mountains cold, Goes to bring his
2. Patient-ly the own - er Seeks with earnest care, In the dust and
3. Lov-ing-ly the Fa-ther Sends the news a-round : "He once dead now

CHORUS.

lost one Back to the fold. Seek-ing to save, Seek-ing to save,
darkness Her treasure rare.
liv-eth—Once lost is found."

Lost one, 'tis Je - sus Seek-ing to save: Seek-ing to save,

Seek-ing to save, Lost one, 'tis Je-sus Seek-ing to save.

88

At the Cross I'll Abide.

I. B.   "And many women were there."—Matt. xxvii. 55.   I. BALTZELL.

1. O Jesus, Saviour, I long to rest Near the cross where thou hast died;
2. My dy-ing Je-sus, my Saviour God, Who hast borne my guilt and sin,
3. O Je-sus, Saviour, now make me thine, Never let me stray from thee;
4. The cleansing pow'r of thy blood apply, All my guilt and sin re-move;

For there is hope for the ach-ing breast, At the cross I will a-bide.
Now wash me, cleanse me with thine own blood, Ever keep me pure and clean.
Oh, wash me, cleanse me, for thou art mine, And thy love is full and free.
Oh, help me, while at thy cross I lie, Fill my soul with perfect love.

CHORUS.

At the cross   I'll a-bide,   At the cross   I'll a-bide,
At the cross   I'll a-bide,   At the cross   I'll abide;

At the cross I'll abide, There his blood is applied; At the cross I am sanctified.

By permission.

The Numberless Host.

F. A. B.

F. A. Blackmer.

1. When we enter the portals of glo - ry, And the great host of ransom'd we see,
2. When we see all the saved of the ages, Who from cruel death partings are free,
3. When we stand by the beautiful river,'Neath the shade of the life-giving tree,
4. When we look on the form that redeem'd us, And his glory and majesty see,

As the numberless sand of the sea-shore, What a wonderful sight that will be!
Greeting there with a heavenly greeting, What a wonderful sight that will be!
Gazing out o'er the fair land of promise, What a wonderful sight that will be!
While as King of the saints he is reigning, What a wonderful sight that will be!

CHORUS.

Numberless as the sand of the sea - shore, Numberless as the sand of the shore;

Numberless as the sand,

as the sand of the shore;

Oh, what a sight 'twill be, When the ransom'd host we see,

As numberless as the sand of the sea-shore.

Every Day.

Rev. E. H. Stokes, D. D.   Wm. J. Kirkpatrick.

1. Though there may be shades of sadness Ev'ry day, ev-'ry day, There are
2. You may have your little crosses Ev'ry day, ev-'ry day; You may
3. Seek to lighten some one's sorrow Ev'ry day, ev-'ry day; This will
4. Life may have its ho-ly pleasures Ev'ry day, ev-'ry day; And the

golden gleams of gladness Ev'ry day, ev-'ry day; There is joy a-mid the
meet with little loss-es Ev-'ry day, ev'ry day; Never mind! each cross will
bring a sweeter morrow Ev-'ry day, ev-'ry day; Faint, it may be, yet pur-
heart find richest treasures Ev'ry day, ev-'ry day; See, the skies are growing

rit.

sighing, Laughter ringing thro' the crying, Love to love with smiles replying, Ev'ry
lighten, Grief in all your losses brighten, If your hold on God shall tighten Ev'ry
suing, All the christly graces wooing, And some little good be doing, Ev'ry
clearer, Dear ones all becoming dearer, And our home is so much nearer, Ev'ry

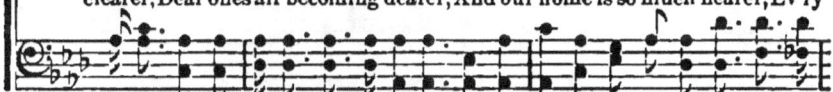

CHORUS.

day, ev-'ry day. Ev-'ry day, . . . while on our way   Thro' the

while on our way

world, . . . let come what may,   Going forth with strong desire, To the

let come what may,

DO RE MI FA SO LA SI

greatest good aspire, From the high, still rising higher, Ev'ry day, ev'ry day.

Jesus, I come to Thee.

FANNY J. CROSBY.   WM. J KIRKPATRICK.

1. Je - sus, I come to thee, Long-ing for rest; Fold thou thy
2. Je - sus, I come to thee, Hear thou my cry; Save, or I
3. Now let the rolling waves Bend to thy will, Say to the
4. Swift-ly the part-ing clouds Fade from my sight; Yon - der thy

CHORUS.

wea - ry child Safe to thy breast. Rocked on a storm-y sea,
per - ish, Lord, Save or I die.
troubled deep, Peace, peace be still.
bow ap- pears, Love - ly and bright.

Oh, be not far from me. Lord, let me cling to thee, On - ly to thee.

Why Do You Wait?

G. F. R. "Arise, he calleth thee."—Mark x. 49. Geo. F. Root.

1. Why do you wait, dear brother, Oh, why do you tarry so long? Your
2. What do you hope, dear brother, To gain by a further de - lay? There's
3. Do you not feel, dear brother, His Spirit now striving within? Oh,
4. Why do you wait, dear brother, The harvest is passing a - way, Your

Saviour is waiting to give you A place in his sanc- ti- fied throng.
no one to save you but Je - sus, There's no other way but his way.
why not accept his sal - va - tion, And throw off thy burden of sin?
Saviour is longing to bless you, There's danger and death in delay?

CHORUS.

Why not? why not? Why not come to him now?

Why not? why not? Why not come to him now?

DO RE MI FA SO LA F

Seeking for Me.

93

E. E. HASTY.

1. Jesus, my Saviour, to Bethlehem came, Born in a manger to sorrow and shame;
2. Jesus, my Saviour, on Calvary's tree, Paid the great debt, and my soul he set free;
3. Jesus, my Saviour, the same as of old, While I did wander afar from the fold,
4. Jesus, my Saviour, shall come from on high, Sweet is the promise as weary years fly;

Oh, it was wonder-ful, blest be his name, Seeking for me, for me.
Oh, it was wonder-ful, how could it be? Dy-ing for me, for me.
Gent-ly and long he hath pled with my soul, Calling for me, for me.
Oh, I shall see him descending the sky, Coming for me, for me.

for me, ... for me; ....

Seeking for me, seeking for me, Seeking for me, seeking for me
Dy-ing for me, dying for me, Dy-ing for me, dying for me;
Call-ing for me, calling for me, Call-ing for me, calling for me;
Com-ing for me, coming for me, Com-ing for me, coming for me;

Oh, it was wonderful, blest be his name, Seeking for me, for me.
Oh, it was wonderful, how could it be? Dy-ing for me, for me.
Gent-ly and long he hath pled with my soul, Calling for me, for me.
Oh, I shall see him descending the sky, Coming for me, for me.

From "Good Will," by per.

94 Is there Any One Here.

MARTHA J. LANKTON. WM. J. KIRKPATRICK.

1. Is there an-y one here that is will-ing to-day On Je-sus the
2. Is there an-y one here that is try-ing to-day The fet-ters of
3. Is there an-y one here that is wea-ry to-day, Or la-den, or
4. Hear the Saviour's sweet voice while he calls thee again, O come, and be-

Lord to be-lieve? Is there an-y poor soul that is longing to-day The
e-vil to break? An-y read-y to fol-low the Saviour to-day, And
sor-row oppressed? Is there any sad heart that is praying to-day To
lieve and o-bey, He is waiting to bless, he will comfort thee now! He

CHORUS.

gift of his grace to re-ceive.   Come   un-to me,
take up the cross for his sake.
find in the Sav-iour a rest.
nev-er turned an-y a-way.   Come un-to me,   come un-to me,

Come   un-to me;   Je-sus is call-ing,
Come un-to me,   come un-to me;

ad lib.

call-ing now to thee, Come, oh, come un-to   me. un-to me.

DO RE MI FA SO LA SI

Keep Step Ever.

C. R. BLACKALL.　　　　　　　　　　　　　　　　　　　　H. R. PALMER.

1. Would you gain the best in life? Win the prize 'mid all the strife? Hold your
2. Life is more than i - dle play; It will quickly pass away; Use a-
3. Look beyond the present hour; Nev-er yield to Satan's power; Tho' a-

place thro' troubles rife? With the right keep step! Know the world is watching you;
right each golden day; With the good keep step! There are earnest pressing needs,
bove the clouds may lower, With the truth keep step! Onward press! nor, on the way,

Be sincere in all you do; With the good, the pure, and true, Ever firm keep step!
Filled alone by purest deeds; Happy he the call who heeds—With the true keep step!
Loiter once or waste the day: God and truth and right all say, Strong in faith, keep step!

CHORUS.

Keep step, keep step ev-er, Keep step, keep step ev-er,

Keep step, keep step, Keep step, keep step ev-er.

By permission.

Into His Image.

E. R. Latta.   Wm. J. Kirkpatrick.

1. In - to his im - age to grow   Ev - er my purpose shall be,
2. In - to his im - age to grow,   Ev - er resembling him more,
3. In - to his im - age to grow,   Out of the likeness of sin;

Who from the courts of the sky   Came as a ran-som for me:
As in his footsteps I tread,   Seeking the heav-en-ly shore:
Trusting, thro' mer-its of his,   Glo-ry e-ter-nal to win:

Like as a servant he came,   Bear-ing my guilt and my shame;
Yea, I will ear-nest-ly plead, Plead to be like him in-deed,
Per-fect in faith and in love, Meet for his kingdom a-bove:

Bear-ing my bur-den of woe;   Lov-ing and suf-fer-ing so!
Who, up-on Cal-va-ry's tree,   Purchased sal-va-tion for me.
This the dear wish of my soul, Now to be per-fect-ly whole.

REFRAIN.

Lov - - ing and suf-fering so,   Lov - - ing and suf-fering so!
Loving, yes, lov-ing   Loving, yes, lov-ing
Pur - chased salvation for me, Pur - chased salvation for me,
Purchased salvation,   Purchased salvation,
Per - - fect in faith and in love, Meet . . . for his kingdom above;
Perfect, yea, perfect   Meet for his kingdom,

Bearing my burden of woe, . . . Loving and suf-fering so.
Bear - - - ing my bur-den of woe, suf-fering so.
Who, upon Calva-ry's tree, . . . Purchased salvation for me. . . .
Who, ... up-on Cal-va-ry's tree, sal-vation for me.
This the dear wish of my soul, . . Now to be perfect-ly whole. . .
This . . . . the dear wish of my soul, perfect-ly whole.

Whosoever.

JAMES NICHOLSON.   JNO. R. SWENEY.

1. I praise the Lord that one like me For mercy may to Je-sus flee,
2. I was to sin a wretched slave, But Jesus died my soul to save;
3. I look by faith and see this word, Stamp'd with the blood of Christ my Lord,
4. I now believe he saves my soul, His precious blood hath made me whole;

He says that whoso - ev - er will May seek and find salva - tion still.
He says that whoso - ev - er will May seek and find salva - tion still.
He says that whoso - ev - er will May seek and find salva - tion still.
He says that whoso - ev - er will May seek and find salva - tion still.

CHORUS.

My Saviour's promise faileth never; He counts ME in the Whoso-ev-er.

By permission.

Christ Arose!

R. L. By per.   "He is not here, but is risen."—Luke xxiv. 6.   Rev. Robert Lowry.

Slow.

1. Low in the grave he lay—Je-sus, my Sav-iour! Waiting the coming day—
2. Vainly they watch his bed—Jesus, my Sav-iour! Vainly they seal the dead—
3. Death cannot keep his prey—Jesus, my Sav-iour! He tore the bars away—

CHORUS. *faster.*

Je - sus, my Lord! Up from the grave he a-rose, he a-rose, With a

might-y triumph o'er his foes; he a-rose! He a-rose a Victor from the

dark do-main, And he lives for-ev-er with his saints to reign: He a-

rit.

rose! he a-rose! Hal-le-lu-jah! Christ a-rose!

He a-rose!   he a-rose!

DO RE MI FA SOL LA SI

Walk in the Light.

Asa Hull.   Isaiah ii. 5.   Geo. C. Hugg.

1. Walk in the light the Lord hath given,   To guide thy steps a - right; His
2. Walk in the light of gospel truth, That shines from God's own word ; A
3. Walk in the light! tho' shadows dark, Like spectres cross thy way; Dark-
4. Walk in the light! and thou shalt know The love of God to thee; The

CHORUS.

Holy Spirit sent from heaven, Can cheer the darkest night.   Walk   in the
light to guide in early youth The faithful of the Lord.
ness will flee before the light Of God's e - ter - nal day.
fellowship, so sweet below, In heaven will sweeter be.   Walk in the light, in the

light, ... walk . . . in the light, ...
beauti - ful light of God,   Walk in the light, in the beauti - ful light of God,

Walk . . in the light, ... Walk in the light, the light of God.
Walk in the light, in the beautiful light of God ;

The Healing Touch.

"When she heard of Jesus, came in the press behind, and touched his garment."
Mark v. 27.

Mrs. E. C. Ellsworth.   Wm. J. Kirkpatrick.

1. An ea - ger, restless crowd drew near, And round the Saviour pressed;
2. The mul - ti - tude, with curious eyes, Just gazed up - on his face;
3. Oh, near to Christ the man - y came, In that most fa - vored hour!
4. Of all who throng his courts to-day Who shall re - ceive his word?

But one, with warm and lov - ing faith, His heal - ing power confessed.
But she glanced up with hope and love, To feel his sav - ing grace.
But one stretched out the hand of faith, And touched his healing power.
Who shall reach forth with faith sincere To touch the heal- ing Lord?

CHORUS.

She had touched the hem of his garment, Trusting with all her soul;
last v. Come and touch the hem of his garment, Trusting with all your soul;

For ev - 'ry touch of the lov- ing Je-sus Can make the wounded whole.

Come to the Arms of Jesus.

Rev. M. L. Hofford.   " To-day if ye will hear his voice."—Ps. xcv. 7.   T. M. Miller.

1. Come to the arms of Je - sus, O come without de - lay,
2. Come to the arms of Je - sus, Re- cline on his dear breast,
3. Come to the arms of Je - sus, And when the shades of night

Come while the voice of mer - cy Is call - ing you to - day.
Come, for the heav- y la - den Can find no sweet- er rest.
Have wrapped the world in darkness, In him you shall have light.

DUET.

The gold - en gates are o - pen, To your ce - les - tial home,
His lov - ing voice is call - ing, En- treat - ing you to come,
Come while the Spir - it bids you, In sweet - est tones to come;

CHORUS.

The shin - ing ones are wait - ing To hear you say, "I come."
His gen - tle arms are wait - ing To give you welcome home,
The gold - en gates are o - pen To your ce - les - tial home,

The shin- ing ones are wait - ing To hear you say, "I come."
His gen - tle arms are wait- ing To give you wel- come home.
The gold- en gates are o - pen To your ce - les - tial home.

By permission of S. T. Gordon & Son.

102   It Reaches Me.

MARY D. JAMES.   JNO. R. SWENEY.

1. Oh, this ut - ter-most sal - va - tion! 'Tis a fountain full and free,
2. How a- maz - ing God's compassion, That so vile a worm should prove
3. Je - sus, Saviour, I a -dore thee! Now thy love I will proclaim,

Pure, ex-haustless, ev - er flow-ing, Wondrous grace! it reaches me!
This stupend - ous bliss of Heav-en, This un-measured wealth of love!
I will tell the blessed sto - ry, I will mag - ni - fy thy name!

CHORUS.

It reaches me! it reaches me! Wondrous grace! it reaches me!

Pure, ex-haustless, ev - er flowing, Wondrous grace! it reaches me!

DO RE MI FA SO LA SI

The Land Just Across the River. 103

T. C. O'KANE.   By per.

1. On Jor - dan's storm- y banks I stand, And cast a wish - ful eye
2. O'er all these wide- ex - tend - ed plains Shines one e - ter - nal day;
3. When shall I reach that hap - py place, And be for - ev - er blest?
4. Filled with delight, my rap - tured soul Would here no long - er stay;

To Canaan's fair and hap - py land, Where my pos - ses - sions lie.
There God the Son for - ev - er reigns, And scat- ters night a - way.
When shall I see my Father's face, And in his bo - som rest?
Tho' Jordan's waves a - round me roll, Fear - less I'd launch a - way.

CHORUS.

We will rest in the fair and happy land,   Just across on the evergreen shore, . .
by and by,   evergreen shore.

Sing the song of Moses and the Lamb, by and by, And dwell with Jesus evermore.

Bringing in the Sheaves.

Words from "Songs of Glory."

Geo. A. Minor.

1. Sowing in the morning, sowing seeds of kindness, Sowing in the noon-tide,
2. Sowing in the sunshine, sowing in the shadows, Fearing neither clouds nor
3. Go, then, ev-er weeping, sowing for the Master, Tho' the loss sustained our

and the dew-y eves; Waiting for the har-vest, and the time of reap-ing,
winter's chilling breeze; By and by the har-vest, and the la-bor end-ed,
spir-it oft-en grieves; When our weeping's over, he will bid us welcome,

CHORUS.

We shall come re-joic-ing, bringing in the sheaves. Bringing in the sheaves,

bringing in the sheaves,   bringing in the sheaves,
            We shall come rejoicing,   Bringing in the sheaves,

bringing in the sheaves, We shall come rejoic-ing, bringing in the sheaves,

DO RE MI FA SO LA SI

Saviour, Blessed Saviour. 105

GODFREY THWING.   HAYDN.

1. Saviour, blessed Sav - iour, List- en whilst we sing, Hearts and voices
2. Near-er, ev - er near - er, Christ, we draw to thee, Deep in ad - o -
3. Great and ev-er great - er Are thy mercies here; True and ev- er-

rais - ing Prais- es to our King, All we have we of - fer:
ra - tion Bending low the knee: Thou for our re - demp-tion
last - ing Are thy glo- ries there, Where no pain, or sor - row,

All we hope to be, Bod - y, soul, and spir - it,
Cam'st on earth to die; Thou, that we might fol - low,
Toil, or care is known, Where the an - gel - le - gions

CHORUS.

All we yield to thee. Saviour, bless - ed Sav - iour,
Hast gone up on high.
Cir - cle round thy throne.

Listen whilst we sing, Hearts and voices rais - ing Praises to our King.

Clinging to the Cross.

FRANK GOULD.   JNO. R. SWENEY.

1. O, my heart is full of joy, for my sins are wash'd away, Clinging to the
2. I have laid my burden down, I have cast it on the Lord, Clinging to the
3. I have found the hallow'd peace which the world can never give, Clinging to the
4. I am happy in his love, I am safe beneath his care, Clinging to the

cross of Je - sus; I am trusting more and more in his mercy ev'ry day,
cross of Je - sus; I can now believe and claim ev'ry promise in his word,
cross of Jesus; I have promised by his grace while he spares me I will live
cross of Jesus; Tho' temptations I shall meet they shall never harm me there,

CHORUS.

Clinging to the cross of Je - sus. Cling-ing to the cross, where his

blood was shed for me, Clinging to the cross, where the flowing stream I see,

Clinging to the cross, where I come on bended knee; Blessed, blessed cross of Jesus!

DO RE MI FA SO LA SI

Tell Me the Story of Jesus.

FANNY J. CROSBY.   JNO. R. SWENEY.

1. Tell me the sto - ry of Je - sus, Write on my heart ev-'ry word,
2. Fast-ing, a- lone in the des - ert, Tell of the days that he passed,
3. Tell of the cross where they nailed him, Writhing in anguish and pain,

Chorus.—Tell me the sto - ry of Je - sus, Write on my heart ev-'ry word,

Fine.

Tell me the sto - ry most pre - cious, Sweetest that ev - er was heard;
How for our sins he was tempt - ed, Yet was triumphant at last;
Tell of the grave where they laid him, Tell how he liv - eth a - gain;

Tell me the sto - ry most pre - cious, Sweetest that ev - er was heard.

Tell how the an- gels, in cho - rus, Sang as they welcomed his birth,—
Tell of the years of his la - bor, Tell of the sorrows he bore,
Love in that sto - ry, so ten - der, Clear-er than ev - er I see;

D.C.

Glo - ry to God in the high - est! Peace and good tidings to earth.
He was despised and af- flict - ed, Homeless, re - ject- ed and poor.
Stay, let me weep while you whisper, Love paid the ransom for me.

DO RE MI FA SO LA SI

Rise, and Let Me In.

W. A. O.

Andante.

"Behold, I stand at the door and knock."—Rev. iii: 20.   N. E. Townsend.

pp   cres.

1. Lo! a stranger standing there, Knocking, knocking at the door,
2. 'Tis thy Sav-iour wait-ing there, Knocking, knocking at the door,
3. Hear the Sav-iour call to - day, Knocking, knocking at the door,
4. Shall thy Saviour plead in vain, Knocking, knocking at the door?

pp   cres.

Love - ly stranger! wond'rous fair! Knocking, knocking at the door;
Call - ing thee, O wan - der - er, Knocking, knocking at the door;
Do not grieve thy Lord a - way, Knocking, knocking at the door.
Will you slight his call a - gain, Knocking, knocking at the door?

, cres.   cres.

Wait-ing, oh, so pa - tient-ly! Call - ing, oh, so ten - der - ly!
Pleading, oh, so earn - est - ly! Striv-ing, oh, so faith - ful - ly!
Wea -ry, worn, and troub-led breast, Tempt-ed one, with care op - prest,
Will you heed his earn - est plea? "Heav - y la - den, come to me."

Op - en now thy heart to me; Oh, rise, and let me in.
'Tis thy Sav - iour calls to thee; Oh, rise, and let me in.
I will give thy spir - it rest; Oh, rise, and let me in.
Rest and peace I give to thee; Oh, rise, and let me in.

By permission of E. T. Goshus & Son.

Entire Consecration.

FRANCES RIDLEY HAVERGAL. Chorus by W. J. K. WM. J. KIRKPATRICK.

1. Take my life, and let it be Con - se - crat - ed, Lord, to thee;
2. Take my feet, and let them be Swift and beau - ti - ful for thee;
3. Take my lips, and let them be Filled with mes - sag - es for thee;
4. Take my moments and my days, Let them flow in endless praise;

Take my hands and let them move At the impulse of thy love.
Take my voice and let me sing Al- ways, on - ly, for my King.
Take my sil - ver and my gold,— Not a mite would I withhold.
Take my in - tel- lect, and use Ev - 'ry power as thou shalt choose.

CHORUS.

{ Wash me in the Saviour's precious blood, the precious blood,
Cleanse me in its pu - ri - fy - ing flood, the healing flood, } Lord, I give to

thee, my life and all, to be, Thine, henceforth, e- ter - nal - ly.

5 Take my will, and make it thine;
It shall be no longer mine;
Take my heart.—it is thine own,—
It shall be thy royal throne.

6 Take my love,—my Lord, I pour
At thy feet its treasure-store!
Take myself, and I will be
Ever, only, all for thee!

110 When the King comes in.

J. E. Landor. Rev. E. S. Lorenz.

1. Call'd to the feast by the King are we, Sit- ting, perhaps, where his
2. Crowns on the head where the thorns have been, Glo - ri -fied he who once
3. Like lightning's flash will that instant show Things hidden long from both
4. Joy - ful his eye shall on each one rest Who is in white wedding

peo - ple be: How will it fare, then, with thee and me,
died for men; Splendid the vis - ion be - fore us then,
friend and foe, Just what we are ev - 'ry one will know,
gar - ments dressed—Ah! well for us if we stand the test,

REFRAIN.

When the King comes in? When the King comes in, brother, When the King comes

in! How will it fare with thee and me When the King comes in?

From "Songs of Grace," by per.

DO RE MI FA SO LA SI

Redeemed.

FANNY J. CROSBY.

WM. J. KIRKPATRICK.

111

1. Redeemed, how I love to proclaim it, Redeemed by the blood of the Lamb;
2. Redeemed, and so happy in Je - sus, No language my rapture can tell,
3. I think of my blessed Redeemer, I think of him all the day long,
4. I know I shall see in his beauty The King in whose law I de - light,
5. I know there's a crown that is waiting In yonder bright mansion for me,

Redeemed thro' his infi-nite mer - cy, His child and forev - er I am.
I know that the light of his presence With me doth continual-ly dwell.
I sing, for I cannot be si - lent, His love is the theme of my song.
Who loving- ly guardeth my footsteps, And giveth me songs in the night,
And soon, with the spirits made perfect, At home with the Lord I shall be.

REFRAIN.

Re - deemed, re - deemed, redeemed by the blood of the Lamb,
redeemed, redeemed,

Re - deemed, re - deemed, His child and forev - er I am.
redeemed, redeemed,

Copyright, 1882, by WM. J. KIRKPATRICK.

DO RE MI FA SO LA SI

112 He Came to Save Me.

HENRIETTA E. BLAIR.　　　　　　　　　　　　　　　WM. J. KIRKPATRICK.

1. When Je - sus laid his crown a - side, He came to save me;
2. In my poor heart he deigns to dwell, He came to save me;
3. With gen - tle hand he leads me still, He came to save me;
4. To him my faith with rap- ture clings, He came to save me;

When on the cross he bled and died, He came to save me.
O, praise his name, I know it well, He came to save me.
And trust-ing him I fear no ill, He came to save me.
To him my heart looks up and sings, He came to save me.

CHORUS.

I'm so glad, I'm so glad, I'm so glad that Jesus came, And grace is free,

I'm so glad, I'm so glad, I'm so glad that Jesus came, He came to save me.

Hark, Hark, My Soul.

Rev. F. W. Faber.   Arr. from C. C. Converse by Ira D Sankey.

Moderato.

1. Hark, hark, my soul, angelic songs are swelling O'er earth's green fields and
2. Far, far away, like bells at evening pealing, The voice of Je - sus
3. Onward we go, for still we hear them singing, "Come, weary souls, for

ocean's wave-beat shore; How sweet the truth those blessed strains are telling
sounds o'er land and sea, And la - den souls by thousands meekly stealing,
Jesus bids you come;" And thro' the dark, its echoes sweetly ring-ing,

CHORUS.

Of that new life when sin shall be no more. Angels, sing on! your faithful watches
Kind Shepherd, turn their weary steps to thee.
The music of the Gospel leads us home.

keep-ing; Sing us sweet fragments of the songs above, Till morning's joy shall

end the night of weeping, And life's long shadows break in cloudless love.

Temple Songs-H

Behold, the Fields are White.

Rev. M. Lowrie Hofford.   Jno. R. Sweney.

1. Look up! behold, the fields are white, The harvest time is near; The summons of the
2. Look up! behold, the fields are white, The laborers are few, The gath'ring of the
3. Look up! behold, the fields are white, The Master soon will come, And carry with re-

Mas- ter falls Up- on the reaper's ear: Go forth in - to the gold- en grain And
har- vest must By grace depend on you· Go forth throughout the busy world, The
joicing heart His gathered trophies home; And can you stand with empty arms, While

bind the precious sheaves, And garner for the Lord of Hosts The harvest which he gives.
world of want and sin, And gather for the Lord of Hosts Its dying millions in.
glad - ly he receives From others in the harvest field A load of precious sheaves.

CHORUS.

Look up!   look up!   behold, the fields are white,   The harvest time is
Look up!   look up!   be- hold! be- hold! the fields are white, The har - vest

near,   The har- vest time is   near: Look up!   look up!   be-
time is near,   the har - - vest   time is near;   Look up!   look up!

Behold, the Fields are White.—CONCLUDED. 115

hold, the fields are white, Look up! behold, the fields are white, The harvest time is near.

I will Trust in Thee.

In answer to question of leader at Ocean Grove "Who will trust?"
many rose, saying, "I will."

W. H. G.   W. H. GEISTWEIT.

1. Blessed Saviour, my sal - vation, I will trust in thee; I am saved from
2. Sanctify and cleanse me, Saviour, I will trust in thee; Let me know thy
3. Here I stand and thee confessing, I will trust in thee; Pour up-on my

CHORUS.

condemn - a - tion, I will trust in thee. Yes, I will, yes, I will,
lov - ing fa - vor, I will trust in thee.
heart thy blessing, I will trust in thee.

I will trust in thee; Thou, my Strength and Song forever, I will trust in thee.

DO RE MI FA SO LA SI

Meet in the Morning.

H. E. Blair.　　　　　　　　　　　　　　　　　Wm. J. Kirkpatrick.

1. We are marching onward to the heavenly land, To meet each other in the morning;
2. We are trav'ling onward from a world of care, To meet each other in the morning;
3. We are trav'ling onward, and the way grows bright, We'll meet each other in, etc.,

We are pressing forward to the golden strand, Where joy will crown us in the morning.
Oh, the time is coming, we shall soon be there, And joy will crown us in the morning.
Where our friends are waiting, at the gate of life, And joy will crown us in the, etc.,

CHORUS.

In the morning, in the morning, We will gather with the faithful in the morning;

Where the night of sorrow shall be rolled away, And joy will crown us in the morning.

4 Where the hills are blooming on the
　　other shore,
We'll meet each other in the morning!
Where the heart's deep longing will be
　felt no more,
And joy will crown us in the morning.

5 In the boundless rapture of a Saviours'
　　love
We'll meet each other in the morning;
Then we'll sing his glory in the realms
　above,
And joy will crown us in the morning.

Jesus the Rock.

Mrs. C. N. Pickop.   Wm. J. Kirkpatrick.

1. Jesus, the rock on which my feet   May safely and securely stand,
2. Jesus, the rock on which I build, The sure foundation, true and tried ;
3. Jesus the rock stands firm, secure, Unyielding, tho' the storms may beat ;
4. Jesus the rock, blest Saviour, thou Art all I want, and all I   crave ;

While all around me sinks and falls, And scatters like the crumbling sand.
Bright star of hope for   ruined man, Is Jesus Christ, the cruci - fied !
In this sure trust I   anchor fast, And find a blessed safe re - treat.
I trust in thee, for   well I know   Thy mighty power alone can save.

CHORUS.

Jesus the rock, I   cling to thee, Tho' waves and billows 'round me roll ;

Jesus my hope, my on - ly plea, The stay and comfort of my soul.

He Comes.

FANNY J. CROSBY.

JNO. R. SWENEY.

1. Awake! awake! O Zion, lift thy voice! In the Lord thy God forevermore re-
2. He comes! he comes! the faithful watchmen cry; To the hills look up and wave the [banner

Fine.

joice; A - rise! arise! behold, the night is past, And the day has come at last;
high! He comes! he comes! with trumpet tongue proclaim Our redemption thro' his [name.

Let thy harp resound as once it rang In the grand old time of thy strength and prime,
Oh, the songs, glad songs that now we raise In the dear retreat where we love to meet,

When thy soul within thee sweetly sang, Trusting in the promise of the Lord.
In the house of prayer and joyous praise, Singing with the happy ones above.

Hark! O Zi- on, hear the joy-bells ring! Lo, he cometh, thy Redeemer-King!
Crown, oh, crown him, our Deliv'rer-King! Hail, oh, hail him, while our gifts we bring!

He shall reign all glorious, He shall reign victorious O'er the world from shore to shore.
All shall hear his story, All shall see his glory; He shall reign from shore to shore.

D.C.

We Know Not Why.

SALLIE MARTIN.   JNO. R. SWENEY.

1. We know not why our path at times Is one of thorns and sad- ness,
2. We know not why our warning words Seem lost or dis - re- gard- ed,
3. We know not why our brightest hopes Like autumn leaves must perish,

While oth - ers walk a - mid the smile Of con- stant joy and gladness.
While oth - ers reap, from day to day, The fruit of toil reward- ed.
Or why the hand of death removes The friends that most we cherish.

Fine.

D.S.—Though heaven and earth should pass away, His truth shall stand forever!

CHORUS.   *D.S.*

But this we know, the Lord is just, His promise fail - eth nev - er;

4 We know not what our joy will be
  When, in the realms of glory,
  We at the Saviour's feet shall tell
  Redemption's wondrous story.

5 O then, content, we'll walk by faith,
  Our hearts his love possessing;
  We'll praise him for his mercies past,
  And trust for every blessing.

Do Something To=Day.

LANTA WILSON SMITH.   WM. J. KIRKPATRICK.

1. You're longing to work for the Master, Yet waiting for something to do;
2. Go rescue that wandering brother Who sinks 'neath his burden of woe,
3. Go sing happy songs of rejoicing With those who no sorrows have known;
4. O never, my brother, stand waiting, Be willing to do what you can;

You fancy the future is holding Some wonderful mission for you;
A single kind action may save him, If love and compassion you show;
Go weep with the heart-broken mourner, Go comfort the sad and the lone;
The humblest service is need-ed, To fill out the Father's great plan;

But while you are waiting the moments Are rapid-ly passing a-way;
Don't shrink from the vilest about you, If you can but lead them from sin;
From pitfalls and snares of the tempter Go rescue the thoughtless and wild:
Be earning your stars of rejoic-ing While earth-life is passing a-way;

O brother, awake from your dreaming, Do something for Jesus to-day.
For this is the grandest of missions,— Lost souls for the Master to win.
Go win from pale lips a 'God bless you,' Go brighten the life of a child.
Win some one to meet you in glo-ry,— Do something for Jesus to-day.

CHORUS.

Do something,   do something,   Do something for Jesus to - day;

Do something,   do something,

O brother, the moments are passing, Do something for Jesus to - day.

Jesus will Meet You There.

W. L. K.   W. LEWIS KANE.

1. { Come to Calv'ry's mount to - day, Je - sus will meet you there; }
   { Look and live without de - lay, Je - sus will meet you there. }

CHORUS.

Come to Jesus, Don't stay away, my friend; Come to Jesus, He calls to-day.

2 Rest beneath the hallowed cross,
   Jesus will meet you there;
   Saving mercy gained for loss,
   Jesus will meet you there.

3 Come and join his faithful band,
   Jesus will meet you there;
   Take his mighty, helping hand,
   Jesus will meet you there.

4 At the blessed mercy seat,
   Jesus will meet you there;
   Come with this assurance sweet,
   Jesus will meet you there.

5 You'll find rest in heaven at last,
   · Jesus will meet you there;
   And be happy with the blest,
   Jesus will meet you there.

On the Road, Going Home.

P. J. OWENS.   WM. J. KIRKPATRICK.

1. We are go - ing home to glo - ry, Bright a- bode, bright a - bode!
2. We will call to those faint hearted, " Be of cheer, be of cheer;"
3. We will call to souls in blindness, "Come this way, come this way;"

And will gladly work for Je - sus, On the road, on the road.
And to pilgrims who have started, "Never fear, nev - er fear."
We will tell Christ's loving kindness, Ev - 'ry day, ev - 'ry day.

CHORUS.

For his mercy sought and found us, And his blood to service bound us;

So we'll work for all around us, On the road, go - ing home.

4 May our souls with love be yearning
   As we sing, as we sing;
 May our lamps be brightly burning,
   For the King, for the King.

5 We are waiting till his message
   Bids us come, bids us come;
 But we'll live and work for Jesus,
   Going home, going home.

"And I will cause the shower to come down in his season."
Ezekiel xxxiv. 26.

JENNIE GARNETT.   JNO. R. SWENEY.

1. Here in thy name we are gathered, Come and revive us, O Lord;
2. O that the showers of bless-ing Now on our souls may descend,
3. There shall be showers of blessing,—Promise that never can fail;
4. Showers of blessing,—we need them, Showers of blessing from thee;

"There shall be showers of bless-ing" Thou hast declared in thy word.
While at the footstool of mer - cy Pleading thy promise we bend!
Thou wilt regard our pe - ti - tion; Sure-ly our faith will pre-vail.
Showers of blessing,—oh, grant them; Thine all the glory shall be.

CHORUS.

Oh, gracious-ly hear   us,   Gracious-ly hear us, we   pray:
gracious-ly hear   us,

Pour from thy windows upon   us Showers of blessing to - day.
Lord, pour up-on us

Triumph By and By.

Dr. C. R. BLACKALL.　　　　　　　　　　　H. R. PALMER.　By per.

1. The prize is set before us, To win his words implore us, The
2. We'll follow where he leadeth, We'll pasture where he feedeth, We'll
3. Our home is bright above us, No tri - als dark to move us, But

eye of God is o'er us, From on high, from on high : His loving tones are calling,
yield to him who pleadeth From on high, Then naught from him shall sever,
Jesus, dear, to love us, There on high, there on high : We'll give him best endeavor,

While sin is dark, appalling ; 'Tis Jesus gently calling, He is nigh, he is nigh.
Our hope shall brighten ever, And faith shall fail us never, He is nigh, he is nigh.
And praise his name forever ; His precious ones can never, Never die, never die.

CHORUS.

By and by we shall meet him, By and by we shall greet him, And with

1st.　　　　　2d.

Jesus reign in glory, By and by, by and by : Jesus reign in glory, By and by.

E. A. H.   Rev. E. A. HOFFMAN.   By per.

1. Have you been to   Jesus for the cleansing power? Are you washed in the
2. Are you walking   dai - ly by the Saviour's side? Are you washed in the
3. When the Bridegroom cometh will your robes be white, Pure and white in the
4. Lay a- side the garments that are stained with sin, And be washed in the

blood of the Lamb? Are you ful- ly trusting in his grace this hour? Are you
blood of the Lamb? Do you rest each moment in the Cru - ci- fied? Are you
blood of the Lamb? Will your soul be ready for the mansions bright, And be
blood of the Lamb? There's a fountain flowing for the soul unclean, O be

CHORUS.

washed in the blood   of the Lamb? Are you washed   in the
                                              Are you washed

blood,   In the soul-cleansing blood of the Lamb?   Are your
  in the blood,   of the Lamb?

garments spotless? are they white as snow? Are you washed in the blood of the Lamb?

Waiting at the Pool.

Rev. A. J. Hough.   Wm. G. Fischer   By per.

1. Thousands stand to-day in sorrow, Waiting at the pool; Saying they will
2. Souls your filthy garments wearing, Waiting at the pool; Hearts your heavy
3. Thousands once were standing near you, Waiting at the pool; Come their voices
4. Mother leaves the son, the daughter, Waiting at the pool; Calls to them a-
5. Step in boldly—death may smite you, Waiting at the pool: Jesus may no

wash to-morrow, Waiting at the pool; Oth-ers step in left and right,
bur-den bearing, Waiting at the pool; Can it be you nev-er heard,
back to cheer you, Waiting at the pool; Back from Canaan's happy shore,
cross the water, Waiting at the pool; You can nev-er more embrace
more invite you, Waiting at the pool; Faith is near you, take her hand,

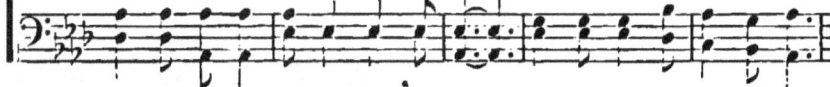

Wash their stained garments white, Leav-ing you in sorrow's night,
Jesus long a-go hath stirred-The wa-ters with his might-y word,
Sor-rows past and la-bor o'er, Where they stand in tears no more,
Moth-er or be-hold her face, If you keep the lep-er's place.
Seek with her the bet-ter land, And no long-er doubting stand

Waiting at the pool, Waiting, wait-ing, waiting at the pool.

In the Shadow of the Cross.

FRANK GOULD.   JNO R. SWENEY.

1. At the cross I found my Saviour, And my boasting there shall be,
2. At the cross I cried for mer-cy, Jesus heard my humble prayer;
3. At the cross he gave me com-fort, In my darkest hour he came,
4. When among the just made perfect My Redeem-er I shall see,

For my man-y sins are pardoned Through the blood he shed for me.
I was wretched, weak, and helpless, Till on him I cast my care.
And my faith looked up and saw him, Hal-le-lu-jah to his name!
I will tell, through endless a-ges, What his love has done for me!

CHORUS.

O my soul in him rejoic-es, And the world I count but dross,—

I am walk-ing, dai-ly walking In the shadow of the cross.

Glory to God, Hallelujah!

FANNY J. CROSBY.   WM. J. KIRKPATRICK.

1. We are nev-er, nev-er wea-ry of the grand old song; Glo-ry to
2. We are lost a-mid the rapture of redeem-ing love; Glo-ry to
3. We are go-ing to a palace that is built of gold; Glo-ry to
4. There we'll shout redeeming mercy in a glad, new song; Glo-ry to

God, hal-le-lu-jah! We can sing it loud as ever, with our faith more strong:
God, hal-le-lu-jah! We are rising on its pinions to the hills a-bove:
God, hal-le-lujah! Where the King in all his splendor we shall soon behold:
God, hallelujah! There we'll sing the praise of Jesus with the blood-wash'd throng:

Fine. CHORUS.

Glo-ry to God, hal-le-lu-jah! O, the children of the Lord have a

right to shout and sing, For the way is grow-ing bright, and our

D.S.

souls are on the wing; We are going by and by to the palace of a King!

Make Room for Jesus. 129

"There was no room for them at the inn."
Luke ii. 7.

Rev. Alex. Clark, D D   Wm. G Fischer.

1. Make room for Je - sus! room! sad heart, Beguiled and sick of sin;
2. Make room for Je - sus! room! make room! His hand is at the door;
3. Make room for Je - sus! soul of mine, He waits re-sponse to-day;
4. Make room for Je - sus! by and by, 'Midst saint and ser - a - phim,

Bid ev - 'ry a - lien guest de-part, And rise and let him in.
He comes to ban - ish guilt and gloom, And bless thee more and more.
His smile is peace, his grace, di-vine, Oh, turn him not a - way.
He'll welcome to his throne on high The soul that welcomed him.

CHORUS.

Make room, sad heart, make room, make room! Bid a-lien guests de - part,

Oh, let the Mas - ter in, sad heart; A-rise, make room, make room!

By permission.   *Temple Songs*—I

Meet me There.

Henrietta E. Blair. Wm. J. Kirkpatrick.

1. On the happy, golden shore, Where the faithful part no more, When the
2. Here our fondest hopes are vain, Dearest links are rent in twain; But in
3. Where the harps of angels ring, And the blest for-ev - er sing, In the

storms of life are o'er, Meet me there; Where the night dissolves away Into
heav'n no throb of pain, Meet me there; By the river sparkling bright, In the
palace of the King, Meet me there; Where in sweet communion blend Heart with

Fine.

pure and perfect day, I am going home to stay, Meet me there.
ci - ty of delight, Where our faith is lost in sight, Meet me there.
heart, and friend with friend, In a world that ne'er shall end, Meet me there.

D.S.—happy golden shore, Where the faithful part no more, Meet me there.

CHORUS.

Meet me there, Meet me there, Where the tree of life is

D.S.

blooming, Meet me there; When the storms of life are o'er, On the

Meet me there;

A little Talk with Jesus.

WM. G. FISCHER.

1. A lit-tle talk with Je-sus, How it smooths the rugged road!
2. Ah, this is what I'm wanting, His love-ly face to see;
3. I can-not live without him, Nor would I if I could;
4. So I'll wait a lit-tle long-er, Till his appoint-ed time,

How it seems to help me on-ward, When I faint beneath my load;
And I'm not a-fraid to say it, I know he's wanting me.
He is my dai-ly por-tion, My med-i-cine and food.
And a-long the upward path-way My pil-grim feet shall climb.

When my heart is crushed with sorrow, And my eyes with tears are dim,
He gave his life a ran-som, To make me all his own,
He is al-to-geth-er love-ly; None can with him com-pare;
There, in my Father's dwell-ing, Where man-y mansions be,

There is naught can yield me comfort Like a lit-tle talk with him.
And he'll ne'er forget his prom-ise To me, his purchased one.
Chief-est among ten thousand, And fair-est of the fair.
I shall sweetly talk with Je-sus, And he will talk with me.

132

FANNY J. CROSBY.

On let us go.

WM. J. KIRKPATRICK.

1. On let us go where the val-ley of Ed - en fair Blooms on the
2. On let us go where the beauti- ful realms above Ring with the
3. On let us go where the weary and toil-oppressed Soon shall for-
4. On let us go where the loving and loved shall meet, Meet on the

bank of the riv - er; On where the fields, in the beautiful robe they wear,
time-honored sto - ry: Saved thro' the might of a blessed Redeemer's love,
get ev -'ry sor - row; On where the soul to a happy and golden rest
bank of the riv - er; There shall they sing at the blssed Redeemer's feet

CHORUS.

Wave in the sunlight for - ev - er.
His be the praise and the glo - ry.
Wakes in e - ter - ni- ty's mor- row.
Songs that shall echo for - ev - er.

On let us go,

On, march on, to the beauti - ful land we go,

On let us go,

On, march on, to the beau - ti - ful land we go,

On let us

On, march on, where the

go,

riv - ers of pleasure flow,

On where the hap - py ones are call - ing.

A Shelter in the Time of Storm.   133

Words arranged.   "My God is the Rock of my refuge."—Ps. xciv : 22.   IRA D. SANKEY.

1. The Lord's our Rock, in him we hide, A shelter in the time of storm;
2. A shade by day defence by night, A snelter in the time of storm;
3. The raging storms may round us beat, A shelter in the time of storm;
4. O Rock divine, O Refuge dear, A shelter in the time of storm;

Secure whatev - er ill be - tide, A shelter in the time of storm.
No fears alarm, no foes af-fright, A shelter in the time of storm.
We'll nev - er leave our safe retreat, A shelter in the time of storm.
Be thou our helper ev - er near, A shelter in the time of storm.

CHORUS.

Oh, Jesus is a Rock in a weary land, A weary land, a weary land; Oh,

Jesus is a Rock in a weary land, A shelter in the time of storm.

134 **Only a Beam of Sunshine.**

FANNY J. CROSBY.   JNO. R. SWENEY.

1. On - ly a beam of sun - shine, But oh, it was warm and bright; The
2. On - ly a beam of sun - shine That in - to a dwell - ing crept, Where,
3. On - ly a word for Je - sus! Oh, speak it in his dear name; To

heart of a wea - ry trav - 'ler Was cheered by its wel - come sight.
o - ver a fad - ing rose - bud, A moth - er her vig - il kept.
per - ish - ing souls a - round you The message of love pro - claim.

On - ly a beam of sun - shine That fell from the arch a - bove, And
On - ly a beam of sun - shine That smiled thro' her falling tears, And
Go, like the faith - ful sun - beam, Your mission of joy ful - fil; Re-

ten - der - ly, soft - ly whispered A mes - sage of peace and love.
showed her the bow of prom - ise, For - got - ten perhaps for years.
mem - ber the Saviour's prom - ise, That he will be with you still.

CHORUS.

On - ly a word for Je - sus, On - ly a whispered prayer

DO RE MI FA SO LA SI

Only a Beam of Sunshine.—CONCLUDED. 135

O - ver some grief-worn spir - it May rest like a sun-beam fair.

The New Name.

J. E. H.   J. E. HALL.

1. We shall have a new name in that land, In that land, that sunny, sunny land,
2. We'll receive it in a pure white stone, And no one will know the name therein;
3. Don't you wonder what that name will be, Sweeter far than aught on earth can be,

Cho.—We shall have a new name in that land, In that land, that sunny, sunny land,

Fine.

When we meet the bright angelic band, In that sunny land.   A new name, a
Only unto him who hath 'tis known, When we're free from sin.   A white stone, a
We will be quite satisfied when we Shall that new name know.   I won- der, I

When we meet the bright angelic band, In that sunny land.

D. C.

new name We'll receive up there; A new name, a new name, All who enter there.
white stone We'll receive up there; A white stone, a white stone, All who enter there.
won- der What that name will be, I wonder, I wonder, What he'll give to me.

Copyright, 1878, by JOHN J. HOOD.

136

My Shepherd.

Rev. Joseph H. Martin.   Ps. xxiii.   Wm. J. Kirkpatrick.

1. The Lord ... is my shep - - - herd, my keep - - er and
2. Whenev - - - er I wan - - - der, and leave . . the true

1. The Lord is my shepherd, my keeper and guide, The Lord is my shepherd, my
2. Whenev - er I wan- der, and leave the true way, When- ev - er I wan- der, and

guide, ... My wants ... he'll sup-ply, ... and for
way, ... And like ... a lost sheep ... from the

keep- er and guide, My wants he'll supply, and for me he'll provide, My
leave the true way, And like a lost sheep from the flock go a - stray, And

me .... he'll pro-vide; ... In midst . . of green
flock ... go a-stray; . . My soul ... he re-

wants he'll sup- ply, and for me he'll provide; In midst of green pastures he
like a lost sheep from the flock go a - stray; My soul he restores to the

pas - - - - tures he makes - - me to lie, ... Be-
stores ... to the path ... that is right, ... He

makes me to lie, In midst of green pastures he makes me to lie, Be-
path that is right, My soul he restores to the path that is right, He

Copyright, 1880, by John J. Hood.

DO RE MI FA SO LA SI

My Shepherd.—CONCLUDED.

side . . the still wa - - ters that gen - - tly pass by. . . .
leads . . me in safe - - ty, I walk - - in his light. .

side the still waters that gently pass by, That gently, that gently pass by.
leads me in safe-ty, I walk in his light, In safety I walk in his light.

CHORUS.

My Shepherd will provide, what - ev - er may be-tide; I am se-

cure, For his promise is sure, The Lord will pro - vide.

3 When called to surrender my faltering breath,
And pass through the vale of the shadow of death,
The presence of Jesus will brighten the tomb,
With hope and with gladness dispelling its gloom.
            With gladness dispelling its gloom.

4 For me his free bounty a table has spread;
And blessings unmeasured he pours on my head;
My cup with abundance and joy overflows;
He dries all my tears, and he heals all my woes.
            He heals all my woes, all my woes.

5 His goodness and mercy shall crown all my days,
My mouth shall be filled with thanksgiving and praise;
I'll dwell in his temple of glory above,
And sing evermore of his grace and his love.
            And sing of his grace and his love.

137

Little Ones Like Me.

JNO. R. SWENEY.

1. Je-sus, when he left the sky, And for sinners came to die, In his
2. Mothers then the Saviour sought In the places where he taught, And to
3. Did the Saviour say them nay? No, he kindly bade them stay, Suffered
4. 'Twas for them his life he gave, To redeem them from the grave, Jesus

CHORUS.

mer-cy passed not by Little ones like me. Little ones, little ones,
him the children brought, Little ones like me.
none to turn a-way Little ones like me.
now will gladly save Little ones like me.

"Suffer them to come." said he; Jesus loves the little ones, Little ones like me.

Copyright, 1880, by Jons J. Hood.

138 Touch and Cleanse Me.

MARY F. MARSH.　　　Matt. viii. 3.　　　WARREN W. BENTLEY.

1. Touch and cleanse me, blessed Sav-iour, I am wea-ry of my sin;
2. Touch and cleanse me, blessed Sav-iour, Humbly now my guilt I own;
3. Touch and cleanse me, blessed Sav-iour, I am poor, and weak, and blind;
4. Thou dost cleanse me, blessed Sav-iour, Light is streaming from a-bove;

Touch and Cleanse Me.—CONCLUDED.

Fine.

I am long - ing for thy fa - vor, Longing to be pure within.
Oh, be- stow thy pard'ning fa - vor! Thou canst save me, thou alone.
Grant me now thy lov-ing fa - vor, Let me now sal - vation find.
Now I feel thy pard'ning fa - vor, Oh, my soul is full of love.

D. S.—Touch and cleanse me, touch and cleanse me, Jesus, save me or I die.
D. S.—Thou dost cleanse me, thou dost cleanse me, Glory be to God on high.

REFRAIN.

D. S.

Touch and cleanse me, touch and cleanse me, Listen to my fee- ble cry,
4th v. Thou dost cleanse me, thou dost cleanse me, Thou hast heard my feeble cry,

139 The Morning Light.

SAMUEL F. SMITH.

Tune, WEBB. 7, 6.

Fine.

D. S.

1 The morning light is breaking;
The darkness disappears;
The sons of earth are waking
To penitential tears;
Each breeze that sweeps the ocean
Brings tidings from afar,
Of nations in commotion,
Prepared for Zion's war.

2 See heathen nations bending
Before the God we love,
And thousand hearts ascending
In gratitude above;
While sinners, now confessing,
The gospel call obey,
And seek the Saviour's blessing,
A nation in a day.

3 Blest river of salvation,
Pursue thine onward way;
Flow thou to every nation,
Nor in thy richness stay:
Stay not till all the lowly
Triumphant reach their home:
Stay not till all the holy
Proclaim, "The Lord is come!"

Leaning on Jesus.

Rev. W. F. Crafts.   Wm. J. Kirkpatrick.

1. Wea-ry with walking a - lone, Long heav-y - laden with sin;
2. Fearing to stand for my Lord, Trembling for weakness in prayer;

Toil-ing all night with-out Christ,—Rest for my soul shall I win,
Yet on the bo - som di - vine Los - ing each sor-row and fear,

Chorus.

Lean - ing on Je - sus, I walk - at his side; . .
Leaning on Je-sus, in him I a - bide. Leaning on Je-sus, I walk at his side;

Lean - - ing on Je - - sus, I trust him, my Shepherd and Guide.
Leaning on Je-sus, what-ev- er be - tide,

3 Anxious no longer for self,
   Shrinking no longer from pain;
Leaning on Jesus alone,
   He all my care will sustain.
     Leaning on Jesus, etc.

4 Leaning, I walk in "The Way,"
   Leaning, "The Truth" I shall know;
Leaning on heart-throbs of Christ,
   Safe into "Life" I may go.
     Leaning on Jesus, etc.

From " Leaflet Gems, No. 2," by per.

Come and See.

CHARLES H. ELLIOTT.

JNO. R. SWENEY

1. There is pardon sweet, at the Master's feet, Come and see, O come and see;
2. There's an easy yoke that you all may bear, Come and see, O come and see;
3. There's a healing balm for the weary breast, Come and see, O come and see;
4. There's a life beyond, 'tis a life di - vine, Come and see, O come and see;

CHORUS.

There's a song of peace that shall never cease, Come, O come and see.   In the
There's a   ho- ly joy that you all may share, Come, O come and see.
There's a tranquil peace and a sa-cred rest,   Come, O come and see.
And the light of faith on your path will shine, Come, O come and see.

precious, precious blood of Je - sus Washed a - way   your sins may be;

You may plunge just now in its cleansing flood,—Come, will you come and see.

DO RE MI FA SO LA SI

142 Wont You Love My Jesus?

SALLIE SMITH.   JNO. R. SWENEY.

1. I have found a friend di - vine, Wont you love him too?
2. Oh, how dear his name to me, Wont you love him too?
3. Heav - y - lad - en, care - oppressed, Wont you love him too?
4. Cast your bur - den at his feet, Wont you love him too?

I am his and he is mine, Wont you love him too?
None can save your soul but he, Wont you love him too?
How he longs to give you rest, Wont you love him too?
There is par - don pure and sweet, Wont you love him too?

CHORUS.

Wont you love my Je - sus, My pre - cious, precious Je - sus?

Wont you love my Je - sus? He is waiting now for you.

Copyright, 1884, by JOHN J. HOOD.

DO RE MI FA SU LA SI

Holy, Holy, Holy!

"They rest not day and night, saying, Holy, holy, holy, Lord God Almighty."—Rev. iv. 8.

REGINALD HEBER.   JOHN B. DYKES.

1. Ho - ly, ho - ly, ho - ly! Lord God Al - might - y!
2. Ho - ly, ho - ly, ho - ly! all the saints a - dore thee,
3. Ho - ly, ho - ly, ho - ly! though the darkness hide thee,
4. Ho - ly, ho - ly, ho - ly! Lord God Al - migh - ty!

Grate- ful - ly a - dor - ing our song shall rise to thee;
Cast - ing down their golden crowns a - round the glass - y sea;
Though the eyes of sin- ful man thy glo - ry may not see,
All thy works shall praise thy name in earth, and sky, and sea;

Ho - ly, ho - ly, ho - ly! mer-ci - ful and might - y!
Cher - u - bim and se - ra - phim fall-ing down be - fore thee,
On - ly thou art ho - ly, there is none be - side thee
Ho - ly, ho - ly, ho - ly! mer-ci - ful and might - y!

God in three per - sons, bless - ed Trin - i - ty!
Which wert and art and ev - er - more shall be.
Per - fect in power, in love and pur - i - ty.
God in three per - sons, bless - ed Trin - i - ty!

144 **The Firm Foundation.**

George Keith.

Tune, PORTUGUESE HYMN.

1. How firm a foundation, ye saints of the Lord, Is laid for your
2. "Fear not, I am with thee, O be not dismayed, For I am thy
3. "When thro' the deep waters I call thee to go, The riv-ers of
4. "When thro' fie-ry tri-als thy path-way shall lie, My grace all suf-

faith in his ex-cel-lent word! What more can he say, than to
God, I will still give thee aid; I'll strengthen thee, help thee, and
sor-row shall not o-ver-flow; For I will be with thee thy
fi-cient, shall be thy sup-ply, The flame shall not hurt thee; I

you he hath said, To you, who for re-fuge to Je-sus have
cause thee to stand, Up-held by my gracious, om-ni-po-tent
tri-als to bless, And sanc-ti-fy to thee thy deepest dis-
on-ly de-sign Thy dross to consume, and thy gold to re-

fled? To you, who for re-fuge to Je-sus have fled?
hand, Up-held by my gracious, om-ni-po-tent hand.
tress, And sanc-ti-fy to thee thy deep-est dis-tress.
fine, Thy dross to consume, and thy gold to re-fine.

5 "E'en down to old age all my people
shall prove [love;
My sovereign, eternal, unchangeable
And when hoary hairs shall their tem-
ples adorn, [be borne.
Like lambs they shall still in my bosom

6 "The soul that on Jesus hath leaned
for repose,
I will not, I will not desert to his foes;
That soul, though all hell should en-
deavor to shake,
I'll never, no never, no never forsake!"

Redeemed, Praise the Lord. 145

ABBIE MILLS.

WM. J. KIRKPATRICK.

1. O happy day! what a Sav-iour is mine! I am redeemed, praise the Lord!
2. O clap your hands, all ye people of God, I am redeemed, praise the Lord!
3. Thanks be to God for the great vict'ry given, I am redeemed, praise the Lord!
4. Glory to God, I would shout ev-ermore, I am redeemed, praise the Lord!

Fine.

All to his pleasure I glad-ly re-sign, I am redeemed, praise the Lord!
Let ev'ry tongue speak his mercy abroad, I am redeemed, praise the Lord!
Now I am free; ev'ry chain has been riven,—I am redeemed, praise the Lord!
O for a voice that could reach ev'ry shore, I am redeemed, praise the Lord!

Key C.

Jesus has taken my burden away; Jesus has turned all my night into day;
His loving-kindness is better than gold; He doth bestow more than my cup can hold;
Out of the pit, and the mire, and the clay, Jesus has borne me in triumph away;
Help me, ye ransom'd, awake, ev'ry string, Let earth rejoice and the whole heavens ring,

Use first four lines as Chorus. D. C.

Jesus has come to my heart,—come to stay,—I am redeemed, praise the Lord!
Wondrous Salvation, that ne'er can be told,—I am redeemed, praise the Lord!
Safe on the rock I am standing to-day,—I am redeemed, praise the Lord!
While we the chorus u-ni-ted-ly sing, I am redeemed, praise the Lord!

Copyright, 1884, by John J. Hood.   *Temple Songs*-K

DO RE MI FA SO LA SI

Trusting in the Promise.

Rev. H. B. Hartzler.   E. S. Lorenz.

1. { I have found repose for my weary soul, / And a harbor safe when the billows roll, } Trusting in the promise of the Saviour;

2. { I will sing my song as the days go by, / And rejoice in hope, while I live or die, } Trusting in the promise of the Saviour;

3. { O the peace and joy of the life I live, / O the strength and love only God can give, } Trusting in the promise of the Saviour;

{ I will fear no foe in the deadly strife, / I will bear my lot in the toil of life, } Trusting in the promise of the Saviour;

{ I can smile at grief, and abide in pain, / And the loss of all shall be highest gain, } Trusting in the promise of the Saviour;

{ Whosoever will may be saved to-day, / And begin to walk in the holy way, } Trusting in the promise of the Saviour;

REFRAIN.

Resting on his mighty arm forev - er, Never from his loving heart to sever,

I will rest by grace in his strong embrace, Trusting in the promise of the Saviour;

From "Songs of Refreshing," by per.

Come to Jesus.

J. H. S.   Rev. J. H. Stockton.

1. Come, ev - 'ry soul by sin oppressed, There's mercy with the Lord;
2. For Je - sus shed his pre - cious blood Rich blessings to be- stow;
3. Yes, Je - sus is the Truth, the Way, That leads you in - to rest;

Fine.

And he will sure - ly give you rest, By trusting in his word.
Plunge now in - to the crim - son flood That washes white as snow.
Be - lieve in him, with - out de - lay, And you are ful - ly blest.

D. S.—He will save you, he will save you, He will save you now.

CHORUS.   *D. S.*

Come to Je - sus, come to Je - sus, Come to Je - sus now!

Second Chorus.

On - ly trust him, on - ly trust him, On - ly trust him now;

4 O Jesus, blessed Jesus, dear,
   I'm coming now to thee;
Since thou hast made the way so clear,
   And full salvation free.

5 Come, then, and join this holy band,
   And on to glory go;
To dwell in that celestial land
   Where joys immortal flow.

By permission.

Come, Humble Sinner.   Tune above.

1 COME, humble sinner, in whose breast
   A thousand thoughts revolve,
Come, with your guilt and fear opprest,
   And make this last resolve:—

2 I'll go to Jesus, though my sin
   Like mountains round me close;
I know his courts, I'll enter in,
   Whatever may oppose.

3 Prostrate I'll lie before his throne,
   And there my guilt confess;

I'll tell him I'm a wretch undone,
   Without his sovereign grace.

4 Perhaps he will admit my plea,
   Perhaps will hear my prayer;
But, if I perish, I will pray,
   And perish only there.

5 I can but perish, if I go;
   I am resolved to try:
For if I stay away I know
   I must forever die. —Edmund Jones.

Let Him In.

Rev. J. B. Atchinson.   E. O. Excell.

1. There's a stranger at the door, Let him in,
2. O-pen now to him your heart, Let him in,
3. Hear you now his lov-ing voice? Let him in,
4. Now admit the heavenly Guest, Let him in,

Let the Saviour in,   let the Saviour in,

He has been there oft be - fore, Let him in;
If you wait he will de - part, Let him in;
Now, oh, now make him your choice, Let him in,
He will make for you a feast, Let him in,

Let the Saviour in,   let the Saviour in,

Let him in ere he is gone, Let him in the Ho - ly One,
Let him in, he is your Friend, He your soul will sure de - fend,
He is stand-ing at the door, Joy to you he will re - store,
He will speak your sins for-given, And when earth ties all are riven,

Je-sus Christ, the Father's Son, Let him in.
He will keep you to the end, Let him in.
And his name you will a - dore, Let him in.
He will take you home to heaven, Let him in.

Let the Saviour in,   let the Saviour in.

"Mine are thine and thine are mine."
John xvii. 10.

"London Hymn Book."   A. J. GORDON. By per.

1. My   Je - sus,   I   love thee, I   know   thou art   mine,
2. I   love   thee be - cause thou have first lov - ed   me,
3. I will love   thee   in   life, I'll   love   thee in   death,
4. In   man - sions of   glo - ry   and   end - less delight,

For thee   all   the   fol - lies of   sin   I   re - sign;
And pur - chased my   par - don   on   Cal - va - ry's tree;
And praise thee as   long   as   thou lend - est me breath;
I'll ev - er   a - dore thee in   heav - en   so bright;

My gra - cious Re - deem - er, my   Sav - iour art   thou,
I   love thee for wear - ing the thorns on thy brow;
And say, when the death - dew lies cold , on my brow,
I'll sing with the glit - ter - ing crown on my brow,

If ev - er   I   loved thee, my   Je - sus, 'tis now.

Whiter than Snow.

"Wash me, and I shall be whiter than snow"
Psalm li. 7.

JAMES NICHOLSON.   WM. G. FISCHER. By per.

1. Lord Je-sus, I long to be per-fect-ly whole; I want thee for-
2. Lord Je-sus, look down from thy throne in the skies, And help me to
3. Lord Je-sus, for this I most humbly en-treat; I wait, blessed
4. Lord Je-sus, thou se-est I pa-tient-ly wait; Come now, and with

ev - er, to live in my soul; Break down ev-'ry i - dol, cast
make a com-plete sac - ri - fice; I give up my - self, and what-
Lord, at thy cru - ci - fied feet, By faith, for my cleansing, I
in me a new heart cre - ate; To those who have sought thee, thou

out ev - 'ry foe; Now wash me, and I shall be whit - er than snow.
ev - er I know—Now wash me, and I shall be whit - er than snow.
see thy blood flow—Now wash me, and I shall be whit - er than snow.
nev - er said'st No—Now wash me, and I shall be whit - er than snow.

CHORUS.

Whiter than snow, yes, whiter than snow;
Now wash me, and I shall be whiter than snow.

151 I am Coming to the Cross.

Rev. Wm. McDonald.   John vi. 37.   Wm. G. Fischer. By per.

1. I am com - ing to the cross; I am poor, and weak, and blind;
2. Long my heart has sighed for thee, Long has e - vil reigned within;
3. Here I give my all to thee, Friends, and time, and earthly store;

CHO.— I am trust - ing, Lord, in thee, Blest Lamb of Cal - va - ry;

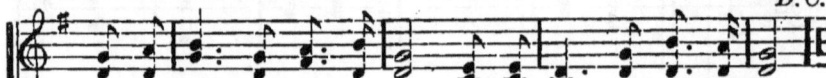

D. C.

I am count - ing all but dross, I shall full sal - va - tion find.
Je - sus sweet - ly speaks to me,— "I will cleanse you from all sin."
Soul and bo - dy thine to be,— Whol - ly thine for ev - er-more.

Humbly at thy cross I bow, Save me, Je - sus, save me now.

4 In thy promises I trust,
Now I feel the blood applied:
I am prostrate in the dust,
I with Christ am crucified.

5 Jesus comes! he fills my soul!
Perfected in him I am;
I am every whit made whole:
Glory, glory to the Lamb.

152 Rest for the Weary.   Rev. Wm. McDonald.

Rev. S. G. Harmer.

1. In the Christian's home in glo - ry There re - mains a land of rest;
2. Pain or sickness ne'er shall en - ter, Grief nor woe my lot shall share;
3. Death itself shall then be vanquished, And his sting shall be withdrawn:
4. Sing, oh, sing, ye heirs of glo - ry; Shout your triumph as you go;

There my Saviour's gone be - fore me, To ful - fil my soul's request.
But in that ce - les - tial cen - tre, I a crown of life shall wear.
Shout for gladness, O ye ransomed! Hail with joy the ris - ing morn.
Zi - on's gates will o - pen for you, You shall find an entrance through.

CHORUS.

{ There is rest for the wea - ry, There is rest for the
On the oth - er side of Jor - dan, In the sweet fields of

wea - ry, There is rest for the wea - ry, There is rest for you— }
E - den, Where the tree of life is blooming, There is rest for you. }

153

Come, Ye Disconsolate.

THOMAS MOORE, alt., and THOS. HASTINGS.　　　SAMUEL WEBBE.

1. Come, ye disconsolate, where'er ye languish; Come to the mercy-seat, fervently kneel;

Here bring your wounded hearts, here tell your anguish;
Earth has no sorrow that heaven cannot heal.

2 Joy of the desolate, light of the stray-
ing,
Hope of the penitent, fadeless and pure,
Here speaks the Comforter, tenderly saying,
"Earth has no sorrow that heaven cannot cure."

3 Here see the bread of life; see waters
flowing
Forth from the throne of God, pure
from above;　　　[knowing
Come to the feast of love; come, ever
Earth has no sorrow but heaven can
[remove.

154

At the Fountain.

OLD MELODY.

CHORUS.

1 Of him who did salvation bring,
　I'm at the fountain drinking,
I could forever think and sing,
　I'm on my journey home.

CHO—Glory to God,
　I'm at the fountain drinking,
　Glory to God,
　I'm on my journey home.

2 Ask but his grace and lo! 'tis given,
　I'm at the fountain drinking,
Ask and he turns your hell to heaven,
　I'm on my journey home.

3 Tho' sin and sorrow wound my soul,
　I'm at the fountain drinking,

Jesus, thy balm will make me whole,
　I'm on my journey home.

4 Where'er I am, where'er I move,
　I'm at the fountain drinking,
I meet the object of my love,
　I'm on my journey home.

5 Insatiate to this spring I fly,
　I'm at the fountain drinking,
I drink and yet am ever dry,
　I'm on my journey home.

CHO—Glory to God,
　I'm at the fountain drinking,
　Glory to God,
　My soul is satisfied.

155 We'll Work till Jesus Comes.

Mrs. ELIZABETH MILLS.   Arr. by W. J. K., 1859.   Dr. WM. MILLER.

CHORUS.

1 O land of rest for thee I sigh,
　When will the moment come,
　When I shall lay my armor by
　And dwell in peace at home?

CHO.—We'll work till Jesus comes,
　We'll work till Jesus comes,
　We'll work till Jesus comes,
　And we'll be gather'd home.

2 No tranquil joys on earth I know,
　No peaceful sheltering dome,

This world's a wilderness of woe,
This world is not my home.

3 To Jesus Christ I fled for rest;
　He bade me cease to roam,
　And lean for succor on his breast
　Till he conduct me home.

4 I sought at once my Saviour's side,
　No more my steps shall roam;
　With him I'll brave death's chilling
　And reach my heavenly home. [tide,

156 Happy Land.

OLD MELODY.

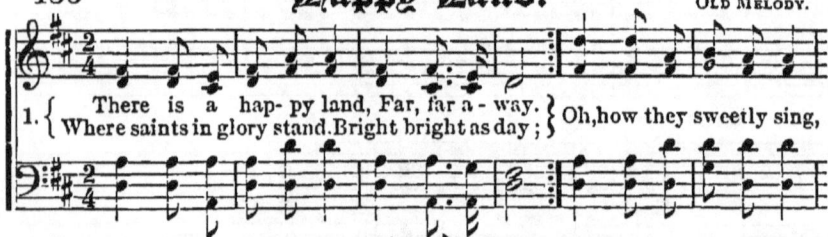

1. { There is a hap-py land, Far, far a-way. } Oh, how they sweetly sing,
   { Where saints in glory stand. Bright bright as day ; }

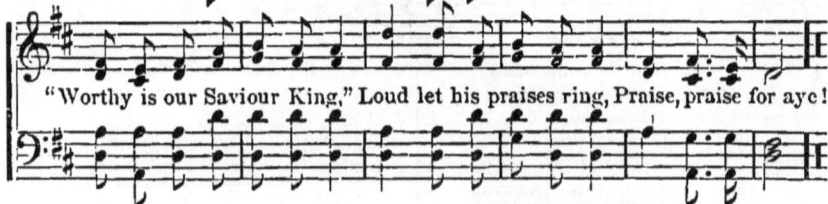

"Worthy is our Saviour King," Loud let his praises ring, Praise, praise for aye!

2 Bright, in that happy land,
　Beams every eye ;
　Kept by a Father's hand,
　Love cannot die.
　On, then, to glory run ;
　Be a crown and kingdom won ;
　And bright, above the sun,
　Reign evermore.

3 Come to that happy land,
　Come, come away ;
　Why will you doubting stand?
　Why still delay ?
　Oh, we shall happy be
　When from sin and sorrow free ;
　Lord, we shall dwell with thee,
　Blest evermore.

153

157 Will You Go?

Fine.

D. C.

1 We're trav'ling home to heaven above,
  Will you go?
To sing the Saviour's dying love;
  Will you go?
Millions have reached that blest abode,
Anointed kings and priests to God;
And millions more are on the road;
  Will you go?

2 We're going to walk the plains of light,
  Will you go?
Far, far from curse and death and night;
  Will you go?
The crown of life we then shall wear,
The conqueror's palm we then shall bear,
And all the joys of heaven we'll share;
  Will you go?

3 The way to heaven is straight and [plain;
  Will you go?
Repent, believe, be born again;
  Will you go?
The Saviour cries aloud to thee,
"Take up your cross and follow me,
And thou shalt my salvation see."
  Will you go?

158 While Jesus Whispers to You.

WILL. E. WITTER.   H. R. PALMER.

1st.   *2d.*

1. { While Je-sus whispers to you, Come, sinner, come!
   { While we are praying for you, Come, ... sin-ner, come!

1st.   *2d.*

{ Now is the time to own him, Come, sinner, come!
{ Now is the time to know him, Come, ... sin-ner, come!

2 Are you too heavy laden?
   Come, sinner, come!
Jesus will bear your burden,
   Come, sinner, come!
Jesus will not deceive you,
   Come, sinner, come!
Jesus can now redeem you,
   Come, sinner, come!

3 Oh, hear his tender pleading,
   Come, sinner, come!
Come and receive the blessing,
   Come, sinner, come!
While Jesus whispers to you,
   Come, sinner, come!
While we are praying for you,
   Come, sinner, come!

159 Crown Him.

"Thou hast crowned him with glory and honor."

Rev. Thos. Kelly. Psalm viii. 5. Arr. by Geo. G. Stebbins. By per

Fine.

1. Look, ye saints, the sight is glorious, See the "Man of sorrows" now.
From the fight re-turn vic-to-rious, Ev-'ry knee to him shall bow.

2. Crown the Sav-iour! an-gels crown him, Rich the trophies Jesus brings,
In the seat of power enthrone him, While the vault of heaven rings.

D. C.—Crown him! crown him, angels crown him! Crown the Saviour King of kings.

REFRAIN.

D. C.

Crown him! crown him, angels crown him! Crown the Saviour King of kings;

3 Sinners in derision crowned him,
Mocking thus the Saviour's claim,
Saints and angels crowd around him,
Own his title, praise his name.

4 Hark! the bursts of acclamation!
Hark! these loud, triumphant chords,
Jesus takes the highest station,
Oh, what joy the sight affords!

160 My Faith Looks Up to Thee.

Ray Palmer. L. Mason.

1 My faith looks up to thee,
Thou Lamb of Calvary,
Saviour divine!
Now hear me while I pray;
Take all my guilt away;
Oh, let me from this day
Be wholly thine!

2 May thy rich grace impart
Strength to my fainting heart,
My zeal inspire!
As thou hast died for me,
Oh, may my love to thee
Pure, warm. amd changeless be—
A living fire!

3 While life's dark maze I tread,
And griefs around me spread,
Be thou my guide;
Bid darkness turn to day,
Wipe sorrow's tears away,
Nor let me ever stray
From thee aside.

4 When ends life's transient dream,
When death's cold sullen stream
Shall o'er me roll,
Blest Saviour! then, in love,
Fear and distrust remove;
Oh, bear me safe above—
A ransomed soul!

161 He is Calling.

FABER.　　Arr by S. J Vail.

1. { There's a wideness in God's mercy, Like the wideness of the sea : }
   { There's a kindness in his justice Which is more than } li - ber-ty.

CHORUS.

He is call-ing, "Come to me!" Lord, I'll gladly haste to thee.

2 There is welcome for the sinner,
  And more graces for the good ;
  There is mercy with the Saviour ;
  There is healing in his blood.

3 For the love of God is broader
  Than the measure of man's mind ;

And the heart of the Eternal
Is most wonderful and kind.

4 If our love were but more simple,
  We should take him at his word ;
  And our lives would be all sunshine
  In the sweetness of our Lord.

162 The Golden Key.

"Prayer is the key to unlock the door, and the bolt to shut in the night."　J. R. S.

1. Prayer is the key For the bending knee To open the morn's first hours;
2. Not a soul so sad, Nor a heart so glad, When cometh the shades of night,
3. Take the golden key In your hand and see, As the night tide drifts away,

See the incense rise To the star-ry skies, Like per-fume from the flow'rs.
But the daybreak song Will the joy prolong, And some darkness turn to light.
How its blessed hold Is a crown of gold, Thro' the weary hours of day.

4 When the shadows fall,
  And the vesper call
Is sobbing its low refrain,
  'Tis a garland sweet
  To the toil dent feet,
And an antidote for pain.

5 Soon the year's dark door
  Shall be shut no more :
Life's tears shall be wiped away
  As the pearl gates swing,
  And the gold harps ring,
And the sun unsheathe for aye.

From "Goodly Pearls," by per.

156

DO RE MI FA SO LA SI

Cleansing Wave.

Mrs. J. F. Knapp.

CHORUS.

1 Oh, now I see the cleansing wave!
  The fountain deed and wide;
Jesus, my Lord, mighty to save,
  Points to his wounded side.

Cho.—The cleansing stream, I see, I see!
  I plunge, and oh, it cleanseth me!
  Oh, praise the Lord! it cleanseth me;
  It cleanseth me—yes, cleanseth me.

2 I rise to walk in heaven's own light,
  Above the world of sin,   [white,
With heart made pure and garments
  And Christ enthroned within.

3 Amazing grace! 'tis heaven below
  To feel the blood applied;
And Jesus, only Jesus, know,
  My Jesus crucified.

164

Doxology.

Words arr. by B. M. A.   Melody by J. R. S.   Harmony by W. J. K.

Slow, with dignity.

Glo - ry be to the Fa - ther, Glo - ry be to the Son,

Glo - ry be to the Ho - ly Ghost; As it was in the be - ginning,

Is now, and ev - er shall be, World without end. A - men, a - men.

INDEX.

·FINIS·

www.ingramcontent.com/pod-product-compliance
Lightning Source LLC
Chambersburg PA
CBHW020847270326
41928CB00006B/591